THE INTERNET

An Introduction to New Media

Lelia Green

BERG

Oxford • New York

English edition
First published in 2010 by
Berg
Editorial offices:
First Floor, Angel Court, 81 St Clements Street, Oxford OX4 1AW, UK
175 Fifth Avenue, New York, NY 10010, USA

Berg is the imprint of Oxford International Publishers Ltd.

Library of Congress Cataloging-in-Publication Data

Green, Lelia, 1956-
    The internet : a[n introduction to new media] / Lelia Green.
    p. cm. — (B[erg new media series])
Includes bibliogra[phical references]
ISBN 978-1-8478[8-298-1 (cloth) — ISBN 978-1-84788-299-8 (pbk.)]
1. Internet—Social a[spects. 2. Computers and civilization.] [3. Informati]on society. I. Title.
HM851.G744 20[10]
302.23'1—dc22
                                                                                                    2010004767

British Library Cataloguing-in-Publication Data

A catalogue record for this book is available from the British Library.

ISBN   978 1 84788 298 1(Cloth)
          978 1 84788 299 8 (Paper)
e-ISBN 978 1 84788 769 6 (institutional)
          978 1 84788 798 9 (individual)

Typeset by JS Typesetting Ltd, Porthcawl, Mid Glamorgan
Printed in Great Britain by the MPG Books Group, Bodmin and King's Lynn

www.bergpublishers.com

For Linda Jaunzems who helps me keep all the balls in the air

CONTENTS

ILLUSTRATIONS

TABLES

DIAGRAMS

FIGURES

ACKNOWLEDGEMENTS

I am extremely grateful to my employer, Edith Cowan University, who allocated the study leave which allowed this book to be written, and particularly to Professors Arshad Omari, Clive Barstow, Brenda Cherednichenko and Julie Warn who approved and managed my absence.

Professor Brian Shoesmith, and my PhD supervisors Professors Tom O'Regan and Bob Hodge, first encouraged my interest in this area. Dr Ann Willis, Dr Danielle Brady and Julie Dare have all supported and developed the teaching of units in the discipline, and I've learned a lot from working with them. A number of Australian Research Council (ARC)-funded projects have informed the research communicated in these pages and I acknowledge the ARC's support, and that of my co-Chief Investigators including Professors Robyn Quin and Mark Balnaves, Associate Professor Trevor Cullen, Dr Debbie Rodan, Dr Leesa Costello, Dr David Leith and industry partners Maurice Swanson, Steve Furmedge and Vanessa Bradshaw. Dr Anne Aly, Jack Seddon, Donell Holloway, Christine Teague and Lynsey Uridge were all involved as Research Assistants or PhD candidates with the ARC research. My co-supervisors, postgraduate students and research associates contribute a continuous stream of relevant, fascinating, information and opinion so I also mention Associate Professor Maggi Phillips, Dr Julie Robson, Dr Teresa Maiolo, Dr Kay Hearn, Dr Uta Daur, Julie Johnson, Jason Noble, Robyn Torney, Christopher Phillips, Alex Bradley, Christina Ballico and Catherine Gomersall.

Warm thanks to Dr Judy Clayden for the index. Judy was also generous in sharing a librarian's approach to finding quality information on the web, and helpfully critiqued my punctuation. Ken Gasmier was more patient than I deserve as my specialist librarian. Jude Elund crafted the diagrams in the book, and she and Sharron Snader also provided other help. Dave Batley, proving that Wikipedia discussion lists do work, reviewed them from the perspective of a computer programmer and theoretical physicist, although any errors remain my own.

I am fortunate to be involved as a joint Chief Investigator in the ARC Centre of Excellence for Creative Industries and Innovation. This has brought me into contact with a number of exceptional academics whose work is relevant here, including:

distinguished Professors John Hartley and Stuart Cunningham; Professors Jock Given, Gerard Goggin, Greg Hearn, Catharine Lumby and Alan McKee, Associate Professor Axel Bruns, Dr Jean Burgess and Dr Kate Crawford. My international colleagues on the *Asia-Pacific Digital Review*, but especially Professor Claude-Yves Charron, and volume editors Chin Saik Yoon, Professor Felix Librero, Shahid Akhtar and Associate Professor Patricia Arinto have, since 2003, provided me with an illuminating introduction to the digital divide as it operates in most areas of the globe, for the majority of the world's population.

As a member of the International Advisory Panel of the EU Kids Online project, 2006–9, I was among the first to see the exciting outputs of that 21-nation research network. I'm grateful to Professor Sonia Livingstone and Dr Leslie Haddon for the opportunity to take part. Dr Haddon is also one of the two editors of the Berg New Media series, with Dr Nicola Green, and was particularly generous in his support and unstinting in his feedback: thank you Leslie. Commissioning Editor Tristan Palmer was wonderfully flexible in calling in my deadlines and Emily Medcalf intuited a fabulous cover. I am grateful to them, to the Berg Production staff, and to the anonymous reviewers whose comments both challenged and inspired me. Linda Jaunzems, like Dr Haddon, was indispensable to the eventual completion of this book, offering support, assistance and one-stop expertise. This volume is dedicated to her, and to her family.

My life is sustained by a network of friends, many of whom have already been mentioned and others of whom include: Claire Andrews, Jenny Benjamin, Jeanette Connolly, Carmel Elwell, Professor Nadine Henley, Dr Larissa Hjorth, Dr Kara Jacob, Heather McLean, Joan Smith, Emily Walker and Susan Young.

My mother, also Lelia Green, has fuelled this work with food, drink and love and by creating a refuge from other demands to allow me time to commit myself to writing. My sister, Ginny Weston, has supported me throughout this and other journeys. Anna Weston, Mark Weston and Paul Schutz, all of whom have an important place in my life, have offered feedback from the 'students' viewpoint'.

My final acknowledgement must go to my two wonderful children, Carmen and Ben Guinery. They grew up digital and generously shared the excitement of so doing, together with some details of the journey. They tolerated the progress of this book, and others of my consuming passions, with open-minded good humour and large bowls of vegan pasta. They tell me this is an Oscar acceptance speech. I would be lost without them. Thanks, kids.

PERMISSIONS

I am grateful to the following authors and publishers for permission to reproduce their work. For Table 4.1 and Table 4.2, Sr Enrique De Argaez, Editor and Webmaster, *Miniwatt Marketing Group and World Internet Stats*, published June 30 2009, http://www.internetworldstats.com; reproduced with permission from World Internet Stats. For Table 4.3, Louise Budde of Paul Budde Communication Pty Ltd, 2009, trading as BuddeComm, http://www.budde.com.au, regarding 2009 data from Point Topic on behalf of the Broadband Forum, based on self-reporting by carriers and defining broadband as 144Kb/s; reproduced with permission from Paul Budde Communication Pty Ltd. For Figure 5.1, Jean-Nöel Jeanneney, author of *Google and the Myth of Universal Knowledge: A View from Europe*, 2006, The University of Chicago Press, for permission to create a figure based on Jeanneney's arguments; reproduced with permission from the University of Chicago Press. For Figure 6.1, Gareth Morgan, author of *Images of Organization* (revised edition), 2006, Sage Publications, for permission to create a figure based on the Contents pages of Morgan's book; reproduced with permission from Sage Publications. For Figure 7.1, Axel Bruns, author of *Blogs, Wikipedia, Second Life and Beyond: From Production to Produsage*, 2008, Peter Lang Publishing, for permission to create a figure based on pp. 19–20 of Bruns's book; reproduced with permission from Peter Lang Publishing. For Figure 9.1, Uwe Hasebrink, Sonia Livingstone, Leslie Haddon and Kjartan Ólafsson, editors of *Comparing Children's Online Opportunities and Risks Across Europe: Cross-National Comparisons for EU Kids Online* (2nd edition), 2009, the London School of Economics and EU Kids Online for permission to adapt two figures on pp. 8–9 of the second edition of Deliverable D3.2 of the EU Kids Online project; reproduced with permission from EU Kids Online, the London School of Economics and Political Science, London.

1 INTRODUCTION

This book explores the internet as an introduction to new media. It does so by looking backwards to examine the history of the internet, and by looking forward to its emerging future. It draws upon current evidence from around the world to illustrate different aspects of internet use as these reflect a range of social, political and economic circumstances. It uses case studies, many based on new research, some of it unpublished, to reveal important aspects of the internet for comment and analysis. While the internet is too big a subject for any book to provide a complete review of its past, present and future, insights from case studies provide a series of snapshots which taken together create a broad picture of the contexts of internet use and illustrate what is happening, how and why.

The Internet (as) *An Introduction to New Media* examines the internet as itself, but is also a way of examining our everyday lives through our uses of the internet, and linking the internet with aspects of other new media. Many changes wrought by new media swiftly make their way into popular culture, both reflecting and building the excitement about new possibilities. Old media – the press, radio and television – discuss the innovations, and new media become the central element of novels and films. One example of this, within a popular culture context, would be the film *You've got mail* (Ephron 1998).

The type of context chosen is itself important when considering the internet, since a historical context will provide different information, and raise different questions, compared with a social context, for example. The diverse range of case studies covered in this book makes a number of different contexts visible. These include the way that the internet is used in everyday western life, as well as its technological, political, economic and global contexts. What becomes clear is that the internet, like other new media, is a site of constant reinvention. It has energised creativity, collaboration and novel models for commercialisation. At the same time that the internet makes possible new ways for us to seek information and relate to others, it also offers another technological medium through which individuals and societies can express themselves and their priorities.

In many western countries, the internet is pervasive. That is to say, almost everybody who wants to do so can access the internet (but see Chapter 4). This access will not necessarily always be in the time and place and circumstances that a person chooses, but there are comparatively few people who lack the skills and support to use an internet terminal in a library. It is important to remember, however, that the situation is very different in most parts of the world where the internet is still generally restricted to the richer, better educated, younger, males in the community. This also used to be the pattern of access in the West up until the early 1990s. The huge growth in take-up of the internet has both raised interest and created anxiety, a pattern common to each new medium as it is taken up and diffuses through society. When printing first started, and when telephones, radio, the cinema and television all became integrated within everyday life, the lawmakers and regulators of the day were concerned. Even while people are excited by new possibilities and potentials, as we will see later in the book, they may simultaneously be worried about risks, dangers, control, and relative advantages and disadvantages. For these reasons, new media are often associated with fear and panic, and a concern that the technology is 'too big to regulate'.

Given the numerous ways in which a book about the internet could be structured, this chapter explains why this book has been approached as it has. The explanation includes not only why there is a focus upon case studies, but also the logic behind the structure of the book. First, we start off with consideration of the internet as an introduction to new media, including a definition of the internet, in order to understand what we are focusing upon in this volume of the Berg 'new media' series.

The digital is a critical component of new media, and characteristics of digital goods are compared and contrasted with physical goods. The chapter goes on to consider how societies choose to use technology and explains the 'social shaping of technology' approach, which is the major conceptual framework used. This approach is complemented by the theory that technologies are 'consumed' by the people who use them and become part of a revised, enlarged conception of that person's sense of self. The benefits of consuming a technology are often communicated through 'social constructions' of that technology, the meanings and understandings about that technology which circulate in the relevant society, while a particular strand within that approach – Actor-Network Theory – positions people as key actors in networks which form integrated wholes related to technology use.

The internet can be explored using a wide range of theoretical frameworks and while the social shaping approach is not the only method used in this book, it is the main one. To illustrate the ways in which a particular framework makes some research and some evidence more or less important, the discussion of the social shaping of technology is developed in Chapter 2 through the use of a feminist approach. Partly as a way of considering the predominantly male history of the early internet, we examine Wajcman's (1991) argument that technology is a 'masculine culture'. This is contrasted with the requirements of a more traditional historical analysis, such as that which characterises most of the material in Chapter 2, which positions key inventors and industrialists as the 'heroes' of innovation.

Empirical research forms a vital part of this book and, consequently, there is a brief introduction to case study research methods relevant to a social shaping framework. This allows readers to understand the ways in which case studies draw upon and showcase relevant evidence concerning people's uses of the internet. This introduction concludes with a description of the chapters that follow and suggests ways in which readers might like to use the book, since it has been designed to be read in bits and chunks, as well as a single narrative. A dot-point summary draws the threads of the chapter together, and sets the scene for the chapters to come.

THE INTERNET AS AN INTRODUCTION TO NEW MEDIA

The term 'the internet' is used here to cover:

- the interconnected and networked technological infrastructure that supports the World Wide Web;
- proprietary sites linked into the web (such as that maintained by The Louvre, the world-famous French museum);
- open and closed source software and architecture (e.g. Firefox, Wikipedia, Internet Explorer, Google);
- computer and everyday languages in terms of making the internet accessible to people of many cultures and literacies;
- email, chat and instant messaging (e.g. AOL, MSN);
- blogs and social networking sites (e.g. Facebook);
- games, communities, environments and worlds (e.g. World of Warcraft, Second Life);
- the many ways in which digitally mediated communication has become domesticated and pervasive within the everyday.

Not all of these aspects of the internet are given equal attention in this book since many areas, such as computer games and digital arts, are covered in companion books in the series. However, an inclusive notion of the internet, as indicated above, provides the blueprint for this volume. While it is expected that readers – not only students and educators but also researchers and policy makers – will be familiar with using aspects of the internet, this book encourages a critical examination of such individual experiences and places them into a context which includes the past and the future of the internet; as well as the technical and social implications of internet use.

A new media approach to studying the internet recognises that digital technologies and environments are convergent. When technologies converge they take on and share the capacities and characteristics of other technologies alongside the core technology. This contrasts with everyday goods from pre-digital life, which had separate functions and separate technical characteristics. In the early days, television could not be used as a radio; a telephone could not work as a camera. Once information is digitised, however, it can be handled in consistent and effective ways which allow a blurring of functions and the emergence of hybrid technologies. For example, early computers had started as number crunchers, but became word processors as well as calculators. Increasingly, new media technologies can perform more functions in more varied contexts; such as accessing the internet from a mobile phone to post digital pictures to a social network profile, even as the event recorded is still happening.

Reflection: Convergent technologies

Can you think of a technology in your life that used to be two or more separate technologies? What advantages do you find to having a number of functions combined in the same technology? Are there disadvantages?

In addition to recognising convergence in the functions of end-user technologies, new media perspectives acknowledge that formerly distinct industries also converge, partly to position themselves strongly as competitors in emerging markets. The internet itself is sometimes positioned against a background of 'old media': print culture, which started in about 1439 with Johannes Gutenberg's invention of printing using movable type; and broadcast culture, which is a little over a century old. While old media do offer starting points for understanding the internet and the World Wide Web (WWW), these perspectives are more relevant to 'Web 1.0' than they are to 'Web 2.0', or than they will be for 'Web 3.0'. It might be worth noting here that the internet is not the WWW, although it provides the technological structure which makes the WWW possible. Web 1.0 refers to a stage in its evolution when the internet could be used to access information and relatively static web pages, while Web 2.0 recognises that online environment now offers opportunities for social connection and interactivity for example, through blogs, wikis and social networking systems and technologies. For people in western countries, Web 2.0 has become increasingly prominent since the new millennium, although the organising principles of both print and broadcasting culture dominate many aspects of corporate content production.

As well as including aspects of both print and broadcasting culture, the internet marks a major development in the fields of information technology (IT) and telecommunications. One of the reasons for this huge growth in hybrid and convergent products, services and markets has been the impact of the digitisation of information in comparison to older analogue broadcasting technologies. When audio, video, data, graphic and multimedia applications are all designed to process digital information then those audio, video and data services can also be manipulated, stored and communicated via computers and telecommunications. The underlying digital structure of these different applications allows the outputs to be delivered through a variety of channels including cable, satellite, microwave and other telecommunications systems, with the platform of delivery being less relevant in terms of access and use than the bandwidth capacity of the delivery channel. New media are digital media, they tend to be information and communication technologies (ICTs) and they are hybrid to their core. The relevance of their digital nature lies in differences between the characteristics of digital goods and services, and material goods.

HOW DIGITAL INFORMATION DIFFERS FROM PHYSICAL GOODS

In the physical world, if a package is lost in a journey between London and New York, there is a problem. If it cannot be found, it may have to be replaced. In the digital world, if a packet of information is lost it will be re-sent, automatically, without anyone being aware that the packet has gone 'missing'. This is partly because digital information is kept by the source at the same time that it is sent to the receiver. In the digital world you can have your cake, and eat it too! Four characteristics of digital information differ dramatically from the characteristics of physical goods, as identified by Japanese futurist and information scientist Yoneji Masuda (1981).

First, information is not consumable: it continues to exist after it has been used, and different people can use the same information multiple times. Second, information is non-transferable: this means that the information can be passed onto others and yet still be retained by the original user. Third, information is indivisible. Every fourth letter-space-punctuation in this book, for example, would fail to communicate a quarter of the meaning. Fourth, information is accumulative. As information is used, for example, entered into a database and then processed using statistics software such as SPSS, so it becomes more relevant and accessible for a range of purposes. Usually the processing information makes it more useful: it adds value. This is because 'accumulation of goods is by their non-use, but information cannot be consumed or transferred' (Masuda 1981: 77), thus as information is accumulated, so it has greater use; and as it is being used, so more information is accumulated. Masuda adds that the quality of accumulated information is increased through the addition of further high quality information.

This is the opposite of material goods, where consumption equates with destruction. The use of digital technologies to process data magnifies the benefits of these four properties of information. New information can multiply both the value and the amount of existing information through the creation of new knowledge.

Reflection: How does digital information compare with:

- printed information
- personal knowledge
- material goods?

Are all four characteristics of digital information used in internet communication?

Masuda (1978, cited in Jones 1995: 186) demonstrates that other astonishing things happen when digital information is combined with information technology. He notes that while 'information has always had the property of self-multiplication, computer-communication technology has rapidly increased the speed and quality of self-multiplication because the technology itself has added four more properties to information: (1) concentration, (2) dispersion, (3) circulation, and (4) feedback'. To these four functions we can, following the invention of the WWW, add (5) searchable.

1. Concentration occurs because ICTs store digital information more efficiently than any other means. This results in ICT operators being able to work effectively with multiple data sets using just one piece of technology.

It also allows many people simultaneously to access huge databases from remote terminals, e.g. international ATM access to credit card accounts.

2. Dispersal allows information to be exported to many different sites. Together with inconsumability, this capacity of ICT permits information to be incorporated into a variety of data storage systems for multiple uses by many people.

3. The circulation of information provides users with additional choices. Even if information is not downloaded onto a drive (as, for instance, would happen with dispersal), access to that information circulates via emails, web-links, etc.

4. Feedback allows ICTs, via their data protocols, to verify that all the information sent has been safely received and reassembled. If the sending machine does not receive appropriate feedback verification, it automatically re-sends the data: hence the missing packet is replaced before anyone notices it is missing.

5. Searching for data using WWW search engines allows access to constantly multiplying amounts of information, prioritised according to the searcher's key requirements. This aspect of ICTs will be examined closely in Chapter 2's case study of Google.

THE SOCIAL SHAPING OF TECHNOLOGY

Having established some key features of the digital information handled on the internet, we now move on to examine the main theoretical frameworks drawn upon in later chapters. The social shaping of technology approach to new media studies takes a fundamental pair of questions as its starting point: 'Does technology shape society?', or, 'Does society shape technology?'. Once people have started looking at these questions they find others also emerge: 'How does the shaping process happen?' and 'Is technology neutral?'. These questions and the discussions arising from them provide a starting point for thinking about the internet and other new media. They offer a way of talking about where people experience power and powerlessness in their uses of technology (MacKenzie and Wajcman 1999).

Some people's everyday experience is that technology changes too fast for their comfort. They prefer the old ways of doing things and feel disempowered when asked to carry out their everyday activities online. They resent that bank branches are closed down because more people are using internet banking. They feel disadvantaged when airline companies offer special fares for booking on the web. They can't believe that a smart-phone menu ('Press 1 for ...; Press 2 to ...') offers customer service advantages over the real person who used to answer when they called a company's office. Such people might feel that the technology itself is behind the changes that make them uncomfortable.

Some commentators construct technology as the power which drives social change, impacting upon society. It is almost as if the scientific rules behind the development and application of technology are more effective and non-negotiable than the social and cultural dynamics that shape the communities and countries in which we live. Since new media technologies conform to the laws of science – of electro-magnetics, engineering, digitisation – this can be interpreted as indicating that technological change is a given, like gravity. There is no point in arguing about whether gravity is good or bad. According to this approach, the only role for society is to adapt itself to the technology, and come to terms with a future that is driven by technological change. Such a perspective sees technology as shaping society. It is called 'technological determinism' because the technology is positioned as the most important element determining people's lives.

Very few theorists these days argue a pure case for technological determinism. Instead, this perspective tends to be aligned with those who argue that certain technologies are inherently bad, and that this contaminates all uses of the technology. Such a perspective can be found in Theodore Roszak's classic criticism of the computer:

> No matter how high the promise of that [information] age is pitched, the price we pay for its benefits will never outweigh the costs. The violation of privacy is the loss of freedom. The degradation of electoral politics is the loss of democracy. The creation of the computerised war machine is a direct threat to the survival of our species. It would be some comfort to conclude that these liabilities result from the abuse of computer power. But these are the goals long since selected by those who invented information technology, who have guided it and financed it at every point along the way in its development. The computer is *their* machine; its mystique is *their* validation. (Roszak 1994: 233, original italics)

Reflection: Is the internet neutral?

Thinking about your own circumstances, at home and in other locations, what rights and opportunities are implied in your use of the internet?

Do you see your internet use as neutral? Why?

Do you see the internet itself as a neutral technology?

What factors are you taking into account?

Social determinists agree that technology is an important change agent, but they argue it is not developed outside society but is an expression of priorities and choices that are made within social systems. This perspective is part of an overarching philosophy called Social Constructionism, which argues that social forces construct our understanding of the world and frame how we act within it. When discussing the role of technology, social determinists point to the actions of elites in sponsoring, developing and marketing technologies; and claim it is no accident that some technologies are promoted while others never even reach a prototype stage.

This perspective positions technology as having the power to impact upon everyday life, but it also constructs technologies as the result of social processes. When technology is positioned as an outcome of social dynamics, as it is in the social shaping of technology approach, there is the possibility that technological processes can be made accountable and that the development and deployment of technology can be regulated. The social shaping of technology perspective is generally a positive one. It says that technology is not beyond the control of social processes. However, it also argues that since technology is part of society, it tends to express the priorities of elite groups in that society.

The elites typically identified as supporting the development of technology can be remembered using an alphabet mnemonic: the A, B and C of technology change.

A   Armed forces;
B   Bureaucracy; and
C   Corporate power.

These three drivers of technological change are key promoters of new technology development. The US armed forces, for example – in the shape of ARPA, the (then) Pentagon-based Advanced Research Projects Agency – commissioned the work which led to the start of the internet. Bureaucratic drivers are behind innovations such as online tax returns and government portals delivering information and services. The UK Pension Service (http://www.thepensionservice.gov.uk) would be a contemporary example of a bureaucratically-driven investment in technological development, which would include design and usability studies. Corporate power notes that companies also seek out and develop new products for new markets. Google would offer many examples of corporate power driving development (Chapter 2). Even where universities are the powerhouses for innovation, the funding for their research tends to come either from defence, the (civilian arm of) government or business.

Traditionally, the A, B, C of technology change ended with these three categories. Latterly, however – and excitingly – it has become appropriate to acknowledge a D and an E. These are less clearly elites, but may be seen as comparatively small groups of people within their societies who have special skills and a passion for new media. The D and E that should be added to the mnemonic are

D   Distributed collaborators; and
E   Everyday innovators.

It is not the case that D necessarily comes before E (or that A came before B and C) and many would argue that everyday innovators have always been active in customising technology for their own purposes (Marvin 1990; Haddon 1988).

The acknowledgement of distributed networks of collaborators allows recognition of the creative power of 'harnessing the hive'; the community of people engaged in a shared activity. We see these alliances of enthusiasts working creatively and productively in gaming contexts, in wikis and on fan fiction sites – to name but a few. An everyday innovators category acknowledges the creativity of new media adopters in finding novel applications for emerging technologies unsuspected by the technology developers. This was the case, for example, of SMS texts and the adoption of texting by Finnish teenagers as their major mobile application once it became clear how much cheaper it was to communicate in this way rather than by voice (Kasesniemi and Rautianinen 2002). These examples make clear the possibility that the elite associated with a technology can change over time: the corporate designers were supplanted by the cash-poor teenagers who fashioned the uses of the mobile phone to suit their lifestyles, their budgets, and to circumvent the usual communication patterns of their parents and teachers. (See the separate book in this series on *Mobile Communication* for more.) Clearly some internet advances can be attributed to Distributed and Everyday groups, and the internet is rarely conceptualised solely in terms of its Armed forces-sponsored beginnings.

These examples introduce the fact that the social shaping of technology approach is an umbrella concept for a range of specific micro-theories. Theories of specific relevance to the social shaping of technology approach include the 'Theory of Consumption', the 'Domestication of Technology' framework, the 'Social Con-struction of Technology' (SCOT) and 'Actor-Network Theory' (ANT).

The theory of consumption, developed by Daniel Miller (1987: 178–217) argues that 'Mass goods' ... are an integral part of that process of objectification by which we create ourselves as an industrial society: our identities, our social affiliations, our lived everyday practices' (ibid.: 215). This has been stated more simply as: 'social identity can be interpreted as a function of consumption' (Hearn et al. 1997: 106). Essentially, to the world outside, we are what we consume in terms of products, services and technologies (Green 2001). We fashion our identities in part according to whether or not we go online and what we go online to do. We also change our homes, our schools and our workplaces by engaging in voluntary consumption practices in those spaces. Since the home is the least (externally) regulated of all the places we inhabit, consumption in domestic spaces is particularly indicative of identity. The domestication of technology is consequently of great significance in understanding its consumption.

In suggesting that technology is 'domesticated', the 'Domestication of Technology' framework (Silverstone et al. 1992: 15–31) implies that the technology in question goes through a process of being tamed to serve the needs of those people inhabiting that domestic space. The classic model, originally focusing on domestication in the home, has four elements and proposes that the households concerned have a porous boundary with the wider society. The process of appropriation includes developing awareness, interest and desire for the technology, culminating in the action of procuring it for use in the home. Objectification involves the creation of a physical space, often within the home, for using the technology. In parallel, incorporation describes how the technology is integrated into the rhythms and the time structures of the household, and the individual lives of the people who belong to it. Finally, conversion explains how the people who consume the technology use it to construct and develop their social identity. This may be, for example, by developing good online search skills and becoming not only a better student, but the natural leader in group projects. Alternatively, it may be used to develop an identity as a gamer, or a fan fiction writer. Chapters 8 and 9 address these issues in much greater depth.

SCOT is generally associated with the work of Trevor Pinch and Wiebe Bjiker (Pinch and Bjiker 1984; Bjiker, Hughes and Pinch 1987) and offers both a theory and a methodological approach which sets out a series of steps to follow when analysing the uses of a technology. Whereas I have used the term social elites in my brief introduction to the social shaping of technology, Pinch and Bjiker discuss 'Relevant social groups'. Principally the producers and users of a technology, such relevant social groups can also include, for instance, regulators and journalists. One criticism of the SCOT approach is that there are no objective tests as to what constitutes a relevant social group. Instead, the identification of any relevant social group is itself the outcome of social constructionist processes.

Bruno Latour's work on Actor-Network Theory offers the provocative idea that non-humans are 'actors' in a network alongside humans, and that networks combine different entities (human and non-human) to form a unified whole which can itself be an actor in a network. Thus 'the internet' might include technology, systems, designers, programmers and users; it might also be an actor in the network of people and things that make up a national health system. This theory does not assume that networks, once formed, are stable and tends to focus on how networks evolve and disintegrate. It accepts that networks may be temporary, and it assumes that networks are characterised by conflicts as well as by collaboration. Both human and non-human network actors are implicated in these conflicts. Carefully grounded in qualitative case studies, the early formation of ANT culminated in Latour's 1987 book, *Science in Action: How to follow scientists and engineers through society*. Within the social shaping of technology framework, then, SCOT charts the importance of relevant social groups while ANT sees people and non-human actors forming and reforming critical networks of relevant technological activity.

The discussion so far has used a somewhat inclusive notion of technology. As well as assuming that all new media have a technological dimension, this book treats programs and practices as part of the technological whole: alongside the technological product. The object itself, the systems (e.g. electricity, software) through which that object is made functional as well as the (human) knowledge, skills and expertise through which the technology and its systems are harnessed to create activities and outputs; are all implicated in this inclusive notion of technology. These three levels of understanding technology (Wajcman 1994: 6) together constitute one way to consider the question of whether technology is neutral. At the level of an object – where an object is as inert as a sculpture with no sense of what it was made for or how it is used – technology might be seen as neutral. However, it would be hard to recognise such an inert and mysterious entity as a technology: technologies necessarily have a use. Once that use is known, neutrality becomes impossible as a result of the technology being associated with certain elites, users, outcomes and processes. Further, only certain people have the know-how to use a new technology. When consideration is given to the individuals or groups empowered to use a technology, in which circumstances, in regards to which groups of people, a technology becomes imbued with issues of power, privilege, gender, nation and education: entirely embedded in social and cultural processes.

CASE STUDIES

We now turn from the analytic frameworks used in this book to consider the role of the case studies that it draws upon. These examine many aspects of internet use as a way of addressing and illustrating the relevance of the internet and new media to everyday life. They allow us to explore both the breadth and the depth of current and classic research and this approach is one way to deal with the huge diversity of the global experience of new media. By using research-based case studies, people's uses of the internet are thrown into focus. Readers can examine evidence from their own lives to gauge their experience of the internet compared with other people in terms of points of similarity and points of difference. As the book progresses, students and other readers will learn from the examples given, and analysis offered, how to construct their own case studies around uses of the internet.

Yin identifies three kinds of case study: exploratory, explanatory and descriptive, commenting that the focus should be on 'a contemporary phenomenon with some real life context' (Yin 2003: 1), and that case studies are particularly useful when 'the boundaries between phenomenon and context are not clearly evident' (ibid.: 13). This method of presenting research draws upon a wide variety of materials and evidence: 'documentation, archival records, interviews, direct observation, participant-observation, and physical artifacts' (ibid.: 83); and is particularly indicated when matters of 'how' or 'why' are being addressed (ibid.: 9).

The 'triangulation' of research findings is particularly relevant here (ibid.: 97–99), where two or more research methods are used to illuminate the same issue. Also important is the complementary use of qualitative and quantitative research. A quantitative study may follow on from a qualitative finding in order to investigate how widespread a particular practice or belief may be in terms of a specific population. Similarly, a qualitative investigation, answering 'how' and 'why' questions, is often used to investigate in depth a finding that is uncovered through a quantitative study, which deals with 'how many' and 'how often' issues. For example, we might find via a quantitative survey that people over 75 with children are more likely to be internet users than people over 75 without children. Using in-depth interviews, which are a qualitative tool, we could then discover that a major motivator for over-75 internet use is the desire by seniors to keep in touch with adult children, and that these children are often mentors for their parents in terms of helping them develop internet skills. In a case study of over-75s' internet use, these two data sources, surveys and interviews, would triangulate to support a finding that family communication is an important promoter of internet use among older people.

Among other benefits, triangulation comes into its own when data from a range of different sources or perspectives give similar or overlapping indications as to 'how' or 'why'. Indeed, many detailed case studies try to include a number of different sources to make triangulation possible. In terms of this book, a range of data will be addressed in the case studies, but the case studies themselves are also a research tool to consolidate and integrate available evidence in order to triangulate theories about the role and relevance of the internet across a variety of cultures and contexts.

Yin's view (2003: xiv) is that there are three steps in a case study: defining and designing the study; preparing, collecting and analysing the data for the case study; and drawing conclusions. In the case of this book, considering the internet as an introduction to new media, the case studies have been defined and designed to illustrate the multi-faceted nature of the internet, and give some indication of the range of ways in which organisations, cultures, consumers and prosumers (producer-consumers, e.g. Hartley 2006) use it. A list of case studies is included in the contents section and each case study is also accessible via the index.

A case study approach can be criticised since each study is necessarily short, and to some degree partial, since these 'abbreviated vignettes' are part of a larger consideration of the internet itself (a 'cross-case analysis' in Yin's terms (2003: 148)). However, these studies also mark a starting point upon which further research can be based. All the case studies can be expanded by further research to build additional insights and knowledge. Such further research can be carried out as part of the engagement with the book and will add value to the case studies included here, especially if, paraphrasing Yin, all the evidence gleaned is attended to; alternative interpretations are adequately considered; the finding(s) of greatest significance to the researcher are identified and addressed; and if the elaborated case study builds upon your own area of interest and expertise (Yin 2003: 137).

Reflection: Yourself as a case study

If you were writing a study of your own use of the internet, where would you start?
What motivated you to learn how to use the internet?
Who and what influenced you as you developed your skills and knowledge?

THE STRUCTURE OF THIS BOOK

The book's structure is pivoted around Chapter 4. Chapters 1–3 introduce the internet by examining key concepts and theories, the history of the internet and the important policy dimensions that impact upon its use. Chapters 5–9 start wide and gradually become more specific in focus, beginning with how the internet is customised for specific purposes (Chapter 5); attempts to regulate the internet (Chapter 6); the relevance of the internet to the public sphere (Chapter 7); communities (Chapter 8) and the internet in family life (Chapter 9). Chapter 10, the book's conclusion, ties the different strands together and also looks forward to the future. Within this structure, Chapter 4 uses one example of a policy issue, the 'digital divide', as a bridge to move from the policy focus to research upon how and why people do or do not access the internet. A slightly expanded account of the contents of each chapter follows.

Chapter 1 introduces this volume and explains some key terms which are constant throughout the book. These include the importance of a research-driven approach and the predominant use within the book of the theories of consumption, domestication and the social shaping of technology. Reference to new media implies that we are talking about digital media, and we have introduced some key characteristics of digital information that have helped to promote the dynamic momentum of convergence that underlies many current new media technologies.

Chapter 2 is a gallop through the history of the internet in terms of people and places. It uses a vignette and snapshot approach to a story which could be told as a 35mm feature film, so it is necessarily an overview, with pointers for further research. The chapter outlines central moments and key people in the development of the internet as we know it today, and takes us to the late-2000s, with more recent material included in the case studies.

Chapter 3 provides a technological and policy focus. It examines the policy debates around the internet and introduces and defines major terms in those debates. It explores the implications of the outcomes of such debates through an examination of the policy environments of Australia and China. A glossary of abbreviated and technical terms is also included at the end of the book.

Chapter 4, focusing on the 'digital divide', includes a consideration of tele-communications policy in the US and the UK. Its case studies examine a range of people who may be seen as falling 'on the wrong side' of the digital divide. These include homeless people in Scotland, people in Britain who are the primary carers of (typically) a family member with a disability, and US residents who do not have an internet connection.

Chapter 5 examines attempts to customise the internet and develop aspects of it to serve a specific purpose. These processes are illustrated through considering the development of an Irish Gaelic web, the Francophone (French-speaking) resistance to the dominance of English in the western world's use of the internet, and a vision for the future: 'Web 3.0' and movements towards 'the Semantic Web'.

Chapter 6 considers the challenges of regulating the internet and raises questions of legal jurisdiction over individuals' behaviour online. It does this through two case studies. The first is a look at the pornography industry; the second is an example of cyber-stalking and online defamation. Chapter 7 looks at the contribution of the internet to the development of the public sphere in terms of free speech (as illustrated by *A declaration of the independence of cyberspace*). It also includes case studies on Wikipedia and YouTube.

Chapter 8 addresses the search for community both on- and off- line and points to the many cases in which online activity is a way of bonding more closely with existing friendship networks. It does this through three case studies, two of them gendered. The first concerns young males and online gaming culture; the second looks at young women and fan fiction writing in the Harry Potter fandom. The final case study focuses on ethical issues in researching online communities and centres upon the creation of a community to support recovering heart patients.

Chapter 9 zeroes in on the family. It examines an attempt within a US family to regulate what they see as an 'internet addiction', and looks at families that commit to continuous upgrading of their internet experience. Finally, it considers the role of the internet for some of the poorest families in the world: those that depend upon remittances.

Chapter 10 brings together the various threads running through the book. It examines what we have learned about the internet in terms of the individual, the household and the community; technology, policy, society and culture. This chapter forms the conclusion to the book whilst also acknowledging that the internet continues to develop and the readers of this book are well positioned to analyse how this is happening, and the implications of these changes for themselves and their communities.

READING THIS BOOK

Finally, we can draw attention to how the design of the book enables it to be read in a variety of ways. The book has a semi-modular structure and a detailed index. Through the use of the contents table and index, readers can pinpoint particular case studies and examples, reading the book actively to answer specific questions. Topics and case studies can provide short-cuts to discovering more about aspects of the internet independently of what precedes and follows the section in question. Such an approach requires the reader to mine information by cross referencing the index with the contents, and with the case studies. This strategy requires a more active exploratory reading style than simply turning the pages, but a combination of this active searching and conventional reading practices delivers the most detailed and useful way of working with the book.

Active reading systems vary (see, for example, Kump 1999) but, to summarise, they include suggestions that the reader can scan, survey, mine, check, recall and review the information required. This strategy presupposes that the reader is purposefully looking for something in particular out of their reading experience – this makes it easier to note or dismiss the information presented. The reflection boxes and the questions and exercises for each chapter may provide useful prompts.

   1. Scanning is a skim or flick through technique, to get a feel for a book. Does it have many diagrams, boxed sections, indented quotes, illustrations? Are

the chapters very different in length, and do they share the same kind of structure? Is there a contents section, an index, subheadings, summaries, references, exercises? You might scan a book in the library or bookshop before deciding whether or not to take it.

2. Surveying goes back over the material to mentally map out the terrain of the book. If the scan indicated that the information required was placed in one or more locations, these are found and noted. This is also a chance to look for other relevant areas. The survey clarifies the features of the book and can include, for example, checking the index and browsing the introductions and summaries of chapters that may include the information required to locate the area(s) where it is dealt with.

3. Mining is the in-depth investigation of the required information, read carefully, and with links to other related topics followed through if useful to the matter at hand.

4. Checking is a quick examination of those areas of the book that were not mined, to make sure that no relevant, or contradicting, information has been missed. This deepens the understanding of the context offered by the book for the core information required.

5. Recall includes writing down the information discovered. It occurs best and most effectively with the book shut. Here it is helpful to remember and link the information found with the reasons why it was sought; connecting these together with other relevant ideas and information. Mind maps (Buzan and Buzan 1996) can be a useful strategy for doing this.

6. Review is a final corrective where the reading has been done with a specific output in mind (a research report, or an essay). The book is opened again and the mind map checked. This step ensures that information has been correctly recalled and notes the location at which the information was found: page number, chapter, and details of the book's title, author, publisher and copyright date.

Schema such as this one can help navigate the contents of a book more effectively than passively reading from the first page to the last. These strategies also have useful parallels with the way we follow an information trail on the internet. Indeed, it was the idea of using a hypertext link to locate, access and open a document on another computer anywhere else on the network that led to Tim Berners-Lee creating the WWW (Chapter 2). In doing this, Berners-Lee not only responded to his way of searching for information, which has parallels with the conventional index, he also patterned some aspects of the internet in a manner that encouraged users to follow suit.

Summary

- This chapter places the internet in the context of other new media and reminds us that the experience of the internet will vary considerably depending upon where in the world you live, and upon your social, economic and educational circumstances. It introduces the concepts of digitisation and of convergence as these apply to the internet in particular and to new media more generally.

- By explaining the importance of research for offering a detailed understanding about how we and other people use the internet, the chapter introduces a range of theoretical frameworks which are used in the case studies that follow. In this book these have been generally subsumed under the heading of a social shaping of technology approach. They are: the theory of consumption; the domestication of technology; the social construction of technology and actor-network theory.

- Case studies are critical to the way in which this book examines the internet. The use of case studies allows a rich, deep investigation of specific aspects of the internet. It also means that there are areas not investigated, and important aspects of global history (such as the Cold War) which are examined only in passing, or through the lens of one or more case studies. Any single volume that deals with the internet and its history struggles to reconcile breadth, depth and completeness. This book has chosen to value breadth and depth and indicate the gaps in completeness by drawing its case study examples from a wide variety of countries and contexts. An active reader will finish this book with tools which they can use to develop their own case studies of aspects of the internet that they wish to probe further.

- The chapter ends with an overview of the structure of the book and a suggestion as to an alternative, or supplementary, way in which to read it. In offering a thumbnail sketch of the chapters to follow, this introduction provides a survey of material in the book and an idea of the journey ahead.

Chapter 2 offers a brief history of the internet and introduces some key moments, movements and technologies through which it was developed.

2 HISTORY

INTRODUCTION

New media studies is the exploration and investigation of digital culture. It is an evolving area since the field is characterised by innovation and rapid change. Nowhere is this clearer than in the history of the internet. As one aspect of new media, the internet is important to all aspects of social, political and civic life; and behind every technological story lies a human story. As this book is written, Google remains in the ascendant and has been, for the best part of a decade. Vise recounts a rueful comment by Microsoft founder, Bill Gates: 'Google is still, you know, perfect ...', Gates had sarcastically told the journalists and technology experts 'The bubble is still floating. You should buy their stock at any price. We had a ten year period like that' (Vise 2006: 252). And Gates is right. Both Microsoft and IBM were once where Google are now.

Three of the short stories in this chapter relate to companies which achieved overwhelming high technology market dominance: IBM with hardware, Microsoft with software and Google with search. These companies achieved virtual monopolies to the point where IBM and Microsoft were both prosecuted for using unfair business practices, such as providing services virtually for free that sent competitors broke. Google is next in line (Schonfeld 2009), and as future innovations emerge and dominate so Google will also be knocked off its perch. When we look to the future we need a sense of history to understand what is possible. That sense of history includes knowing about companies that dominated the market, but it also includes an appreciation of key points of transformation. Alongside these companies and the beginnings of the internet itself, this chapter covers the invention of the World Wide Web, the emergence of the open source movement, and considers the notion that 'technology is a masculine culture'. Even so, the chapter provides a partial and incomplete picture of a complex history. Completeness is impossible, and this chapter is a starting point for further investigation and discussion.

The internet is pivotal to the way in which people living in the western ('minority') world relate to one another. Government policy takes it seriously (see Chapter 3), as do stock markets; but it is also important to individuals and families. In domestic contexts we make decisions about whether to get a computer, desktop or laptop and which brand; whether to subscribe to dial-up or broadband; whether to have a wireless or cabled network or a single computer online; and how to decide who uses the computer, and when. Such discussions would have been unthinkable in the middle of the twentieth century, which is when people began to think of building the internet; and they remain equally unthinkable in the majority of the world today. The history of the internet is generally told as a US-based story of individual heroes and heroic places: places where teams of people made things happen.

As a tale, the history of the internet tends to start with a tiny group of (almost all) men who were fascinated by an incredibly expensive, rare, exotic technology: the computer. It was a time when hardware components still needed a soldering iron if functional changes were required; even changes which would later be achieved by software. The drama took place against the background of a life-and-death fear of nuclear war between the United States and the Union of Soviet Socialist Republics (USSR), and the birth of the internet was heralded by two critical international events:

- The launch by the USSR of Sputnik 1 on 4 October 1957. This proved the Soviet Union to be capable of making a satellite that could orbit the earth. The R-7 rocket launched the Sputnik satellite and was a prototype intercontinental ballistic missile designed to be able to carry nuclear warheads. The realisation that the USSR had beaten the US to this critical milestone made the political bureaucracy and the science community (especially specialists in physics and maths) fearful. The Sputnik launch triggered a series of changes in nationally-funded projects and priorities. One of these responses was NASA (the National Aeronautics and Space Administration agency), while another was ARPA – the Advanced Research Projects Agency. Both agencies were established in 1958. ARPA was eventually to project manage the formation of the internet. By the end of 1969 it had masterminded the building of a four-node proof-of-concept network known as ARPANET.

- The Cuban missile crisis between the US, USSR and Cuba. This started on 15 October 1962 and ended thirteen days later on 28 October 1962. Aerial photographs taken by US spy planes indicated that Soviet missile bases were being built in Cuba. The revelations triggered a high-stakes stand-off between the US and the USSR, and President Kennedy reiterated the Mutually Assured Destruction (MAD) philosophy concerning nuclear weapons. Intensive diplomacy involving the United Nations was brought to bear. This period has been described as 'the days the world held its breath'. The possibility of computers across the United States needing to retain 'control and command functions' (discussed below) is one reason given for the development of the internet as a distributed network without a central command hub that could be obliterated in a nuclear attack.

The 'heroic' tale of the internet is used here as a means of defining, describing and discussing various components of internet, its architecture and history.

A BRIEF HISTORY OF THE INTERNET

The internet's twenty-fifth anniversary was celebrated in 1994 at an event billed as the 'history of the future' (Hafner and Lyon 2003: 260). The celebrations were hosted by American consulting company BBN: Bolt Beranek and Newman Inc., which was keen to claim credit for itself as a cornerstone of the internet development project. Although ARPA, the Advanced Research Projects Agency at the US Department of Defense, is generally credited with founding the internet, BBN believe they also deserve to be recognised for their 29 October 1969 achievement in installing the first ARPANET (Advanced Research Projects Agency Network) link between two computers; one at a University of California Los Angeles site (UCLA), and the other at Stanford Research Institute (SRI).

The first 1969 ARPANET connection was not the first time a link had been made between computers, but it was the first time a link had been constructed in a proposed network. It was also the first link to utilise a switched-packet system which allocated bandwidth on the connecting communication cables in response to the requirements of the message to be sent ('dynamic allocation techniques'). Prior to switched-packet systems, the usual way to link computers was through pre-allocating a dedicated channel to the connection. Not only were the links fixed, they were not interconnecting. They could not talk to each other and this made building a network extremely complicated. To become efficient and effective, the network commissioned by ARPA had to solve issues of interconnectivity by connecting each computer to many others, and find a way in which those connections could be simultaneously shared by multiple users.

Computers in those early decades were almost custom-made machines. The way in which an operator programmed a computer, or accessed the information held on it, depended upon the manufacturer and varied with each maker and each model. Indeed, sometimes a computer had to be physically rebuilt to modify its function. Computers were also very expensive. They were a rare commodity, and it was a highly specialised skill to use them.

Although computers had entered popular culture on television with the UNIVAC prediction of the 1952 US Presidential Election results, and through the publicly viewable working computers in the ground-floor display of IBM's Madison Avenue offices, the number of engineers, physicists and mathematicians keen to use them outstripped the supply of available machines. One of the major computing advances pioneered by BBN and MIT prior to the ARPANET link had been the first public demonstration of computer time-sharing in 1962, using a DEC (Digital Equipment Corporation) computer: the PDP-1 (BBN 2008). In those days, people wanting to use a computer had to guess the amount of time that was required and book access in advance. Time-sharing meant that a number of different computer users, working at separate workstations linked to the same magnetic drum memory, were able to access the computer as if they had the machine to themselves. Partly because of time-sharing, computer scientists were often interested in queuing theory and how queues could be made less likely to block efficiency in processing. These studies led to the idea of creating packets of information of a fixed size which could be handled routinely and very quickly by the message processors.

Another problem with the incompatible range of computers in the early 1960s was that every time there was an advance made by one computer, additional work had to be done to duplicate that advance elsewhere, or harness it to the benefit of users of other computers. Hafner and Lyon (2003: 44) comment that software programs 'were one-of-a-kind, like original works of art'. They explain the implication of this as being: 'If the scientists doing graphics at Salt Lake City wanted to use the programs developed by the people at Lincoln Lab, they had to fly to Boston [where Lincoln Lab was based, at MIT]'. There was no easy way to send programs backwards and forwards. Hafner and Lyon comment that if the visiting scientists 'wanted to start a similar project on their own machine, they would need to spend considerable time and money duplicating what they had just seen' (2003: 44). ARPANET was designed to overcome the lack of interconnectivity between different kinds and models of computers, and allow computer users to share resources, software and ideas.

IBM

The technological system underpinning the internet starts with hardware, the actual machinery involved. Historically, the abiding brand in computers has been IBM, also known as 'Big Blue' and the 'PC', the 'personal computer'. IBM was founded in 1924 by Thomas J. Watson (Snr) as the latest incarnation of a company that had started in 1896 as the Tabulating Machine Company. IBM machines in the 1920s were not electronic computers, they were punch card processors: 'elecromechanical contraptions that sorted, counted, and manipulated data stored on rectangular cards punched with holes' (Maney 2003: xxiii). Even so, the processors could handle so much data, so quickly, that the press referred to them as 'thinking machines' and 'electric brains'. They made information processing far more efficient than was possible by clerical work unaided.

The first modern computer 'to use binary, on-and-off switches to make calculations' (Maney 2003: 332) was invented in 1939 by John Atanasoff, an academic at Iowa State University, together with graduate student Clifford Berry. Initially their machine used physical switches to make the changes between on–off, which was much slower than when vacuum tubes were used to perform the same binary functions in an electronic-digital mode. The vacuum system was used by the pioneer machine ENIAC, the Electrical Numerical Integrator and Calculator, but the ENIAC patent of 1947 was eventually overturned in the 1970s as being too much based on Atanasoff and Berry's work. In 1939, as Atanasoff was developing his machine, Watson was being briefed on how vacuum tubes might be applied to IBM's business. Watson was not a technological visionary. He moved slowly, seeing threats as well as value in much speedier calculations. Even so, Watson decided to invest in electronics.

IBM's first electronic calculator was the 603, launched in 1946 at the New York National Business Show. Its successor, the IBM 701, was developed to compete with Remington Rand's UNIVAC. Instead of being a room-sized computer, like UNIVAC, the 701 was a collection of modularised fridge-sized components that could be plugged together into a working assembly. By 1955, IBM had established a lead over Remington Rand in the emerging computer market. At the same time, IBM's near-monopoly in business calculating equipment had become untenable. In January 1956 Watson's son Tom Watson (Jnr) settled a four-year federal antitrust case alleging anti-competitive practices. Following settlement, IBM sold their machines as well as leased them, licensed patents, and allowed competitors to make compatible punch cards.

The focus of IBM on the business market meant that a raft of computers targeted at domestic users could be introduced by other companies, almost into a product vacuum, and this happened increasingly from the 1970s onwards (Haddon 1988). New brands included the 1977 Trinity, Tandy Radio Shack's TRS-80, Apple II and Commodore PET, all of which were 'ready-to-run', a step beyond the self-assembly soldered models aimed at electronics hobbyists.

Domestic computers often relied upon the home television set as a monitor, but were more versatile than the popular games consoles which were marketed in parallel with computers. Models powering the take-up of domestic computing in the UK as well as the US included the Sinclair ZX80 (1980, the first UK computer priced at under £100) and its successors, the ZX81 and the Spectrum; the BBC Acorn; the Atari; the Commodore 64 and the Amstrad. Some of these, the Commodore in particular, were marketed directly to domestic customers in consumer stores, not purely in electronics outlets (Haddon 1988). Operating these computers could be a challenge, however. Murdock, Hartmann and Gray (1992: 149) cite the experience of one woman who 'had seen her husband and son lose interest: "they were going to do great things with it [the computer], and make programmes and use it in all sorts of ways. But then they realised what a long time it was going to be to learn to do this, and a long time putting the programme in. They haven't had the time"'.

Leaving aside business machines, which had been IBM's special focus, the burgeoning development in computers for domestic applications fragmented the market, allowing many other brands to gain critical mass. 'From a high of $68.9 billion in revenue in 1990, [IBM] sales figures began to slip and profits crumpled. IBM lost $2.8 billion in 1991; $5 billion in 1992, and $8.1 billion in 1993' (Maney 2003: 444). CEO Lou Gerstner was able to turn the company around after taking it over in 1993 (Gerstner 2002), but the move to personal computing for a range of non-business applications had already changed the landscape. New media had become domesticated, Tim Berners-Lee had woven the WWW, and the global internet revolution was just beginning.

Larry Roberts, an MIT-trained electrical engineer, was hired by Bob Taylor of ARPA to prove that the concept of an interconnected multi-computer network could work. Roberts was helped by Paul Baran's work at RAND Corporation (Research ANd Development) in Santa Monica, California, which had carried out substantial research for the US Air Force. Baran had been born in Poland in 1928, and his birthplace was under Soviet occupation. He was particularly concerned about security risks to the 'Command and Control functions' of US strategic weapons; indeed, he was concerned about the risks of a few strategic strikes upon any centrally organised communications system. The vulnerability here was that a Soviet missile attack, such as that feared in 1963 during the Cuban missile crisis, could break down the US communications system underpinning strategic weapons deployment. Such a collapse would compromise the US President's capacity to Command a retaliatory attack, or Control (call off) illegitimate and piecemeal responses. RAND had already decided that US long-distance telecommunications systems were vulnerable to a missile strike: Baran's vision was to create a robust computer network that could survive one.

The traditional response to the vulnerabilities of a centralised hub-and-spoke system was to construct a range of sub-hubs, each supporting a number of connections (see Diagram 2.1). This conferred some protection but meant that each sub-hub was vulnerable and a target, while the viability of communication with each spoke entirely depended upon the safety of the hub to which they were connected. Baran's idea was to link all the computers in the system via a distributed network, with each computer operating as a node and having several connections into the network (see Diagram 2.2). In effect, every computer would be linked to three or four other computers. This meant that if one link were broken, there would still be a range of ways to move a communication forward since every computer would be networked to a number of others. 'Even low-cost, unreliable links would suffice as long as there were at least three times the minimum number of them' (Hafner and Lyon 2003: 59). This idea builds 'redundancy' into the network, since there are several times the connections required. It is a very safe approach, but it took several years for Baran to persuade RAND to adopt his vision.

Baran's other idea was that each message should also be fragmented into 'packets'. This idea built on advances in queuing theory developed by Leonard Kleinrock at UCLA. Baran's research was carried out independently of, but parallel to, similar work in the UK by Donald Davies, who coined the term 'switched-packet network'.

The idea of a distributed switched-packet network was that each message would be broken up into small packets of information with a standardised header containing information about destination and the sequence for reassembling the whole massage. The header was communicated along with the data segment transferred in

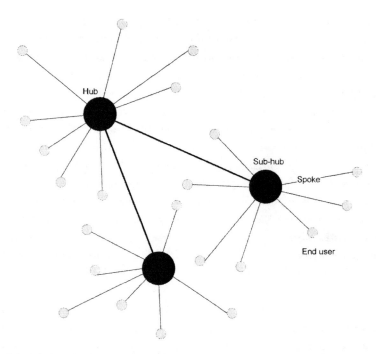

Diagram 2.1: A hub and spoke system with sub-hubs

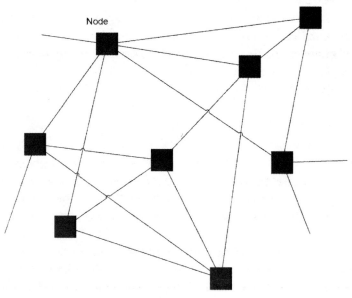

Diagram 2.2: A distributed network

the packet. It was the header which switched the packet along different links in the network to maximise the efficiency of the transit, and each processor in the network would handle this small packet of information very quickly. Each packet would find its own way through the distributed network to the final destination, and would be reassembled there by the receiving message processor.

The transfer of information across the network would be a little like sending a largish library of books from the Pentagon in Washington DC to Los Angeles in California. The library would not travel as an entity: it would be divided into truck-loads, and the number of trucks would be noted. Each truck would be given the destination address and would travel a different route to arrive there, in accordance with the driver's preferences, weather and road congestion, the towns to be passed through, and so forth. Once safely at the new location it would be easy to check that the right number of trucks had arrived. Finally, the cataloguing system applied by the sender library (for example, the Dewey decimal classification system) would mean that all the books could be efficiently reassembled into a functional collection in their new location.

The value of packet switching across a distributed network had several elements. It was more secure, since the message was diffused; and it was also more efficient, since many messages could share the same network at the same time, with each message broken into properly labelled information packets. Further, in the digital domain, unlike the Pentagon library, the sending computer retains the information forwarded (see Chapter 1 for how the properties of information differ from physical goods). After checking all the received information, the receiving message processor would contact the sender machine to confirm all the elements had been received. Without a confirmation, the sending computer keeps re-sending the message until it gets through.

Microsoft

Microsoft, from *Micro* computer *Soft*ware, is the creation of Bill Gates and Paul Allen, who formed Traf-Data while they were still at school. The program helped to control traffic flows in their native Seattle. When Gates was 15, he and Allen sold the company to city administrators for $20,000. The two entrepreneurs formed Microsoft in 1975 to market a simplified version of the BASIC programming language for the Altair 8800, an early self-assembly microcomputer.

If hardware is a vital part of the internet technological system, software is the element which affects most users' relationship with their computer. Microsoft changed the business model by establishing that, for most users, 'usability' was more critical than hardware specifications. Wohl, referring to the early days of the PC comments:

[W]e were asked to design classes for senior executives—each to spend three days learning about the PC and then to take one home. The client ... wanted the executives to learn how to program their PCs. Later we learned that of the several hundred executives who took the course, fewer than 10 ever used their PCs. Programming is not intended to be part of the business user's PC experience. (Wohl 2006: 89)

'Microsoft became one of the most valuable companies in the world by relentlessly focusing on its core mission of a computer on every desk, and Microsoft products running on every computer', says Battelle (2006: 248). In 1981, IBM contracted the recently-incorporated Microsoft to develop an operating system. That IBM application became MS-DOS, the Microsoft Disk Operating System. By 1983 the IBM PC, operating MS-DOS, had become the industry standard and Microsoft persuaded IBM that it should be permitted to licence its MS-DOS operating system to manufacturers of PC clones. Microsoft then went on to supply the operating system at a very low unit cost, allowing it to be bundled with virtually all PC-compatible machines sold. Partly because of the interaction of the PC platform and the MS-DOS operating system, PCs held the majority market share in the personal computer market from 1986 onwards (Reimer 2005).

Microsoft's first word processor, Multi-Tool Word, was launched in 1983. This software developed into Microsoft Word, the core of an integrated suite of office applications, noted for its commitment to 'what you see is what you get' (WYSIWYG). This meant that the printed document strongly resembled the document as it appeared on the screen: a bonus since the program was the first PC-based application to offer easy changes in font and typeface. Additionally, Word made use of a wheel-mouse, a Microsoft innovation, and customers could purchase a mouse-plus-Word package. Initially, these products were not directly marketed to consumers, but were licensed to other parties for sale under their own brands for a range of machines and platforms.

When Microsoft developed the Windows 3.0 operating system for its 1990 introduction, it did so partly as a way of distancing itself from the IBM alliance. Windows 3.0 was to become the default operating system of the early 1990s, bundled with almost all non-IBM PC clones, much cheaper and more versatile than the IBM products, and it also supported a large range of hardware which made it more attractive to domestic users. By the time Windows 95 was launched, the WWW had captured popular attention and the launch was also used to promote MSN, the Microsoft Network, which by 1997 included MSN Hotmail and, from 1999, MSN Messenger. Microsoft's Internet Explorer 1.0 was initially available as add-on software for Windows 95 and both the Windows and Explorer applications were typically bundled with new PC clones. Early browsers, such as Netscape Navigator (see the World Wide Web, below), had been used prior to Internet Explorer and the aggressive marketing of Internet Explorer, especially when bundled with Windows which supplied no uninstaller, led to what have been called the 'browser wars' (Wang, Wu and Lin 2005).

The US Justice Department filed an antitrust suit against Microsoft in 1998, the year Netscape officially closed doors and was bought by AOL (America Online), and the year Google was incorporated. In June 2000, a federal court judge found that the 'bundling of the Internet Explorer browser within the Windows operating system violated antitrust laws. During the trial, Microsoft founder Bill Gates was depicted by prosecutors as a bully and a monopolist' (Vise, 2006: 96). The European Commission, starting with a 1993 complaint from Novell, also sought to make Microsoft build their products to allow compatibility with other companies' software. In 2003 they found Gates guilty of anti-competitive practices.

Reflection: Is market dominance inherently unfair?

Why do you think that regulators in the US and EU thought that Microsoft's near-monopoly was a problem?
Do you think that the bundling of software gives them an unfair advantage?
What are the implications of your views?

To get over the problem that different computers could not communicate with each other, the scientists building the internet decided that the network would operate with a sub-network. According to a scheme proposed by Wes Clark, who had built the TX-2 at MIT's Lincoln Lab, each computer would have its own IMP (Interface Message Processor). IMPs were initially based on the early Honeywell 516 computer. Effectively, the host computer only had to communicate with its own IMP; not the other computers. The IMPs formed a sub-network which was interconnected but autonomous, with each IMP separate from (but linked to) its host computer(s), and with the network under the control of ARPA. IMPs operated like modern day routers. They didn't read the message itself: only the header concerning sender, receiver, packet order and data integrity. This made it simpler for each packet to be pulled into the IMP, processed quickly and sent on its way. Sub-network elements were invisible. This design made the network 'fast, free of congestion and extremely reliable' (Hafner and Lyon 2003: 99).

Roberts published a groundbreaking position paper on ARPANET in 1967. The fact that this project was open for discussion, rather than top secret, meant it could inspire excitement throughout the computer science community. His paper (Roberts 1967) explained that as each packet arrived at the IMP, it would instantly send a copy forward to the next IMP on its way to the destination computer. The forward node switched to by the sending node was eventually 'based on a continuous evaluation within the network of the least-delay paths, considering both line availability and queue lengths' (Roberts 1978). This process was called 'hot potato routing' because no machine held the information for very long. The effect was near-instantaneous. 'Data would zip in and out of the nodes so quickly, and the response time from a human perspective would be so rapid, that it qualified as a real-time [system]' (Hafner and Lyon 2003: 75). The receiving machine would check that no errors had crept into the data and confirm safe receipt, stopping the node from re-sending the data. This error-checking process employed a technique called 'checksum', in which the received data is checked to ensure that it 'sums' to a given amount. The same system is often used with bar codes to confirm accurate scanning.

In 1968 BBN won the contract to build the IMP network from existing documents and ideas, and began publicising the initiative among graduate students around the US. Young computer scientists at the first node, UCLA, were particularly excited. Starting a collaborative consultation process that still thrives in computing circles, Steve Crocker, a UCLA graduate student, initiated the first ever 'Request for Comments': RFC1. Crocker's RFC concerned the host-to-host protocols to get host computers talking to their IMPs, and thus to each other. The first applications written were for 'login' and 'file transfer', and the full host-to-host protocol was named the Network Control Protocol (NCP). The student–faculty–business–military collaboration worked well. By the end of 1969, BBN had added UC Santa Barbara and the University of Utah to the first link between the Sigma-7 host (at UCLA) and a SDS 940 at SRI.

BBN itself was the fifth ARPANET site, connected into the network early 1970, and the first on the East Coast. As well as featuring a robust matrix of interconnections with the redundancy provisions originally envisaged, BBN's design also featured diagnostic elements and allowed for some remote maintenance (Hafner and Lyon 2003: 162). This speeded up further development and improved reliability, also enabling the network engineers to spot when the problem lay with the telecoms connections or signal quality, rather than with the IMPs themselves. The network was adding about one node a month and by the end of 1970 the BBN contract with ARPA had been extended, and the network had moved from an experimental to an operational system. Meanwhile demand for greater access per IMP led to the development of Terminal IMPs (or TIPs) enabling the network to be accessed from terminals, rather than solely via mainframes. This meant that a number of terminals could connect to an individual TIP.

It was decided that 'the first International Conference on Computer Communication [would] be held in Washington in October 1972' (Hafner and Lyon 2003: 176). This was the ideal opportunity for a public demonstration. At that point there were 29 nodes to the network with multiple terminal connections per node and people had begun to refer to the system as the Net, rather than ARPANET. The demonstration was a huge success; for hundreds of participants it brought to life the potential offered by computer networks. 'It was almost like the rail industry disbelieving that airplanes could really fly until they actually saw one in flight', said Kahn (Hafner and Lyon 2003: 185). The same could be said about electronic mail. Although the network had not originally been designed with email in mind, this application was soon generating huge quantities of traffic and made the internet a sociable and lively place to be.

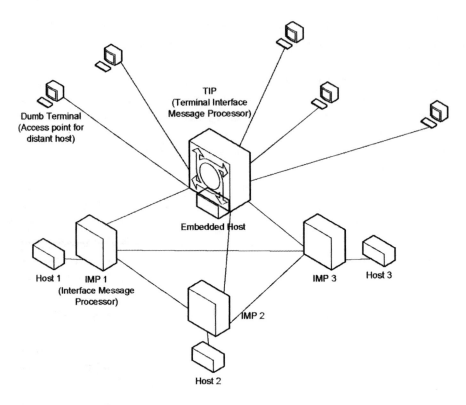

Diagram 2.3: How IMPs and TIPs link to each other, and to hosts

Reflection: The genesis of the internet

The internet started life as a military project.
Have the millions of different uses and users changed its character?

The ARPANET was not the only developing computer network. In particular, Davies's UK network had started at NPL, the National Physical Laboratory, and was growing strongly, as was the French equivalent, Cyclades. Named after the group of 220 Greek islands which interconnect as a functioning whole, Cyclades was the brainchild of French computer scientist Louis Pouzin (1973). It had grown out of Pouzin's early association with MIT's work on CTSS, a Compatible Time-Sharing System, and Pouzin had a strong positive relationship both with European researchers and with his counterparts in the US. Cyclades's operating principle was opposite to

ARPANET's, however, in that host computers were responsible for checking the data transmitted had been safely received. The host computer would keep sending out full copies of the data, broken into packets, until it received information from the destination computer that the message had been safely received and reassembled, with all elements checked and found present. The original ARPANET design had made data integrity a part of the IMP's store-and-forward role, but Cyclades's end-to-end protocol greatly simplified the packet switching operations of the network. The UK and the French systems were interoperable, and by 1976 Cyclades had 20 nodes plus connections to the British and Italian networks.

Meanwhile, work in the Hawaii archipelago had made it clear that networks could operate using a range of communication platforms. Across the US island state, it didn't matter whether nodes were connected by cable, microwave radio, satellite or (later) by fibre optics, digital information could pass between connection points and then use a different platform for the next leg of the journey. The Hawaiian experiments also had implications for connecting the US armed services during manoeuvres: an important priority for ARPA in the Vietnam era. The desire to see all available networks capable of talking to each other prompted the creation in 1972 of the International Network Working Group.

BBN's mathematician Bob Kahn had moved to ARPA, (now DARPA, Defense Advanced Research Projects Agency) in early 1972. Kahn and Vint Cerf, one of the original UCLA grad students who had worked on the protocols for the first ARPANET link, collaborated on the challenge of integrating the diverse international networks. Links between networks had to be transparent to users re-gardless of the communication platform they used, the equipment they ran and the speed at which they operated. ARPANET, Cyclades and NPL had to be able to interconnect. Kahn and Cerf came up with the idea of a 'gateway' which would look like a straightforward host computer to each of the different networks, but which would allow messages to pass between networks. The problem was the different organising principles of the separate networks. Intrigued by Pouzin's success with Cyclades they looked carefully at the French system. By May 1974, having discussed their ideas with British and French collaborators, their paper was ready. They called it 'A protocol for packet network intercommunication' (Cerf and Kahn 1974).

The idea was to adopt several principles from Cyclades and invert the ARPANET model to minimise international differences. The host computer was to keep a copy of the entire message while the packets traversed the system, and would re-send it as necessary. All computers on the internet would wrap their messages inside a protocol which would be recognised at gateways and handled efficiently. This meant that it did not matter if the ways in which messages were communicated differed, providing they were contained in the standard envelope.

Kahn's new system was called the Transmission Control Protocol (TCP), but slowed down message transmission at the point where a message moved from one network to another, because it involved the gateways performing more tasks than solely routing the message. Having moved to DARPA in 1976 to work with Kahn, Cerf continued to work on the problem and it was eventually decided to split the part of the protocol dealing solely with the movement of the packet through the gateway into a smaller program to be called the Internet Protocol (IP). This meant that gateways between the networks were cheaper and easier to build since all that was required of them was to receive a packet from one network and pass it into the next one. All other issues to do with standardising packet sizing, sequencing and confirmation, so that each packet could travel any network, were to be handled by the host using TCP. By 1978 TCP/IP – Transmission Control Protocol/Internet Protocol – had been proposed as the universal standard. It was the 'internet' in 'Internet Protocol' that was to give the internet its name (Hafner and Lyon 2003: 244).

In 1983 every ARPANET computer switched from using the initial Network Control Protocol to the new TCP/IP. Even though some governments and European users favoured a rival protocol (OSI: Open Systems Interconnection), TCP/IP was tried and tested, bundled with a number of popular computers and was eventually adopted universally. By the time that TCP/IP had been totally accepted, ARPANET had been closed down: it was no longer needed as a research project. In 1989, around the twentieth anniversary of the beginnings of ARPANET, all the IMPs and TIPs were decommissioned from the network and the computers were migrated across to bigger, faster networks like NSFNET (the National Science Foundation Network). At this point Tim Berners-Lee was pondering the possible implications of integrating HTML and computer networks and was on the verge of creating the WWW. The internet as we know it today was about to take shape.

The World Wide Web

Tim Berners-Lee, the inventor of the WWW, believed it should be available to everyone. Berners-Lee was British, a physicist by training, and the key elements of his 1990 invention were put in place while he was working at CERN, a European particle physics research centre based near Geneva on the French–Swiss border.

Michael Dertouzos (1999: x), director of the MIT Laboratory for Computer Science where Berners-Lee now works comments: 'Thousands of computer scientists had been staring for two decades at the same two things – hypertext and computer networks. But only Tim conceived of how to put those two elements together'. The

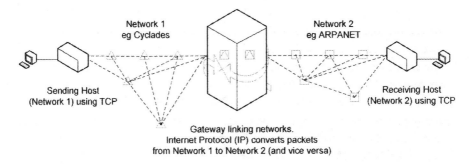

Network 1
eg Cyclades

Network 2
eg ARPANET

Sending Host
(Network 1) using TCP

Receiving Host
(Network 2) using TCP

Gateway linking networks.
Internet Protocol (IP) converts packets
from Network 1 to Network 2 (and vice versa)

Diagram 2.4: A schematic representation of TCP/IP

difference between the pre-1990s version of the internet and one with the web lies in Berners-Lee's realisation of the internet's potential for providing an accessible, connected web of information with pieces scattered on many different computers. This vision depended upon the standardisation of relevant protocols so that travel between networks, servers and documents could be seamless. All networked computers should be able to contribute to the web; and all information should be accessible to any user.

People were interested but apart from Robert Cailliau, a colleague at CERN, generally unconvinced. There had been previous unsuccessful attempts to achieve this kind of idea, and Berners-Lee had yet to prove that it could work. In 1990 Berners-Lee used a NeXT computer, an innovative machine from a new company set up by Steve Jobs co-founder of Apple Computer Inc, to start mapping out the programs and protocols needed to link information held on different machines. The functionality he wanted to achieve was 'a point-and-click browser/editor' (Berners-Lee 1999: 29), so that a user would be able to click on a 'hypertext' link within a web page to move through to a different page with more detailed information. The person creating the hypertext link did not need to have created the page that it clicked through to, nor would it matter where in the world that page was held, so long as it was accessible.

Berners-Lee started by building 'the client', the software shell into which he would fit the other elements of his system. The client program would establish that his computer was requesting information from another machine. The next element on Berners-Lee's 'to do' list was the writing of HTTP: Hypertext Transfer Protocol. HTTP allows the client machine to use Transmission Control Protocol (TCP) to request access to a hypertext document held on a website located on a remote server. It's through HTTP that one machine accesses the material held on another. The server machine then communicates back to the user-client, ideally providing access to the web site or the document requested. (There are a number of HTTP error codes for when things go wrong, including the frustrating '404 Not Found' response.) Berners-Lee's point-and-click browser/editor, running HTTP, would only work if it was possible to identify the location where the information wanted was held. A destination had to be given when requesting access to material, so Berners-Lee developed the URL, or Uniform Resource Locator, in order to identify each destination uniquely. Every site to be included on the web would require its own URL, so that the client machine could use the HTTP language to access information held there. Each URL provides details of exactly where the desired information is stored and typically starts with http://.

Next, Berners-Lee wrote the HyperText Markup Language (HTML) program to make the web pages containing hypertext links. HTML allows a person reading a web page to click through to another document or website. Following the HTML protocols, Berners-Lee wrote the software for the web server, defining which part holds the materials to be accessed by other people using the web. Finally, he set up the first website: http://info. cern.ch. (It still exists.) At this point, Berners-Lee's NeXT machine held the only web browser, and was both the first client and the first server on the web. It was time for the next step. Robert Cailliau 'bought his own NeXT machine and we revelled in being able to put our ideas into practice: communication through shared hypertext' (Berners-Lee 1999: 29). The program-writing period had taken three months, October through to December 1990. It had been a busy time!

There was another problem. Berners-Lee wanted people accessing the web to find something worth reading. He reprogrammed his web browser, which had been designed to work with Macs, PCs, mainframes and all other computers, to access FTP (file transfer protocol) materials as hypertext. FTP resources included many public posts and discussion forums occurring within established networks, often using the decade-old Usenet system. This step meant that people who were accustomed to the complexities of accessing Usenet materials were able to experience the functionality of the web, as well as discovering that much more information was accessible.

Within the first months several servers were set up across Europe by CERN collaborators. A year later, December 1991, the first US server was established at the Stanford Linear Accelerator Center. In November 1992 the worldwide number of servers had risen to 26; by the start of 1993 there were approximately 50 web servers in the world (Berners-Lee 1999: 67), and 'by late 1993 there were over 500 known web servers, and the WWW accounted for 1% of internet traffic, which seemed a lot in those days! (The rest was remote access, e-mail and file transfer.)' (CERN 2008). Between 1991–93 the hits on Berners-Lee's CERN server increased exponentially:

100 hits per day in Summer 1991
1,000 hits per day in Summer 1992
10,000 hits per day in Summer 1993 (Berners-Lee 1999: 75)

In 1993, Marc Andreessen, a student at the National Center for Supercomputing Applications (NCSA, University of Illinois at Urbana-Champaign) and Eric Bina, a faculty member, created the web-browser Mosaic. Andreessen went on to develop Netscape which was publicly launched in 1995, with its share price more than doubling on the first day of trading from US$28 to $71 (Berners-Lee 1999: 106). The browser was much more developed than Berners-Lee's had been. It made the web much more accessible. By the end of 1994, according to Burman, there were about '10,000 servers connected to the Web, and as many as 10 million users worldwide' (2003: 25). Battelle comments that: 'from 1993 to 1996, the web grew from 130 sites to more than 600,000' (2006: 40). The introduction of the web marked the transition from an internet designed predominantly 'for universities, researchers and larger organisations' (Berners-Lee 1999: 80) to one which could be used at home by individuals. The WWW reached across the globe and into people's homes and everyday lives.

As the European Union makes clear in its rulings against Microsoft, it is extremely important that there is enough information about the internet's software and hardware components for entrepreneurs to create compatible new products. No company will purchase a new media player, for example, if that means that all their existing computers need to be changed. The 'barriers to entry' become too great to allow new manufacturers to produce products, and this breaks some of the rules regulating markets since it prevents the development of a vibrant and competitive industry. Both IBM and Microsoft became big by guarding access to, and secrets about, their products. While this is usual business practice, once a company becomes so big that it almost has an monopoly of an important industry, the regulators become involved. We look at government policy and regulation of access to the internet in Chapter 3, and at attempts to regulate the content of the internet in Chapter 6.

There are also mechanisms for the international regulation of the internet. Even though the internet evolves in unpredictable ways, some critics complain that there are continuing reminders of its US beginnings, and too much opportunity for US control of future development. One recent example is the controversy surrounding the Internet Corporation for Assigned Names and Numbers (ICANN). ICANN was created in 1998 as a way of part-democratising decisions that had previously been the direct responsibility of US government authorities, but the organisation is accused of failing to give sufficient weight to non-US perspectives. One example is given by Coopersmith (2006: 13): 'In 2005 the George W. Bush administration upset [ICANN] by refusing, at the last stage of the process, to allow ICANN to issue an ".xxx" domain, rising anew concerns about American dominance'.

The Bush administration intervened because the proposal for an 'Adults only' .xxx generic top-level domain (gTLD) was a highly controversial one for some US citizens and lobby groups. The news that ICANN had approved it triggered 'an "unprecedented" level of protest' within the USA (*Wired* 2005). This protest was strengthened because people believed that the US administration had the power to stop the .xxx plan. *Wired* comments that the US Department of Commerce has 'veto power over ICANN decisions given the US government's role in funding early development of the internet' (*Wired* 2005). Critics of the .xxx proposal argued that, since the Bush administration could stop the creation of an 'adults only' domain, it would show US government support if it went ahead. There were some other international concerns as well as the US domestic protests, but when ICANN effectively reversed its earlier position and did not create the .xxx gTLD this was seen as a sign of US control.

Following the .xxx debates and other controversies around ICANN's cost structure and the pricing of services, there was speculation that the UN might try to take over ICANN. Given US opposition to such a UN takeover, this proposal triggered fears of 'splitting the internet'. Instead, the 2005 World Summit on the Information Society called for an international Internet Governance Forum, IGF, which first met in 2006. The IGF has an advisory mandate, rather than a decision-making one, but is structured to be a strong influence on ICANN's activities. The IGF is further evidence of the importance placed by global users of the internet upon having a voice as part of policy-formation and decision-making processes.

Google

As the internet grew to include unimaginable amounts of information, it needed a way for people to find what they were looking for, even if they did not know where to look. This is the role of the search engine. Early search engines included Alta Vista, Lycos, Yahoo and Excite. Like Google, Yahoo and Excite were started by entrepreneurs linked to Stanford University, in the heart of Silicon Valley.

Battelle (2006: 45) comments that there are three elements to the traditional search engine: the spider (or crawl), the index, and the search software and user interface. The 'spider' is a computer program that hunts in a methodical and deliberate way for specific pieces of information, gathering these together for later use. Any terms and all strings of words noted during the spiders' crawl across the web can become a point of linkage to a whole document. These items are indexed for subsequent use. Powerful search engines scour their indexes of all words in sequence on all pages of the web. There may be thousands of documents found, however, so a search engine also needs to rank results according to importance. If I put 'we want our notion of "relevant" to only include the very best documents' into Google's Advanced Search using the 'this exact wording or phrase' option, for example, I discover the words are from *The Anatomy of a Large-scale Hypertextual Web Search Engine* (Brin and Page, n.d.). Larry Page and Sergey Brin invented Google, and their paper relates to the theory behind the way it works.

Today's search engines link web users with the words of all accessible pages. Apart from password protected and secure content, search engine indexes provide links to the words, phrases and complete contents of all websites. Critical alongside the frequency and accuracy of the spider's crawl, and the power of the engine's index, is the speed of response. Users don't want to wait for long. They also want the best sites for their purposes to come up first. For example, searchers will almost always want to access the original Brin and Page paper, rather than documents that refer to it, like this one. Google's first impact was the way it ranks sites in its search results. It ranks each site according to the number of other sites which are linked through to it. The number of sites linking to a site or document was taken to indicate its relative importance.

Larry Page and Sergey Brin launched their prototype search engine via their uni website in 1996. Both were graduate students in the Computer Science Department at Stanford University. Their fascination for mathematics was clear from the start, and 'Google' is a play on 'Googol', the mathematical term for 1 followed by 100 zeros, which is a Very Large Number. Page's PhD research was into web page linkages. When someone surfs the web they follow the links forward, but Page was intrigued by the fact that there was no way to search backwards. For any specific web page it was impossible to tell how many other pages linked through to it, or which pages these were. In 1995 Page addressed this problem by developing a crawler to find the links to each page. The crawler was called 'BackRub' and its role was to identify every link in the entire web. 'At one point the BackRub crawler consumed nearly half of Stanford's entire network bandwidth ... . And on at least one occasion, the project brought down Stanford's internet connection altogether' (Battelle 2006: 78).

Brin, intrigued by the scale and ambition of the project, got involved. Both inventors soon decided they needed to value links differently. One link might be from a school kid, another from a University and it was important to differentiate between the two. 'Page and Brin's breakthrough was to create an algorithm — dubbed PageRank after Page — that manages to take into account both the number of links into a particular site, and the number of links into each of the linking sites'. The effect of this was that 'more popular sites rose to the top of their annotation list, and less popular sites fell toward the bottom' (Battelle 2006: 75, 76).

The measure of a site's relative importance, alongside its search engine function, became Google's unique selling point. In 1998 Page and Brin incorporated their company as Google Inc and concentrated on their business venture rather than their PhDs. Vise (2006: 214) suggests this date of incorporation was the reason why Microsoft didn't target Google early on. He comments that Microsoft's 1998 antitrust lawsuit, resulting from the bundling of the Internet Explorer browser with Windows 95, 'hung over the company and distracted senior Microsoft management as Google seized the Internet'. Google's growth has continued ever since, and has the dual strategy of fostering new products inside the company while also buying successful start-ups. For example, Google purchased YouTube in 2006. The launch of the G1 Google phone in 2008, with accessible software to allow user-innovation, is a direct response to Apple's iPhone; while Google Desktop Search challenges Microsoft's dominance over the internal operations of individual computers.

In 2004 Google went from being a company owned by Page and Brin and their venture capitalists ('angel investors') into one in which people and companies can hold shares. This was done by an IPO (Initial Public Offering) which took the form of a geek in-joke when the company announced it had $2,718,281,828 worth of shares to sell. It was a seemingly meaningless sum which was instantly recognisable to serious math enthusiasts as the first ten digits of the mathematical number for e, an 'irrational constant' and the base of the natural logarithm. Within a year the company was worth over $70 billion; about a quarter of the market capitalisation of Microsoft (Vise 2006: 251).

Such success comes at a price, however. Google's workplace motto 'Don't be evil' was adopted back in 2001, before it was a listed company, before it grew tenfold, and before it had acquired many of its current business initiatives and international links. The slogan became far more controversial following Google's move into China (see Chapter 3), with organisations such as Amnesty International using it to challenge Google and try to call it to account. There are also concerns over products such as Google Maps' 'Street View': 'Privacy groups are up in arms because Google has not made a firm commitment to obscure faces and number plates', says Moses (2008), referring to the 'highly detailed, panoramic photos' which provide a street-level view of cities the world over, and which have led to a number of people being 'unwittingly snapped in embarrassing or compromising positions'.

Google, listing after the dot.com crash in 2000, is the newest mega-player in internet start-ups. Battelle, comparing Google's experience with Yahoo's, comments that Yahoo was humbled by its experience of the 'tech-wreck' days. It 'had to watch its stock drop from highs of more than $500 to lows of less than $10 ... Google has never known anything but success. The only thing Google has failed to do, so far, is fail' (2006: 236).

Reflection: The ethics of success

Is it possible to be a globally successful company and hold fast to a 'don't be evil' philosophy?

TECHNOLOGY AS A MASCULINE CULTURE

This history of the internet almost entirely features men. This domination by one gender is not accidental. Judy Wajcman's ground-breaking book *Feminism Confronts Technology* (1991) uses both a social shaping of technology framework and feminist analysis. At that time, two things were already clear to feminist researchers. First, computers were a vital part of society, and second, they were used overwhelmingly by white, middle-class, well-educated men living in western economies. Wajcman's argument is that women are excluded from involvement in emerging technologies because of the ways in which society creates meanings around ('constructs') technology and gender; and controls and allows access to new technologies primarily for the benefit of men. She comments (1991: 144) that 'In our culture, to be in charge of the very latest technology signifies being involved in directing the future and so it is a highly valued and mythologised activity'. Essentially, argues Wajcman, high-technology use is a masculine activity.

One reason for this dominance of men in technological fields is that the construct of 'woman' is oppositional to 'man'. Wajcman (1991: 159) sums up the situation as being: 'Technical competence is central to the dominant cultural ideal of masculinity, and its absence is a key feature of stereotyped femininity'. Men hold greater power in society and claim a range of attributes as being particularly male. One such aspect is technological competence. Feminists argue that men see themselves the dominant 'given' in terms of gendered behaviours, while women are positioned as 'other'.

This division between men/technological and women/not-techological is underlined in our social systems in two main ways. First, technological skills that are culturally assigned to women are not defined as technological: for example, cooking, knitting, using domestic machinery: Gray's 'technologies of service' (1992: 169). Second, access to high technology is expensive, restricted and requires training and resources which are disproportionately assigned to men. This is not to say that it's impossible for women to work in high technology or contribute to the develop-ment of hi-tech inventions, but it is to say that women who manage these feats have to overcome a range of challenges and constraints not faced by men in equivalent situations.

In her more recent writings, Wajcman (2004: 14) discusses why repeated at-tempts to recruit women to hi-tech careers in computing, programming, network and systems development, etc., have not been more successful. Suggesting that most strategies to promote such careers construct the problem as being women's 'social-ization, their aspirations and their values', she comments that these approaches do not 'ask the broader questions of whether, and in what way, technoscience and its institutions could be reshaped to accommodate women'. Wajcman notes (2004:. 14–15) that most women who work in fields such as computer sciences are required:

> to exchange major aspects of their gender identity for a masculine version with-out prescribing a similar 'degendering' process for men. For example, the current career structure for a professional scientist dictates long unbroken periods of intensive study and research that simply do not allow for child care and domestic responsibilities. In order to succeed, women have to model themselves on men who have traditionally avoided such commitments.

Some of these issues will be highlighted in future case studies.

Open Source

The growth of the internet has led to the recognition of a new phenomenon: the productivity of skilled people who are willing, indeed eager, to work on a shared task for uncertain benefits. Herz (2002) has called the process of building products using a collaborative dynamic 'Harnessing the hive'; and she refers to the benefits produced as 'harvesting the honey'. Bruns talks about 'large communities of users, who act without an all-controlling, coordinating hierarchy [and] operate along lines which are fluid, flexible, heterarchical, and organized *ad hoc* as required by the ongoing process of development' (Bruns 2008a: 2). In contrast to a pyramid-like hierarchy of power; heterarchy describes a fishnet-like arrangement of workers who are theoretical equals. In heterarchical structures no-one is given a position: roles are developed as a result of ability and commitment.

We will be considering some heterarchical communities later in the book, in terms of gamers and fan fiction writers, as well as through some of the internet's newest and most vibrant brands. These include Flickr and YouTube, Facebook and Twitter. At this point we address the first 'hive' communities to develop, the pro-am (*pro*fessional-level skills acting in an *amateur* capacity) prosumers who continuously improve open source software. The term 'open source' refers to a situation where the source codes for a software program have been made openly available. Open source software is developed for people to share by programmers whose own software development processes include sharing their successes and problems.

Open source is often linked to socially friendly versions of the hacker movement, and to the 'more or less continuous and self-conscious technical culture of enthusiast programmers, people who built and played with software for fun' (Raymond 2001: 3). Talented software developers are frustrated that the source code behind proprietary systems like Microsoft's Windows can't be legitimately accessed. People can't legally share proprietary programs with friends. Further, bugs in licensed software take a long time to fix, compared with what some programmers think should be possible. In 1983 Richard Stallman, a software developer with MIT, formed the Free Software Movement. He resigned from his programming job in 1984 in order to write GNU to be a 'complete Unix-compatible software system which ... can be given away free to everyone who can use it' (GNU n.d.). GNU stands for Gnu's Not Unix, and in 1985 Stallman founded the charitable Free Software Foundation (www.fsf.org), which attracted widespread voluntary involvement from other software developers.

In addition to working on completely copyright-free software, such as GNU, communities of programmers formed around specific software products, or categories of software, such as operating systems. Linux, which has its roots in GNU and in Unix-compatibility, is one well recognised example of such software. Developed from work by Finnish software developer Linus Torvalds in 1991, Linux is the current leader in open source software platforms for operating systems, alongside 'Apache for Web servers ... MySQL for databases, Firefox for browsers and the World Wide Web itself' (Tapscott and Williams 2006: 22). Controversy continues over the magnitude of the debt owed by Linux and other open source software to GNU. Commenting on this controversy in 1999 while a visiting scientist at MIT, Jim Gettys of Compaq said, 'There are lots of people on this bus; I don't hear a clamor of support that GNU is more essential than many of the other components; can't take a wheel away, and end up with a functional vehicle, or an engine, or the seats. I recommend you be happy we have a bus' (Gettys 1999).

Eric Raymond's online analysis of the dynamic nature of the development of Linux is distilled in *The Cathedral and the Bazaar: Musings on Linux and open source by an accidental revolutionary* (Raymond 2001, rev. edn). Streeter (2003: 659), analysing Raymond's metaphors, comments that 'the core trope is to portray Linux-style software development like a bazaar, a real-life competitive marketplace'. A bazaar is a market of separate, yet complementary, traders each displaying their wares and trying to compete with others. This contrasts with 'Microsoft-style software production [which] is portrayed as hierarchical and centralised — and thus inefficient — like a cathedral'.

The open source movement has been credited with influencing Netscape to release the source code for its browser in 1998. Why would companies, talented software developers and gifted amateurs donate their work in this way? Raymond (2001: 53) thinks that part of the answer lies in 'ego satisfaction and reputation among other [peers]'. Essentially, open source operates as a gift economy where developers gain recognition for their talents, and also get personal satisfaction at having solved a problem or written 'beautiful programmes' (2001: 68). 'Voluntary cultures that work this way are not actually uncommon ... e.g. science fiction fandom, which unlike hackerdom has long explicitly recognized 'egoboo' (ego-boosting, or the enhancement of one's reputation among other fans) as the basic drive behind volunteer activity' (Raymond 2001: 53).

Summary

- Chapter 2 examines the history of the internet. It does this in two ways: through a narrative of the development of the first ARPA network and through five snapshots of key technological developments and affiliations related to the internet: hardware, software, the World Wide Web, search and the open source movement.
- The internet has its roots in the Cold War between the western world and the communist bloc, primarily between the USA and the USSR. A response to the Soviet launch of the first Sputnik rocket in 1957 and to the Cuban Missile Crisis of 1962, the internet was originally developed as a US military project. Some people think that the USA administration still controls aspects of the internet.
- The history of the internet's development, and of many web-based brands, mostly involves the work of men. This has led some feminists to question the ways in which power in society is reflected in terms of access and opportunity in relation to high technology.
- In terms of an account of the history of new media, this book is positioned to complement other volumes in the series which deal with mobile phones and communication; interactive gaming; new media, arts and cultural production; and digital broadcasting.

Chapter 3 examines policy, offering a comparative study of internet policy in Australia and China as well as considering the relevance of telecommunications infrastructure and pricing.

3 POLICY

INTRODUCTION

In every country there are policies in place that decide who provides internet services, who can access the internet, and what the costs are. In free market economies, these policies have often been formulated following public debate and with the input of committees and hearings. Unfortunately, many people find policy debates boring or irrelevant. To them, these debates may simply be about politicians arguing that their ideas are better than anyone else's. This perception may mean that everyday citizens are put off getting involved in policy debates.

Policy is a vital element of any technology take-up. It's also a riveting indicator of what aspects of technology the powerful and privileged elites in a society think are important. The sorts of priorities that influence the policy agenda include national interest issues such as defence, and social priorities such as the opportunity for people to benefit from technology to improve their own circumstances and to increase the country's wealth.

As we see below, social policies, including issues of civil liberties and human rights, can also impact in unexpected ways upon a nation's ability to be creative and to innovate, in technology as well as in the arts. Indeed, a landmark book by Richard Florida, *The Rise of the Creative Class* (2002), argues that economic development and creativity is highest in areas that embrace cultural and social diversity in terms of acting inclusively towards people of different backgrounds, sexuality and 'bohemian' lifestyles. Florida (2002: 249) suggests that 'Technology, talent and tolerance [are] the 3 T's of economic development ... Each is a necessary but by itself insufficient condition: To attract creative people, generate innovation and stimulate economic growth, a place must have all three'. The social impacts of policy and regulation also affect creativity and technological development.

When we look at the history of a technological development, as we did in Chapter 2, we might usefully ask ourselves what kind of policy environment supported the developments in question. There is a problem here, however. The retracing of the historical events that lead over time to the emergence of a technological development seems to create a single path from the present back to the past without acknowledging the many points at which things might have turned out differently. Science historian and philosopher Thomas Kuhn wrote an influential book called *The Structure of Scientific Revolutions*, originally published in 1962. In that book Kuhn noted (1996: 1) that public ideas of science are drawn 'mainly from the study of finished scientific achievements' even though, he adds, 'a concept of science drawn from them is no more likely to fit the enterprise that produced them than an image of a national culture drawn from a tourist brochure'. If Kuhn is correct, there is no inevitable path of progress: it just seems that way looking back. In contrast, Florida suggests that certain circumstances can help foster creativity and innovation. We start this chapter by examining the possibility that, with different policy circumstances, computers and the internet might have first been developed in the UK.

Policy issues impact upon levels of creativity and innovation. They also impact the regulatory environment. Legislators in most western countries respond to changing circumstances by tailoring the development of policy and regulation to maximise benefits, as they see them, and to minimise harm. This is fundamentally a reactive model with seven components. It is a continuing process with components overlapping and with the sequence repeating, as outlined in Figure 3.1.

Each component in the cycle constitutes a sequential *focus*, rather than an ordering of absolutely separate/sequential events. Thus the establishment of desirable outcomes and the first steps in formulating policy may well be undertaken alongside information gathering. In democratic countries, regular elections give people the choice of supporting different parties which identify certain issues as important and

1. Identification of problems
2. Information gathering regarding the problems
3. Identification of desired outcomes
4. Formulation of policy to achieve desired outcomes
5. Enactment of policy
6. Implementation of policy and regulatory regime
7. Evaluation of policy outcomes

which leads to:

1. Identification of problems
2. Information gathering regarding the problems
   [etc.]

Figure 3.1: An indicative framework for regulation (based on Green 2002: 135)

then put forward possible policy responses to them. For example, in many countries a growing problem has been recognised with some people not having access to the internet, while a majority of the population does. This situation has been called 'the digital divide' and it is the major focus of Chapter 4. After looking at the history of Alan Turing and how the internet might have been developed outside the US, this chapter goes on to consider aspects of Australian public policy regarding access and infrastructure for internet use and compares the Australian situation with that of China. The aim here is to show how countries differ in the ways they handle matters of policy, and also to demonstrate in context the technical terms generally used in the debate so that readers of this book are better placed to contribute to policy discussions.

The final case study in this chapter, setting the scene for discussions on the digital divide in Chapter 4, concerns telecommunications policy and provision in the UK and the USA, with a brief glimpse at India. International debates provide pointers to issues which drive policy development in other nations. Some terms in this chapter may seem very technical. They are explained as they arise, but they are also included in the Glossary, at the end of the book.

ALAN TURING AND THE AUTOMATIC COMPUTING ENGINE

Could the internet have developed outside the United States? Some people think it almost did. From the 1940s to the 1960s, at the time when modern computers and the internet were in conceptual and physical development in the US, parallel research was going on in Britain. One example of this was Alan Turing's secret work on code-breaking at Bletchley Park during WWII (the background to the movie *Enigma* (Apted 2001)), and his pre-war theoretical work on 'computable numbers' and a 'universal machine' which could be programmed to work with different rules (Turing 1936). These ideas developed into plans for ACE, the Automatic Computing Engine, which ultimately informed the development of a 'Pilot ACE' computer in the UK in 1950. Turing's ideas arguably pre-dated work by John Atanasoff and Clifford Berry who, in 1937, developed the Atanasoff–Berry Computer (ABC). This was subsequently identified as the first computer since it was built and shown to work in 1942. It was not programmable, however, and served primarily to prove that the concept worked.

Although Turing was excited, after the end of the war, to be joining the UK's National Physical Laboratory (NPL), work on the realisation of the ACE ground to a halt, stifled by bureaucracy and secrecy. Even so, Turing's work in the NPL brought him into contact with a young scientist called Donald Davies whose work on computer networks became important from the 1960s onwards. In the 1960s, Davies's exploration of ways to transmit data down existing telephone lines led to the concept of 'packet switching'. The same kind of research, with a different rationale and name, was being carried out in the US by Paul Baran. Baran's work eventually informed plans for the interconnected matrix of ARPANET computers which seeded the internet.

Davies's work doesn't generally get much recognition in accounts of the internet's formation (but see Roberts 1978) because the internet is a US invention and US researchers tell its story. British scientists and researchers have parallel stories about conceptual developments which, due to government policy including the Official Secrets Act, lack of investment and other inhibitors, were destined never to realise their full potential. Polish scientists, meanwhile, argue that British accounts of Alan Turing's secret code-breaking successes at Bletchley Park do not acknowledge adequately the work of the Polish Cipher Bureau, which was first to crack the Enigma code and which passed on vital details to France and Britain in the weeks leading up to WWII.

How might the US environment in which the internet was eventually developed differ from that in the UK at that time? Some people trace the foundation of the Advanced Research Projects Agency, which funded the development of the internet, to President Eisenhower's appreciation of scientists and his keenness, as a man with a military past, to separate some American scientific enquiry from direct military control. Eisenhower's lead science adviser, James R. Killian, had been recruited from his role as President of the Massachusetts Institute of Technology, and he attributed past US science achievements to 'the free wheeling methods of outstanding academic scientists and engineers who had always been free of any inhibiting regimentation and organization' (Killian, cited in Hafner and Lyon 2003: 18). Effectively, this creative approach is in line with Florida's ideas for promoting innovation.

Circumstances in which the ARPA scientists were to work, collaboratively involving graduate students and networking with business and academia, were very different from the situation in the UK. In the post-WWII years, for example, not only was Alan Turing's theoretical work on the ACE computer classified as secret but, even so, he was forbidden from incorporating his Bletchley Park experience since this would have revealed his secret code-breaking background. He had to pretend to have a purely theory-based knowledge. These regulations added to the frustrations of several years' delay in building the ACE prototype. Impatient, Turing left NPL in 1947, moving to the University of Manchester in 1948 to work there with Professor Max Newman, who had been Turing's mentor during his studies in Cambridge and had worked alongside him at Bletchley Park. While NPL had floundered, Manchester had built the 'world's first stored-program digital electronic computer – the Manchester "Baby"' (Anderson 2007: 76). At Manchester, Turing used the computer to investigate artificial intelligence. From there he went on to explore pattern formation in nature, especially as this relates to Fibonacci numbers, where each number in the sequence is the sum of the preceding two.

The secrecy regime was not the only issue Turing had with the UK authorities. Turing was homosexual, which was illegal in England and Wales until 1967. In 1952 he was charged and convicted of 'gross indecency', the legal term used at that time. His security clearances were removed, meaning that he was no longer able to collaborate with a number of other scientists in his areas of interest, since they remained bound by the Secrets Acts and Turing was now classified as a risky contact. This happened even though Turing had been meticulous about keeping secrets secret, and even though he was so open about his homosexuality that there was no real prospect of his being a blackmail victim. As an example of his absolute discretion in terms of national secrets, the judge knew nothing about his Bletchley Park role in breaking the Enigma code, which could have made him a national hero. That remained hidden until the 1970s. Turing preferred to accept 'treatment' for his homosexuality rather than a prison sentence. In 1952 such 'treatment' involved an experimental oestrogen regime, which worked as a chemical castration, psychoanalysis and probation. Turing had been a world-class marathon runner, but his lean body grew fat and he developed breasts and became depressed. He committed suicide by eating a cyanide-laced apple in 1954 (Hodges 1992; Holt 2006).

Turing's prosecution, his problems with the UK's secrecy regime and his loss of security clearances are not raised here as part of a debate about whether the UK or US was more or less homophobic. The USA was also homophobic at that time. The reason for including this section is to illustrate how regulation and policy debates may seem unexciting but can have far-reaching and sometimes unexpected implications. It is intriguing to speculate, for example, whether different UK policies on security, secrecy and technology in the late 1940s and early 1950s might have led to different outcomes in the development of computers and networks. In particular, had Turing's time at NPL been productive, and his work with Donald Davies prolonged, and if that collaboration had become the magnet for the post-Bletchley code-breakers, instead of Manchester, then events might have progressed differently.

By the late 1950s to 1960s, the US situation had become entirely unlike that of Turing's post-war UK. Killian's views about collaborative work, the involvement of 'learner' graduate students in the ARPANET project, and the harnessing of outside opinions and ideas through strategies such as Steve Crocker's open 'Request for Comments' all provided a creative milieu which, for their day, aligns well with Florida's 3 Ts: technology, talent and tolerance.

Reflection: Links between social diversity and creativity

Why might Florida and others argue that societies that embrace diversity and difference support creativity and innovation?

Why might creativity and innovation be important in today's society?

REGULATING THE INTERNET: A COMPARATIVE EXPLORATION OF AUSTRALIAN AND CHINESE APPROACHES

Can you imagine the effect upon the internet if every website needed approval before it could be posted, or if voluntary moderators required a specialist qualification – say in technology, ethics and psychology – before they were allowed to host a chat room or discussion board? Perhaps under-18s should get their parents' consent before going online, or have the internet equivalent of a driver's licence before surfing the web? These kinds of restrictive regulations could have meant that the internet's explosive growth might never have happened. They would characterise a highly restrictive regulatory regime. The fact that our experience of the internet is very different is a reflection of the policy approach our governments take, and the regulations that put those policies into operation.

This is not to say that the internet is unregulated in the western world. Prosecutions of people who use the internet to access child pornography, for example, demonstrate that web traffic is closely monitored by police where law enforcement authorities have reason to suspect that a crime is being committed, such as in creating and circulating images of child sexual abuse. Even so, control of the internet in most free market societies is via 'light touch' regulation. Light touch regulation means that an activity is essentially self-regulated by the industry concerned, usually under the scrutiny of a statutory body. A statutory body is an organisation set up by the government to regulate an industry. It usually includes industry and consumer representatives on its committees. The process of self-regulation means the system requires no intervention beyond the consumer, the service provider and the industry body unless the consumer is unhappy with the response or the manner in which the response is handled, in which case they would typically contact an elected representative, or write to the papers or take legal action against the regulator.

In Australia, for example, light touch regulation means that industry bodies such as the Internet Industry Association are required by the regulatory (statutory) body, the Australian Communications and Media Authority (ACMA), to draw up codes of practice and minimum standards. All Internet Service Providers (ISP) within Australia, and other industry players with Australian connections, must subscribe to these codes and standards as part of their industry membership. If the public have complaints, they pursue these through the relevant industry association. Once regulators have approved the codes of practice and the dispute resolution processes, the statutory body only become involved when industry self-regulation fails and consumers have a legitimate complaint that has not been addressed, relating to content that falls within Australia's jurisdiction (ACMA 2008).

Often, where a complaint might be legitimate, the offending material is produced by a non-Australian company and held on a server outside Australian control: in that case Australian law allows the server to be blocked, making it inaccessible to Australian ISPs. Policy-makers are out of the communication loop unless an issue is identified that is not covered by the codes of conduct and which the industry body is unwilling to address voluntarily. Critics of this model of regulation argue that it is unfair that individual citizens are required to battle industry associations since the relative difference in power and resources is so great.

In western nations, the emphasis is generally on encouraging people to use the internet, not stopping them from doing so. This is not the situation in many countries with different legal and regulatory systems. Highly regulated countries include Myanmar (Burma), Saudi Arabia, Iran, North Korea, China and Vietnam, where citizens have been arrested and imprisoned for a range of activities which would be permitted in western countries, including claiming the right to free speech to criticise their government.

Although Australian law allows the blocking of some content from outside Australia, the system of waiting for a complaint before action is taken means that some forbidden content is occasionally seen by some people. The 2007 Australian election saw the Labor Party pledge to introduce an ISP-level internet filter to eliminate 'illegal' content from the internet. However, the definition of illegal was unspecified and later seemed to constitute the kinds of materials which ACMA has blocked in the past or required to be taken down. Since very few of these cases are prosecuted, their illegality has not been tested in court. A conservative regulatory filtering regime effectively removes many freedoms of choice from internet users, as well as slowing internet speeds across the board as a result of a universal ISP-level filtering process. The Labor Party was elected and this proposal caused huge controversy as its implications became clearer. Further, it led to downward pressure on Australia's 'digital freedom rating' on the Harvard–Toronto–Cambridge–Oxford universities-sponsored 'Open Net Initiative'. This international watchdog had already labelled Australia as having 'some of the most restrictive internet policies of any Western nation' (ONI Australia n.d.) on the basis of the blocked internet sites.

Even if Australia is a poor performer in terms of its citizens' digital rights and internet access, it clearly remains in a dramatically different category from the 'heavy' regulation practised by repressive regimes such as China. In the early years of the internet, the Chinese government feared that giving people access to more information would change the political dynamics and risk destabilising the status quo. The authorities tried to anticipate the problems that might arise in order to develop policy and regulations to prevent these problems occurring. 'The first form of internet regulation adopted [in China] was slightly less than total black out of the new technology', says Endeshaw (2004: 41). Strategies for ensuring compliance took the form of laying criminal charges against people for undesirable internet activity, and the use of prosecutions and court cases as means of intimidation.

In terms of the policy cycle (see earlier this chapter), identification of the problem is followed by gathering information to evaluate the extent and seriousness of the issue to be addressed. For many countries, the internet has raised issues in terms of children's use of the technology and their willingness to interact with strangers. The fear is that their openness makes children vulnerable to cyber predators who seek out minors on the net in order to 'befriend' them.

Pornography is a totally separate issue from cyber predators, but it also causes huge concern in some countries. In highly regulated nations like China, Saudi Arabia and Iran, it is illegal to access pornography; no matter whether it is delivered on the internet, or in terms of printed materials or films. In all countries it is illegal to access images of child abuse (although the definition of 'child' may vary in different countries with the legal age of consent). In many countries there are concerns over whether it is 'too easy' for children, including young people under 18 but over the age of consent, to access pornography, on purpose or by mistake – including content which would be legal if it were accessed by an adult. These totally separate concerns about cyber predators, images of child sexual abuse and illegal, inappropriate or accidental access to adult-only content all drive regulatory activity in the East and the West.

Other concerns which have different impacts in different countries include on-line gambling, hate sites with racist or misogynist content, violent images, terror sites and perceived over-use ('internet addiction') of the technology to the point where it interferes with everyday life. Once concerns have been identified and agreed, policy is developed to respond to these concerns and, hopefully, eliminate them. Strategies used to gain support for the enactment of new policy include: public hearings; government committees (some of which may not be public);

harnessing and responding to pressure group advocacy; soliciting comments from individuals, community groups and from elected parliamentary representatives; monitoring debates in the media and other discussion in the public sphere (chat sites, for example, and online petitions). Once new policy is agreed and passed, its effects are evaluated to ensure that it achieves the ends desired and that there are no unintended outcomes.

In China, there were two major problems that arose from the decision to all but ban the internet. Some people continued to use it privately, even though that was against government policy. Also, given the benefits western countries appeared to be gaining, Chinese lawmakers gradually decided that the nation might be putting itself at a competitive disadvantage by forbidding young people to use the internet. 'China soon discovered that its attempt to choke the Internet for fear of what it might do to the political establishment clashed with its commitment to open up the economy to foreign investment and trade' (Endeshaw 2004: 41). China changed it policy. The decision to open up the internet had already seen 137 million Chinese users by the end of 2006 (ONI China n.d.). The number of Chinese citizens online overtook the number of US users in 2008, and China now has more internet users than any other nation on earth.

In terms of embracing the internet in the national interest, China's approach has some similarities with that adopted by Singapore where there is a 'hierarchy of 'heavier vs. weaker' regulation in different social spheres ... Heavier regulation in the home, rather than business, differs from the expected priority of many western countries' (Green 2002: 124). Singapore's reversal of the usual western order, where western regulators see the home as private and thus less regulated than business, reflects Singapore's export priorities and 'recognises that a competitive business strategy might involve businesses operating under a more lenient regulatory regime'. Ang and Yeo (1998: 17) comment that 'Information for the home is considered less critical so censorship of such information is deemed to have less deleterious effect'.

China's policies balance a desire for stability within its national boundaries with an ambition to be hugely influential on the international stage. Leonard (2008a: 113) comments that: 'some Chinese hope to build a global order in China's image'. Given this, there is considerable Chinese eagerness to understand what is currently making the global order tick, and the internet is an important element of that dynamic. Indeed, Ernkvist and Ström (2008: 98) talking specifically about Chinese control of online gaming, in a manner that can be extrapolated to general online activity, argue that there are three critically relevant 'aspects of state policy: (a) information control, (b) technonationalism, and (c) social fears/pragmatic nationalism'. Technonationalism here indicates a Chinese view that since the internet was developed in the US, it needs to be 're-imagined' in a way to make it more culturally Chinese and to ensure that most profits stay in China. Control of digital information, in combination with the promotion of a nationalist ethic, drives much of what China tries to do in its internet policy-making.

Dubbed 'the Great Firewall of China' (e.g. *Guardian* 2008), the nationwide firewall controlling Chinese citizens' access to the internet prevents people reading sensitive information, including: sites run by international human rights groups; accounts of past events such as the Tiananmen Square clampdown; and dissident calls for autonomy and independence for Taiwan and Tibet. Information about Falun Gong has also been banned. Kalathil and Boas (2003: 26) comment that the authorities have adopted 'two main strategies: filtering material and the promotion of self-censorship through regulation, policing and punitive action'. Service providers are required to enforce restrictions: ISPs are forbidden to allow politically sensitive information to be circulated via the internet. They also have to report on internet users. 'Website administrators are required to hire censors, known as 'cleaning ladies' or 'big mammas', to screen for and quickly remove offensive material from bulletin boards and chat rooms' (Kalathil and Boas 2003: 26). Such regulations apply equally to western internet corporations operating in China, such as Google and Yahoo, as to domestic companies. Although innovative libertarians in the East and the West continually develop technology and practices for countering Chinese state censorship, it remains a risky activity for a Chinese citizen to venture beyond the Great Firewall.

Although many countries, like China, have decided that they want more of the next generation of workers to be digitally literate, the appropriate way to achieve that outcome will differ from country to country. In Australia, for example, the Labor government formulated a policy to achieve an 'education revolution' with every schoolchild in years 9–12 (ages 14–17) having access to their own school-based computer: 'computer technology is no longer just a key subject to learn, it is now the key to learning in almost every subject' (ALP 2007). Most western countries aim to educate young people to enter a digital workforce. In China, the desired outcome includes greater business efficiency. Wong and Nah (2001, cited by Endeshaw 2004: 51), comment upon 'China's desire to meet the challenges of the information economy by embracing rapid development of high-technology sectors'. Further, Chinese factories make many components used by other nations to embrace a high-technology future.

Policy formation and policy enactment processes also depend upon the political system in place. The multi-party democratic debate practised in many western nations is entirely at odds with the authoritarian role of the Chinese Communist Party, yet commentators are increasingly indicating that there is considerable debate within the Party. This debate is supported by the outputs of think-tanks and of higher education institutions. A wide variety of opinion seems acceptable, provided the debates do not include a range of taboo topics, from Falun Gong to Tibet, Taiwan and Tiananmen. The 'dignity and interests of the state' (Endeshaw 2004: 46) are also jealously protected.

In 2005, the US internet company Yahoo earned international condemnation by providing Chinese authorities with the details of one of their account holders, Shi Tao, who was subsequently imprisoned by China for ten years for 'illegally providing state secrets to foreign entities' (Amnesty International n.d.). The 'state secrets' concerned a Chinese Communist Party memo to the domestic press warning them against fuelling unrest by reporting social disturbances around the anniversary of the Tiananmen Square massacre. Shi Tao had sent this directive to contacts in the US, who then publicised it. Subsequently, Yahoo, Google, Cisco systems and Microsoft were summoned to explain their companies' policies in China to a US Congress subcommittee. The internet firms argued that 'enabling a censored Internet to grow in China is better than having no Internet at all, or one controlled by Chinese search companies' (Gunther 2006). Opposing this view, Congressman Lantos, a Californian Democrat, commented afterwards: 'These companies tell us that they will change China. But China has already changed them' (Gunther 2006). However, in January 2010 a cyber attack on google.cn prompted it to stop censoring Chinese search results (Zetter 2010).

Although political repression compromises the potential of the internet to liberalise Chinese society, there are signs that a discussion is becoming more open while avoiding the most sensitive topics. Mark Leonard, executive director of the European Council on Foreign Relations and author of *What Does China Think?* (2008b), describes his astonishment during a 2003 trip to discover that the Beijing-based Chinese Academy of Social Sciences (CASS) had '50 research centres covering 260 disciplines with 4,000 full-time researchers' (Leonard 2008a). This contrasted favourably with the sum of all Europe's think-tank researchers, which Leonard estimated as being in the 'low thousands', while his view was that even the US 'think-tank heaven … cannot have more than 10,000'. Further, the 4,000 researchers in CASS are a very small fraction of the Chinese think-tank workforce. There are another 'dozen or so' think-tanks in Beijing alone, along with others elsewhere (Leonard 2008a). In some respects these think-tanks are having a significant impact:

> Inside China – in party forums, but also in universities, in semi-independent think-tanks, in journals and on the internet – debate rages about the direction of the country: 'new left' economists argue with the 'new right' about inequality; political theorists argue about the relative importance of elections and the rule of law; and in the foreign policy realm, China's neocons argue with liberal internationalists about grand strategy. (Leonard 2008a)

It may be a surprise that policy in China is so fiercely discussed. However, disagreement is not readily recognisable as such since certain key issues are not talked about at all; political dissenters face persecution; and the kinds of freedom granted involve the Chinese arguing 'about whether it is the intellectuals that influence decision-makers, or whether groups of decision-makers use pet intellectuals as informal mouthpieces to advance their own views' (Leonard 2008a). In any case, for some aspects of Chinese social and political life, a range of possible options is considered and debated in a more open fashion than might be the case with an adversarial 'Westminster' model of debate. This openness might be attributable to that gap between 'a top-down process' in which the Chinese Communist Party has almost absolute power to implement policy as it sees fit, and the equally important 'negotiated process whereby power is highly fragmented and influenced by a number of actors at different levels with conflicting interests' (Ernkvist and Ström 2008: 102). Think-tank members are some of these influential actors and are experimenting, among other things, with new forms of Chinese-style democratic engagement.

Reflection: How much do we know about China?

China is a huge country with a complex history.

It seems to have the capacity to change very quickly, and appears to welcome a range of social and civic experiments.

If we're surprised to learn about the number of paid 'thinkers' in China, as Leonard seems to be, what does that say about our everyday understandings of the nation?

Surprisingly for many free market nations, some Chinese political scientists and think-tank researchers believe they have identified a range of problems with western democracy. These include: falling election turn-outs; disillusionment with elected leaders; declining political party and trade union membership; and a rise in 'opinion poll' politics. Some Chinese commentators go so far as to suggest that western-style politics is essentially a failing model.

Fang Ning, a CASS political scientist, argues that western democracy is like 'a fixed-menu restaurant where customers can select the identity of their chef, but have no say in what dishes he chooses to cook for them. Chinese democracy, on the other hand, always involves the same chef—the Communist Party—but the policy dishes which are served up can be chosen "à la carte"' (cited in Leonard 2008a). The small town of Zeguo in Wenling City offers one example of this à la carte approach. Zeguo decides its budget priorities on the basis of a model of democratic consultation based upon an original Athenian democratic process called 'deliberative polling' (Fishkin et al. 2006). The results of this experiment with inclusive, community-based democratic engagement have caused significant interest in China and the West, and have clear possibilities for online models of democracy.

As is the case with Zeguo, China's à la carte ideas are often trialled in specific circumstances, such as the Shenzhen economic zone on the border of Hong Kong, with the possibility that they will then be allowed to spread organically. Similarly, a Chinese free-market economy was trialled for many years alongside a state-controlled market 'until by the early 1990s, almost all products were sold at market prices' (Leonard 2008a). In China, the identification of desired policy outcomes and the formulation of policy to achieve these are extensively canvassed by researchers, advisers and intellectuals behind closed doors. To a limited extent such debate is also in public, on the internet, since the internet is generally freer than the print and broadcast media.

In both the West and in China, the enactment of policy and its implementation leads to further consideration of the costs and benefits of these as the implications of policy development and change become visible and are evaluated. In both systems countries seek information about the ways in which other nations have handled the problem. For some Australians, facing the prospect of ISP-level filtering, their government has borrowed too much from the Chinese approach to regulation.

TELECOMMUNICATIONS POLICIES AND TECHNOLOGIES

Good internet services depend upon good telecommunications and, like the internet itself, telecom services are affected by government policies. In most western nations since the 1980s, for example, telecoms monopolies have been broken up. These massive changes in telecom policies were grounded in the 1970s realisations that free-market economies were increasingly information-based (Bell 1973). This meant that the wealth of developed economies was becoming more dependent upon information processing and information-linked employment, including education and management as well as computing and media, than it was upon manufacturing, resources and agriculture. As society became more dependent upon advanced communications to access, manipulate, and add value to important information, so more pressure was placed upon the telecommunications infrastructure. Privatisation of telecoms was one way in which to raise money to power investment. In many majority-world ('developing') nations, by contrast, telecommunications remains a monopoly that is regulated by the government, rather than by market forces.

In richer countries across most of the twentieth century, the 'twisted copper' telephone lines and manually-operated telephone exchanges served the everyday needs of communications across distance. With STD, the Subscriber Trunk Dialling system in the UK, known as DDD or Direct Distance Dialling in the US, a level of automation became possible. These technologies made manual phone exchanges obsolete and enabled the Plain Old Telephone Service (POTS) to support an increased range of applications and automatically connect long-distance calls. With the accelerating transition from analogue communications to digital communications, other ways of moving information could be explored.

Digital information is communicated via an unambiguous sequence of numbers which form a data stream. This differs from analogue information, which resembles the original source characteristics and is continuously variable. Thus an analogue telephone call occurs as a result of the sound waves of the voice causing vibrations which are translated into electronic signals that pass along the wires. In a digital call, the voice is digitised into discrete units of information, with the fidelity of transmission and reproduction depending upon the precision of the samples of information coded. Thus an analogue-to-digital converter that samples 4,000 times per second would have higher fidelity to the original that one which samples 2,000 times per second (Brain n.d.). A communications channel that can handle the digitised version of a voice can also handle other digitised data; for example from a television channel, or email, or any other digital application.

The fact that channels which carried digital voice data could also carry digital information from computers and other communication technologies meant that one channel could handle inputs and outputs from many different information sources, communicated for a variety of different reasons. The technologies themselves began to share important characteristics too, since a key function of digital technologies was the conversion of information into, or from, digital form. Developments in computing and communications in the 1980s and 1990s gave rise to buzzwords such as 'convergence' to note the ways in which more and more information was becoming digitised, and thus amenable to being handled in consistent ways using different technological platforms across a spectrum of uses. Essentially, convergence marked the blurring of borders between:

- Information Technologies (IT: digital processing)
- Telecommunications (information carriage), and
- Media (content – the meaning of what was communicated)

Consistency of handling allowed the packaging and repackaging of digital information within computer networks, and the seamless transfer of data between them, even though the networks could vary in significant ways. Further, the deregulation of telecommunications meant also the de facto deregulation of many elements of media and IT.

Reflection: The Problem of Jargon

Is there a problem with having to learn jargon to take part in policy debates? What happens if policy discussions are restricted to the well-educated?

Increasingly, a differentiation arose between the products, services and data available to consumers with broadband access compared to those with dial-up. Dial-up access depends upon older and cheaper technology, generally using external modems connecting the computer to the analogue phone lines that service an internet connection via access to the consumer's Internet Service Provider (ISP). Modems are *mo*dulator-*dem*odulators, translating the digital information from the computer to an analogue form suited to transfer over the POTS. When received at the ISP in analogue form, the ISP modem translates the information back into digital data for ISP network connection to the internet. Dial-up connections are much slower than broadband and are unsuited to data-intensive services such as streaming video, online game play and the sophisticated graphics and animated sequences of high-specification websites. When they can afford to do so, keen internet users tend to migrate from dial-up services to broadband with the effect that relative US rates in late 2008 indicate the 57 per cent of US citizens have broadband in the home compared with 9 per cent on dial-up (Horrigan 2008a). This is one reason why broadband take-up rates are often used as an indicator of relative economic development. Definitions for broadband services tend to focus on minimum data speeds. Though these have increased over the years and can be delivered at a low level through the POTS, high-speed broadband requires more of the data journey to be via fibre-optics than by cable. Such systems are often referred to by acronyms such as FTTN (fibre to the node). This is not as fast as, but is much cheaper to install than, FTTH (fibre to the home) or FTTP (fibre to the premises). FTTN is cheaper because nodes are junctions which then radiate out to service a range of individual homes and offices, like telephone exchanges do. FTTH takes the high-speed connection that one step further by using fibre to connect the home to the node, as well as the node to the backbone.

At a minimum, broadband requires DSL (digital subscriber line) connection technology interfacing between the domestic computer user and the POTS infrastructure. Alternatively, it may use the bandwidth of cable television services already provided to the home: even though these 'cable' services may actually use satellite delivery (OECD 2008). In contrast to a broadband service, the computer signal travelling via a dial-up service monopolises the phone connection, meaning that the POTS provides either a computer link or a voice link at any one time. With broadband, the DSL operates at high frequency in contrast to the low frequency voice service, so that voice and broadband internet can be accommodated simultaneously.

The West's emerging digital economies in the 1980s and 1990s placed immense pressure upon existing communications networks. The carrying capacity of the older infrastructure elements, such as twisted copper wires, was revolutionised by innovative products. For example, in the 1990s 'Asymmetrical Digital Subscriber Line technology (ADSL) made it technologically feasible and economically attractive to deliver as many as four video channels and high-speed digital data services in addition to voice to the home over the twisted copper networks of the telephone companies' (Estabrooks 1995: 127). ADSL is a particular kind of DSL service that allows greater speeds (hence the 'asymmetricality') of download than of upload, a feature that was initially a problem with peer-to-peer file-sharing software until the development of Bram Cohen's open source BitTorrent protocols in 2001 (Thompson 2005). Whereas twisted copper wires had historically been used to service homes, telecoms providers increasingly laid more coaxial cables. These had previously been used for transmitting large numbers of simultaneous voice calls, for example, in submarine cables with regular booster points, and their use more generally had allowed a dramatic increase in the volume of information carried. Like twisted copper wires, coaxial cabling required physically laying or stringing between points to be serviced, and rewiring cities became expensive. Even so, Estabrooks (1995: 88) comments that: 'the broadband nature of coaxial cable made it feasible to carry as many as one hundred [cable television] channels'.

Although coaxial cable and twisted copper were well-established technologies by the second half of the twentieth century, there were still many places without a cabled infrastructure. Further, the breakthrough which allowed the innovation of new products such as bank Automatic Teller Machines (ATMs), was based on a revolutionary new technology, fibre-optics. These fibres used light signals to transfer data and could 'transmit data at higher transmission rates and with lower losses and [were able] to do this at lower error rates' (Mercury 1992). During the 1990s, older cabling technologies were replaced or augmented by fibre-optics, which also needs laying; and by satellite and microwave communications which work on point-to-point transmission and reception without the requirement for hard-wire connections between those points. Broadband services can be delivered using one of a range of technological platforms (OECD 2008), or a combination of these.

New technologies and technology upgrades magnified the capital cost of providing ICT infrastructure and services, while making them generally more accessible, and growing the market. Governments came under increasing pressure from business and consumers to allocate more money to state-owned monopoly telecoms providers, or to privatise these so that the corporations could raise capital from private investors. These pressures came to a head in the 1980s in the Reagan (US)/Thatcher (UK) era, and over the final decades of that century most of the world's developed nations deregulated. This meant that the telecoms institutions were freer to set their own priorities and invest in the areas which they felt were experiencing greatest demand and offering greatest market growth. Sometimes this kind of deregulation is called liberalisation, since the organisation is freed up to respond to market forces in a 'laissez-faire', or 'let's see what happens', environment. Essentially, liberalisation and deregulation are free market policy approaches that let the ICT market players themselves determine the costs and offerings of telecom products and services, rather than a government deciding these.

For a market to operate freely, which is to say 'unfettered' rather than 'at no cost', there has to be competition. Where competition is lacking, the single business providing the service is called a 'monopoly'. Since it does not have to compete for customers, a monopoly can set its own prices according to how it sees its market. Sometimes a company might decide that it's more profitable to deliver very expensive services to a small number of people or organisations at a high profit per client, rather than delivering more affordable services to a larger number of people at a smaller margin per consumer. This view would have clear implications for economic growth.

In practice, most national telecom companies were heavily regulated by their governments and required to service large segments of their populations. Some people argued that governments were not the best organisations to run telecom companies, and that an organisation with a monopoly becomes inefficient and complacent and is generally unwilling to invest in new technologies. These various considerations meant that many of the traditional monopoly telecom carriers were broken up from the early 1980s onwards with different sections of the fragmented monopoly competing against each other. This was the case with the UK 1981 break-up of the British postal, telegraph and telephone (PTT) service, to form The Post Office and British Telecom (BT). In the US, the break-up of the American Telephone and Telegraph Company (AT&T) had started with an antitrust case in 1974 and resulted in the 1982 division of 'Ma Bell' into seven regional 'Baby Bells'. Additionally, or alternatively, strong telecommunication companies from other jurisdictions were allowed to enter many national marketplaces.

The advantage of monopoly telecom carriers, and one reason why they lasted for so long, was that such companies argued they needed the whole market in order to provide universal service. An early motto of Ma Bell, for example, was 'One policy, one system, universal service' (Nohe 1995). The notion of universal service implied that anyone who wanted a service, in this case a phone connection, could have one for a reasonable charge. Affordability was guaranteed by using general revenue to cross-subsidise hugely expensive connections: for example, remote households in rugged country. For many, this cross-subsidisation was an essential element of the carrier being able to deliver services according to their 'community service obligation' (CSO). As communications became more important in everyday life, so the implications of an individual being excluded from the telephone service (or later, the online environment) became greater. Some telecom carriers described this need to reach everyone as the 'universal service obligation' (USO). While governments generally accepted that it was in the 'public interest' to promote widespread phone access, they began to listen to businesses who argued otherwise.

Corporate customers complained that international competitiveness was threatened because their national telecoms supplier was over-charging for services in order to cross-subsidise unprofitable consumers. They maintained that monopoly providers fail to introduce new technologies quickly and at an appropriate price because they do not need to worry about competition. Further, they suggested that greater public good was achieved where business was as competitive and as profitable as possible, thus employing more people and building local wealth. They argued it was in the public interest to break the telecommunications monopoly.

The breaking-up of monopolies delivered consumer choice at the expense of the principle of universal service. The telephone service was no longer provided as a right to citizens under the USO, instead people qualified for a phone service by having the income and status to be a customer. Desirable customers found themselves benefiting from price competition and service improvements, while less-desirable consumers found themselves waiting a long time for connections and repairs which were only delivered at significant cost. In many countries the government tried to balance the disadvantage experienced by the dismemberment of the monopolies by placing conditions upon telecoms companies as part of the licensing regime. Such conditions might include the maintenance of public phone boxes, or provision of mobile phone services to small communities and isolated homesteaders. Generally this approach has led to conflict, since the telecom carrier argues that such regulation imposes an unfair constraint on trade and profitability. Another approach has been for the government to subsidise the services it wants to see delivered, so that high costs of access are transferred to the tax payer, rather than the individual telecoms customer.

After liberalisation via the break-up of the monopolies, and the introduction of competition, many telecommunications carriers found themselves privatised. This was the case for BT in the UK, and Telstra in Australia, and meant that the capital value of the corporation was divided into shares, which were offered for sale on the local stock exchange. The money raised usually went to the government to offset the public investment in the company which was now owned by shareholders. Privatisation also allowed the previous monopolies to raise money on the stock markets to fund modernisation of their infrastructure and to invest in new products to expand their markets. It is through the mechanism of privatisation that the capital value of publicly-owned (sometime, 'nationalised') companies becomes the property of private individuals and financial institutions, and can be traded on the local stock exchange.

More recently, many of the old telecommunications systems have had their markets decimated by mobile technologies. As Passerini et al. comment, 'Wireless connectivity is driving innovation and business opportunities' (2007: 25). These developments can be dated back to the 1970s and the development of first generation mobile (1G) technology. Second generation (2G) mobile phones allowed voice and SMS/texting services, but change accelerated at the start of the twenty-first century with the introduction of third generation (3G) capability, which marked the introduction of mobile access to the internet and coincided with huge increases in revenues, contributing to the US$1.2 trillion spent on telecommunications in the US alone in 2004 (Passerini et al. 2007: 25). In the early years, 3G capability was promoted as linking subscribers with the 3Gs, 'girls, games and gambling', recognising that these are key drivers for many masculine early-adopters (Layden 2003; Skeldon 2002: 18). Futurists foresee both a 4G (fourth generation) and a 5G before 2020 (Ohmori et al. 2000: 134). With each generation, data speeds increase, as do functionality and choice of features; with dynamic competition between service providers and handset manufacturers prompting spiralling adoption rates.

The discussion of telecommunications deregulation (or 're-regulation' if you see the market as taking over the regulatory driving seat, instead of the government (Palmer 1994)) is an example of changes in policy leading to changes in regulatory practices. Governments attempted to balance different claims upon the public interest, universal service or vibrant industry growth, for instance, with a commitment to protect those most likely to lose from the shift in the market structure. For the majority of people living in western countries, deregulation of telecommunications prompted a dramatic fall in the cost of services and an improvement in service delivery. It also set the stage for the burgeoning growth of the domestic internet. For people in poorer countries, however, it is the continuing growth of affordable mobile communications that has offered the greatest potential to revolutionise lives in terms of digital access, as we discuss briefly now.

In many countries that were too poor to lay traditional telecommunications cables, mobile phones offer a way to bypass piecemeal technological incrementalism. This means that instead of a technical infrastructure being gradually replaced with newer technology, the country has leap-frogged into advanced technology. Passerini et al. argue that the 'rapid adoption of 3G technologies, [means China is] skipping entire generations of technologies and products' (2007: 27). Elsewhere, in the continent of Africa and in India, the adoption of mobile phones has been compared with the invention of the telegraph in terms of its virtually unregulated but revolutionary impact on markets (Carey 1988).

Between 2005 and 2007, the number of mobile subscribers in India doubled, resulting in over 150 million mobile customers compared with fewer than 50 million landline subscribers (Abraham 2008: 9). Abraham's research showed that even 2G capability has the potential to transform markets in poor economies. Specifically, in Kerala, fishermen use their phones at sea to find out demand and price for catch, and then fish 'to order' according to market requirements. This strategy conserves time, fuel and fishing stocks. Out on the water, the fishermen would also 'send out alerts on the mobile phones if large shoals were found ... reducing the number of fishermen who had to spend time idling on shore' (Abraham 2008: 12).

India would be a classic example of a nation which is currently experiencing a digital divide, both internally and between India and the richer countries of the West. At the time of Abraham's research, only 3.5 per cent of India's population was online, and this networked population was judged to constitute 3.7 per cent of global internet users (*Computer Economics* 2007). This compared with 69.9 per cent of the US population, and 62.3 per cent of the UK's (*Computer Economics* 2007). Even though technology users in marginal and emerging markets are comparatively disadvantaged, in India and elsewhere they are resourceful and imaginative, making ICTs work to their benefit. For those unable to take advantage of the ICT environment, however, new media greatly magnify the likelihood and the severity of the digital divide. It is to the social implications of the digital divide that we next turn.

Summary

- Chapter 3 looks at policy as this affects the internet. It started by considering differences in the regulation of social and political life that directly influenced the development of computer technologies in the UK and the US, particularly as these impacted upon one key British scientist, Alan Turing.
- The second case study compared and contrasted aspects of internet regulation in Australia with analogous circumstances in China. Some commentators suggest there is more debate in China than has generally been accepted, as well as some interesting experiments in local democracy. Such comments specifically exclude certain categories of dissent which attract draconian sentences. In contrast, although Australia is generally thought of as a liberal democracy, it seeks to control the internet more than most western nations.
- Finally, we looked at telecommunications policy, which has particular relevance in terms of delivering the internet to consumers. Although the focus of the case study is mainly upon telecom policy in the US and the UK, it also includes an aside about the exciting potential of mobile phones to transform communications in the world's poorer countries.

Chapter 4 focuses on how a 'digital divide' separates rich countries from the poor, and rich consumers from people who cannot afford to consume.

4 THE DIGITAL DIVIDE

INTRODUCTION

Are you a digital native? Do you feel at home on the internet? The chances are that people born since the 1980s, reading this book, have grown up alongside the World Wide Web. Even so, they're only likely to be totally familiar with the internet if they were born into one of the globe's wealthiest countries. According to *Internet World Statistics* (2009), the top 20 countries in terms of their contributions to the overall global population of internet users, account for 76.8 per cent of the world's internet users. This figure demonstrates that some 175 countries between them have the remaining 23.2 per cent of the world's internet users. Interestingly, the total number of countries is a disputed figure. The UN has a total of 192 members, but excludes Taiwan, Kosovo, the Vatican City and some nations like Scotland and Greenland which are not fully independent (UN 2009; Rosenberg 2009).

The table below also uses data from *Internet World Statistics* (2009), but the information has been reworked to put the countries and various non-autonomous regions in order of the percentage of their citizens who have internet access. The top five countries (plus a semi-autonomous region), and the bottom five for which records are available, are shown in Table 4.1.

A country-by-country account of ranked internet participation indicates that internet sources are largely concentrated in a small number of countries, while the huge majority of nations share ever decreasing tiny fractions of overall internet population. Such a distribution graph is described as featuring a 'long tail'. While Table 4.1 indicates that Iceland, Norway and the Netherlands are the three nations with the highest percentage of their population online, with well over 4 in 5 people participating in the internet, a global graph of population participation would have countries like East Timor and Myanmar, both at 0.1 per cent of their population using the internet, close to the end of the tail. Participation here considers 'not just what we possess but also what we can do, the extent to which we can fulfil various social roles – which in itself refers back to older discussions of social rights and citizenship' (Somerville, 1998 cited in Haddon 2000: 389).

Table 4.1: Internet users as a percentage of a territory's population, for 30 June 2009

	Population	*Population using internet*	*% Internet users*
Falkland Islands*	2,483	2,400	96.7
Iceland	306,694	273,930	89.3
Norway	4,660,539	3,993,400	85.7
Netherlands	16,715,999	14,272,700	85.4
Denmark	5,500,510	4,629,600	84.2
Andorra	83,888	70,040	83.5
216 nations and territories [...]			
Ethiopia	85,237,338	360,000	0.4
Sierra Leone	5,132,138	13,900	0.3
Bangladesh	156,050,883	500,000	0.3
Myanmar (Burma)	48,137,741	40,000	0.1
Timor-Leste (East Timor)	1,131,612	1,500	0.1
[...] 15 entities with '0' users			

Source: Data derived from *Internet World Statistics*, 30 June 2009, Miniwatts Marketing Group, http://www.internetworldstats.com/top20.htm. This list includes territories as well as autonomous countries, with [*] indicating a semi-autonomous territory.

Further down this ranked list of percentage of the population participating in the internet, the UK has 79.8 per cent internet users, New Zealand 79.7 per cent, Australia 79.6 per cent, South Korea 77.3 per cent, USA 74.1 per cent and Canada 71.7 per cent. Clearly, percentages differ from raw numbers. If we change the focus from the percentage of each country's citizens that have access to the internet (Table 4.1) and instead look at the top countries in terms of the percentage they contribute to the global community of internet users (see Table 4.2), we see that the lists of countries are very different. The top five countries in each list have no overlaps, implying that it may be easier for smaller, richer countries to reach maximum internet take-up, but very hard for such countries to make much impact on the global population of internet users now that really populous nations such as China and India are coming online. The inclusion of China and India in the top five countries, in terms of their contribution to the overall population of internet users in the world, demonstrates dramatic differences in the percentage of citizens able to access the internet in a national context.

Taken together, these figures indicate interesting information about internet access and opportunity for different people living in different countries. In 2008,

Table 4.2: Percentage of world's internet users, and percentage of a country's citizens using the internet, for the top five countries in terms of numbers of users, 30 June 2009

	% of the world's internet users	% of nation's population using the internet
China	20.3	25.3
United States of America	13.6	74.1
Japan	5.6	74.0
India	4.9	7.0
Brazil	4.0	34.0

Source: Data derived from *Internet World Statistics*, 30 June 2009, Miniwatts Marketing Group, http://www.internetworldstats.com/top20.htm.

China overtook the USA in terms of the number of its citizens online, but only one in four Chinese citizens can access the internet compared with three in four US citizens. India has the world's fourth largest internet-user population, but nine in ten of its citizens (93 per cent) are not online. Such figures address all access to the internet and do not differentiate between dial-up services, which historically have dominated the market, and the more expensive broadband services. Nowadays, broadband take-up is often used as an indicator of economic prosperity and, as Table 4.3 illustrates, the number of broadband subscribers around the world is still comparatively small.

Leaving aside differences between broadband and dial-up, half way through 2009, only 24.7 per cent of the world's population was online (*Internet World Statistics* 2009). Three in every four people globally did not have access to the internet. These global citizens fall on the wrong side of what is termed 'the digital divide': a somewhat problematic term used to indicate that there are 'haves' and 'have-nots' in the digital world. The divide itself marks the parameters which prevent the have-nots from joining the haves. This pattern of relative privilege not only re-inscribes the gender and power debates from the early years of the internet in the West, but offers grounds for an argument of cultural imperialism (see Chapter 5) whereby western patterns of training, behaviour and infrastructure are required to keep, for example, a bank headquarters running, with 24-hour electricity supplies, western-trained technical support, high-level security protocols, and communication and network infrastructures that construct this locale as a node for a network developed and controlled elsewhere. This is the issue identified by Wambi (cited in Bissio 1990), 'Technology is like a genetic material. It is encoded with the characteristics of the society which developed it, and it tries to reproduce that society'.

Table 4.3: Top ten countries worldwide for fixed broadband subscribers, first quarter 2009

Country	Subscribers (million)
China	88
USA	83.9
Japan	30.6
Germany	24.1
France	18
UK	17.6
South Korea	15.7
Italy	12.4
Brazil	10
Canada	9.5

Source: Data from *BuddeComm* (2009), http://www.budde.com.au, Key *Broadband Statistics*, Table 20, Based on Point Topic research for the Broadband Forum, 2009. Broadband defined as a minimum speed of 144Kb/s. 'Fixed broadband' includes wireless but is differentiated from mobile services. Figures based on self-reporting by carriers.

Many nations suffer from being on the wrong side of the digital divide and this lack of e-knowledge and infrastructure has implications for their economy and their society. This is one reason why, as we saw in Chapter 3, China dropped its policy of repressing internet use and moved instead to a policy of heavy regulation of the internet. China, like most growing nations in the world, wants a digitally literate population.

As well as being an issue internationally, the digital divide is discussed here in terms of national policies as a challenge for governments within individual nation-states. Even in wealthy countries like the USA and Japan, the poorest 20–25 per cent of the population is likely to have no internet access (Horrigan 2008b). Although western governments generally want their citizens to participatwe in high technology communications such as internet use, their markets tend to be deregulated. The provision of ICT goods and services is usually left to the big companies that make up the market, moderated on occasion by specific government regulations concerning access and coverage. This approach to providing information and communication goods and services means that the internet becomes available to those elements of national populations which are cost-effective to service, and who can afford to pay. ICTs are not always available to those who need them most. Unlike countries, companies construct their client-base as being 'customers' rather than 'citizens'.

Within the generality of the digital divide there are groups of people who are specifically disadvantaged as a result of changed circumstances (Warschauer 2003; Rooksby and Weckert 2007). These are people who have had access to the internet in the past, but whose circumstances have changed, sometimes termed the *nouveau information poor* (Green 2002: 103–9). Examples would include the newly un-employed, the recently retired on low incomes, some people who are divorced or separated, some migrants, those who relocate to remote or lesser-serviced areas and young people moving away from affluent homes (ibid.: 106–7). These internet-experienced individuals suffer at several levels: not only do they lack access to the internet, they have a clear idea of how the internet could transform their circumstances and, finally, they appreciate how the internet could provide a resource through which other people can offer support while they negotiate the realities of their reduced circumstances.

Every country includes a number of citizens, like those indicated above, who do not make desirable customers for big ICT companies. Such citizens live in inaccessible places, such as in remote locations with residency numbers too small for a viable service, or they are too poor, elderly or socially and culturally marginalised. Typically, these less serviceable citizens are unable to access the internet except through publicly funded resources such as libraries. In this chapter we examine some aspects of the digital divide as it affects people living in wealthy countries. We address digital inequality in the US and we also examine the circumstances of people who care for others in the UK. First, however, we consider the ways that some homeless people in Scotland use ICTs.

Reflection: Being a digital native

Do you think of yourself as a digital native?
How does your communication life compare with that of your parents when they were your age?

ICTS IN THE LIVES OF SCOTTISH HOMELESS

In the context of three in four of the world's population being excluded from the internet, the role of the mobile phone as the globe's major technology for connection and agency should come as no surprise. When we examine the lives of the poorest people in the rich minority world, the same pattern is evident. Claire Bure (2005) carried out a small research project investigating ICT use among homeless people in the Scottish cities of Edinburgh and Glasgow, focussing specifically on mobile phones and internet access. internet access was via a drop-in space for homeless people; mobile phones were usually hand-me-downs, although they may have been gifts from case workers, or sometimes they were stolen.

Homelessness is a name given to a variety of complex circumstances which is generally associated with a heightened level of chaos, vulnerability and unpre-dictability. In some cases the people in Bure's research were living in dormitory or borrowed accommodation; in others they were literally on the streets. In these situations, the mobile offered the valuable benefit of being portable and thus 'at hand', which could be especially important in an emergency or when the user felt under threat. The accessibility of mobiles contrasted with the comparatively fixed locale of internet access points. Phones also had the advantage of tradeability: they could operate as a currency in extremes and be swapped for drugs and alcohol.

Although phones are valuable, there was a preference among the homeless for older, bulkier mobiles. This was because new, smaller phones are highly vulnerable to being stolen by other people, requiring vigilance. For these and other reasons, homeless people moving towards stability in their lives were more likely than the newly homeless to hold onto a phone and experience it as a stable advantage. Consequently the mobile phone also operates as an indicator of status and reliability. The usefulness of the mobile phone as a technology to enable responsiveness is underlined by the description of the lifestyle of homelessness as 'typically transient, nomadic and built on the immediate gratification of needs, so activities tend to be planned on a minute-to-minute basis' (Bure 2005: 117).

The purpose of Bure's study was to investigate whether digital inclusion, which is to say access to ICTs such as mobile phones and the internet, built social inclusion. As Haddon points out (2000: 389), 'The very words "social inclusion" have the merit that they capture this sense of avoiding social isolation'. Social inclusion is the term used for being integrated within wider social and support networks including family, pre-homeless friends, and social and welfare services; participation in everyday public activities such as shopping and conversation; and 'individual agency', experiencing one's life as autonomous and self-directed. The internet was useful in these circumstances, especially for those looking for accommodation, but was comparatively hard to access. It offered homeless people the advantage of an email address as a 'fixed point of contact' in a world where there are few fixed points and not many reliable contact opportunities. On the other hand, the chaos of homelessness introduces its own challenges reminiscent of the illiteracy issues of the majority world: 'one young homeless respondent who admitted that he was a regular drug user claimed that he had five or six (he couldn't be sure) email addresses because he could rarely remember his passwords' (Bure 2005: 119).

A mobile was seen as offering its user a greater opportunity for 'sociality and privacy [and it] allows that person to be contacted, irrespective of their physical location', thus improving the chances of the homeless person being able to maintain their family networks (Bure 2005: 122). Even so, challenges such as battery life, pay-as-you-go costs, and lack of credit mean that access to a mobile is not a cure-all for the communications problems of homeless people, even if other problems of a chaotic lifestyle could be addressed. Bure concludes that 'it is clear that ICTs alone do not provide an avenue to social inclusion, although they may have positive implications' (2005: 125). Nonetheless, access to mobile phones confers more, and more flexible, advantages for those in highly chaotic circumstances compared with the requirements of fixed access to the internet. Typically, this requires hardware, software, a weatherproof location and reliable power. If global use of the internet is going to reach the world's poorer citizens, the chances are it will be via cheap, simple mobile phone access (see Chapter 9, Remittances).

Even with equitable access to telecommunications, which means different things as new technologies become available, a number of issues remain, both for the Scottish homeless and for poorer people across the globe. These challenges include the financial, technological, skills and support resources required to be a competent internet user. In many countries gender is an issue too, with men more able than women to gain access to the resources required to use the internet. Such issues are as much a matter of social policy as technology policy. This kind of digital divide tends to be addressed in two ways. First, people are trained to be internet users through the education system and through work. Second, informal public access and training is encouraged through community locales such as libraries, and through private enterprise such as internet cafés. Additionally, those who feel excluded from online access may lobby and protest so that further avenues for engagement are opened up.

Reflection: Opening up access to the internet

Why do you think that the world's poor are more likely to have access to a mobile phone than access to the internet?

Do you think poor people will eventually be able to access the internet through their phones? Why?

DIGITAL INEQUALITY IN THE US

In the time gap between the election of President Obama, and his inauguration, a number of community associations, pressure groups and research agencies joined industry and business lobbyists in suggesting the kinds of priorities that they would like to see the incoming administration adopt. The Pew internet and American Life Project was one such research organisation. Its website describes its mission as: 'Pew internet explores the impact of the internet on children, families, communities, the work place, schools, health care and civic/political life. The project is non-partisan and takes no position on policy issues' (Pew 2009). Reports date back to 2000 and provide an invaluable source of processed and analysed information, as well as making raw data available to researchers.

In December 2008, identifying a range of ways in which the US had fallen behind leading countries in terms of digital infrastructure, including its fifteenth place in world rankings in terms of broadband take-up, John Horrigan, the Pew internet Project's Associate Director for Research, suggested that there have been four phases of internet development to date. These are:

- A 1990s vision of one-to-many communication (such as telemedicine, or online teaching, where an expert is able to communicate to an audience);
- A late 1990s engagement with many-to-many online communities;
- An early to mid-2000s adoption of 'many-to-many societal conversations', such as blogging; and
- Mid- to late 2000s 'many-to-many collaboration' (Horrigan 2008b).

Whereas it might be hard to see an earlier/later temporal boundary between 'societal conversations' and 'collaboration', with Twitter (2006) more of a conversation than anything else, and Wikipedia (2001) highly collaborative; it is certainly the case that post-2000 has seen a burgeoning of collaborative and Web 2.0 (see Chapter 5) innovations including such phenomena as MySpace (2003), Second Life (2003), Flickr (2004) and YouTube (2005).

Alongside his discussion of the ways in which the internet is being developed by prosumers to address their needs and interests, Horrigan also notes (2008b) that one in four US residents, 25 per cent of the population, do not have online access. He identifies a range of reasons for differences in internet adoption and advancement, including technological availability (some areas do not have the technological infrastructure to offer broadband), and inclination (some people do not see digital connectivity as relevant to them). Horrigan's other two reasons – the costs of internet access, and the difficulties of using the technologies required – are core characteristics of the digital divide. His suggestion is that the Obama program might 'decide that government can play a catalytic role in nudging industry to improve usability and relevance through procurement', thus building the incentive for citizens to be active online and reducing the barriers to doing so (Horrigan 2008b).

In a more detailed study of the respondents who did not use the internet, this population was identified as being older than the norm, with a median age of 61, and 'more than twice as likely as users to live in low-income households' (Horrigan 2008a). Whereas 18 per cent of non-user respondents had used the internet at some time, only 10 per cent of the people who weren't connected indicated that they would want to have an internet service. Further questioning about reasons for a lack of interest indicated that about 9 per cent of people who aren't connected see the internet as too difficult or frustrating, and 7 per cent see it as too expensive. Given that people who are classified as older and poorer are less likely to have the internet connected, how consistent is the data on the opposite population – the people most likely to use broadband in the home?

Totally consistently, over each year from 2005 to 2008, male respondents were always more likely than females to say they had broadband internet. In 2008, males reported 58 per cent adoption, females 53 per cent. Broadband was also consistently associated with age across four age groups. Thus, in the 2008 broadband take-up figures by age, 18–29 year olds had 70 per cent take-up; 30–49 had 69 per cent; 50–64 year-olds 50 per cent, and 65 plus year olds had 19 per cent. The younger the respondent, the more likely they were to have a broadband service. Education was also consistently linked to broadband adoption. This may be partly because advanced education increasingly requires students to master internet skills and use internet equipment to gain a qualification. The higher the level of education, the more likely the respondent is to have adopted broadband. The differential here is 79 per cent for those who have undertaken post-college qualifications, compared with 28 per cent adoption for respondents who did not complete high school.

Income is also consistently linked with home broadband connections. Of upper income US respondents, defined as earning more than $100,000 per year, 85 per cent had a broadband connection compared with 25 per cent of those earning less than $20,000. High income was more likely than age, education or gender to be associated with the take-up of domestic broadband. This 85 per cent adoption rate indicates the potential upper level for interest in the internet if all other factors (such as time, money, support and motivation) could be successfully addressed. The older-age, lower-income profile for non-users suggests that more support to develop relevant skills, and reduced costs combined with content that motivates online engagement, could be key to increasing take-up.

As might be expected, dial-up users are also typically older and less well-off than their broadband cousins, to a slightly less dramatic level than is the case with non-users. Of the dial-up sector, 29 per cent have less than $30,000 per year income compared with 14 per cent of broadband users; the ratio for age is 43 per cent of dial-up respondents were over 50, compared with 29 per cent of broadband users. The Pew internet Project research cited here (Horrigan 2008a) tells us 'how many' and 'what percentage'. The fact that aspects of the research are repeated over time also makes it quasi-longitudinal; we can begin to see how things may have been changing. However, as a quantitative study, this research does not tell us 'why' US broadband users and internet non-users find themselves in their current circumstances.

People prioritise the things that are important to them. For example, as we see in the Chapter 8 case study on HeartNet, older people are more likely to choose email to communicate digitally rather than via blogs, discussion boards or instant messaging. Email is one internet application that is comparatively well-serviced by dial-up. It is possible that this group of dial-up users, being older and more likely to be female, are mainly internet users because they are email users. Until and unless they see a reason to want to do something else with the internet, such as watching television programmes that they have missed, which broadcasters are increasingly making possible (BBC iPlayer 2008), they are content with the level of service provided by dial-up.

Marketers and sales professionals often discuss the pattern of technology take-up in terms of *Diffusion of Innovations* theory (Rogers 2003 [1962]). This theory has also been applied to high-tech situations, with a Silicon Valley-based study published in 1984 (Rogers and Larsen). It was Rogers who first suggested that new ideas and technologies are diffused through a society by a process whereby different proportions of that population, with different characteristics, decide to use the new product or process and then influence others to do so. He identifies five categories of adopter: innovators (first 2.5 per cent); early adopters (next 13.5 per cent); early majority (further 34 per cent); late majority (34 per cent); and laggards (last 16 per cent). The term 'laggards' has a negative tone: it might be just as legitimate to call them 'contents', or 'happy as they are'. Indeed, some people resist getting the internet since they see the impact it has upon friends and families.

A 'content' label indicates that digital divide issues may not always exist as a problem to be solved; at least, not so far as the people themselves are concerned. Sometimes slow technology uptake is an indication that people feel no need to adopt the new technology and cannot see how it will enhance their lives. The challenge of policy designed to minimise the digital divide is that user-choice should be the only inhibition to take-up. Skills development, technology support and affordable pricing should all be built into the adoption packages of policy-makers who would like to see more people able and motivated to use the internet and, ultimately, broadband.

CARING FOR OTHERS IN THE UK: A DIGITAL DIVIDE

In the UK, and in countries around the world, many people with disabilities are cared for in their own homes by close family members who are neither professionally trained, nor professionally paid, for this caring role. Indeed, such families often live in poor financial circumstances. Although the carer may be entitled to some social welfare support from the state, the expenses incurred in supporting a disabled family member are generally very high. When the costs of caring for a disabled person are combined with the financial implications of withdrawing from the workforce in order to carry out the caring, the result is a significantly reduced income. The impact of this reduction is felt both in the present and in the future, since carers are generally unable to contribute towards a personal pension for retirement, and are often at a significant disadvantage if looking for employment, even after their caring role is over. For these reasons, households which include a disabled person and their home-based carer tend to have a lower income and fewer resources than the general population. These factors indicate that carer households are likely to suffer significantly from the digital divide.

Blackburn et al. (2005) carried out research with carers in the UK. They surveyed approximately 8,000 adult carers (the number was uncertain since many question-naires were forwarded through voluntary groups) and received 3,014 responses. These responses indicated that the study cohort included more women and a greater proportion of older carers (over 55) than was generally the case in the UK carer population. Further, there was an over-representation of carers bearing substantial responsibilities (caring for more than 20 hours per week) and carers who had been caring for a long time (more than ten years). All of these dimensions are factors which might be expected to impact upon internet use. At the same time, these factors indicate a population which might especially require information and support delivered in an accessible way to the time and place where it is needed. The lack of resources available to these carers means that they are likely to be 'information poor,' and suffer from 'information poverty'.

Blackburn's study was carried out against the background of a UK government commitment to increase online services for carers. This policy commitment raised some concerns that if new online provision absorbed resources, services provided through other media (for example, print or telephone) might be reduced correspondingly. Information and help is particularly crucial for untrained family-based carers yet Blackburn et al. comment upon 'high levels of unmet need for services' and that 'carers are not provided with essential information at a time when they need it and in a form that they can make use of' (2005: 202). Other studies have associated the carer role with a higher risk of depression and a sense of strain (Molyneux et al. 2008), while Blackburn et al. also suggest that carers are 'vulnerable to isolation and social exclusion' (2005: 202). People suffering from depression often find everyday activities such as shopping and banking highly stressful and this is likely to be made worse if the shopper is also juggling patient care. General online services would help here. Access to the internet has the potential to redress issues such as the lack of information, absent professional support and social exclusion. It would also offer choices to carers and help make their lives easier.

Even so, in Blackburn et al.'s study, with 2003 data, half the 3,014 respondents (50.5 per cent) said they had never used the internet. Of the 1,489 carers who reported using the internet, 896 (29.7 per cent of the total cohort) reported that they used the internet once or more per week. This was judged to be frequent use. Male carers and younger carers were much more likely to use the internet, while people with fewer resources and lower socio-economic status were less likely. 'Not being in paid employment or living in rented or other accommodation reduced the odds by two', Blackburn et al. commented, continuing that 'Age of the person cared for also appeared to be a predictor, reducing the odds by two for those caring for someone aged 18 years or older' (Blackburn et al. 2005: 206). They indicate that carers of children and young people under 18 are more likely to have some free time because of their dependents' educational commitments. Carers of older charges, however, often have extremely limited time for developing and using new skills. The respondents to Blackburn et al.'s study who had never used the internet (50 per cent), or used it only rarely (20 per cent), can be considered substantially disadvantaged.

Reflection: What issues are faced by those who have no access to the internet?

Thinking about your own country, what problems arise, and what issues are faced, by people who do not currently have internet access?

In related US research, a Pew internet and American Life project (Madden and Fox 2006) surveyed adults online to find out how many had helped a friend or loved one cope with a major health crisis or serious health condition in the previous two years. Of the cohort questioned, 12 per cent had offered this kind of help and identified the internet as playing a crucial or important role. These respondents were classified as 'e-caregivers'. Madden and Fox then asked the e-caregivers questions about the specific role played by the internet at the time. Some 36 per cent identified the internet's role in helping to find general advice and support; 34 per cent said it had helped provide specific professional and expert advice, while 26 per cent reported that it provided information and helped the e-caregiver compare options. 'When asked about all of the different sources of information they used, 58 per cent of e-caregivers said the *most important* source was something they found on the internet. Only 38 per cent said the most important source was one they found offline' (Madden and Fox 2006: 2–3, emphasis in original).

The notion of accessing the internet to achieve these positive outcomes of integrating carers within social, professional and informational networks is more than a matter of providing a computer, however. DiMaggio and Hargittai (2001) identified five factors relating to internet inequality: (i) access to appropriate technology and equipment; (ii) autonomous use (the capacity for people to use the internet where and when they wished); (iii) skill levels; (iv) social support in the area of internet use; and (v), the purposes for which the internet is used (where economic drivers might trump social ones, for example). Isolated carers, vulnerable to social exclusion, as well as being older and economically disadvantaged, are likely to rate poorly against these five factors. Blackburn et al. suggest that a range of measures is required to redress the balance. 'Supported access projects for carers who are older adults or in poorer socio-economic circumstances, which provide home-based training and support programmes and cover equipment and online costs may be important ways of widening internet access' (2005: 208).

The take-home message here is that carers represent a population with specific information and support needs. Even though carers are more likely than most to benefit from internet access, Blackburn et al. (2005) indicate that for reasons of age, gender and socio-economic status they are less likely than the general population to be able to access and use digital information. As more services go online, the implication is that existing inequalities will be magnified. Even as the absolute numbers of people excluded from internet access decreases, the relative disadvantage suffered will be greatly increased.

Summary

■ This chapter has moved on from the consideration of policy issues to the discussion of people's lives, and their uses of ICTs. We start our exploration of the internet's importance by noting that many people in the world, in rich countries as well as poor ones, do not have access to the internet. This is the case for three-quarters of the world's population.

■ The first case study in this chapter concerned the relative value of mobile phones and internet access to homeless people in Scotland, and the uses they made of these technologies when they were able to access them.

■ People in the USA who do not go online are often deterred by the costs of internet access and the difficulties of acquiring the skills, knowledge and experience required for proficient internet use.

■ A case study on UK carers illustrates some challenges faced by the information poor. Although internet delivery of information can be very cost effective, this is not a benefit if the key publics to be reached have limited access to the web.

Chapter 5 moves from an examination of people who are excluded from the internet to a consideration of people who feel their culture is absent, or under-represented on the internet. We will also be considering the distinctions between Web 2.0, Web 3.0 and the Semantic Web.

5 CUSTOMISING THE INTERNET

INTRODUCTION

Does your internet use reflect who you are? Is it as individual as your fingerprint? How much is it determined by what you see as your work? How much by your leisure and play choices? This chapter examines what we mean by Web 2.0, and the ways in which we tailor our uses of the internet to express ourselves and to explore the issues and ideas that excite us. Our experience of the internet depends significantly upon our economic resources, education and expectations, and reflects our social, cultural and historical circumstances. We have previously considered some arguments supporting the idea of technology as being socially constructed. These arguments also apply to the internet. Our idea of the internet is, to some extent, what we make it.

This is not to deny the importance of the inventors, developers, designers and manufacturers of the hardware and software we use to engage with the internet. Nor is it to understate the role of the regulator and public policy in reconfiguring the bounds of the internet to which we have access – for example,: in China, as we saw in Chapter 3. Deliberate interventions to customise the web and shape our internet experience have their roots in particular historical and socio-cultural circumstances. Those who design and create internet access tools and experiences for us exercise choice, and do this for political or entrepreneurial reasons. They aim to offer something specific and different from other products available to us. They seek to identify a way to cut through, to reset the 'default activity' of key user groups. This chapter examines some relevant examples – creating a web environment to promote the use of Irish Gaelic, and the struggle by French-speakers to resist the dominance of English.

We recognise our power to choose as part of our participation in markets for goods and services. Brands grow bigger or decline in response to this power, as in 2008 when the number of people using the social networking site Facebook overtook those who use MySpace (Techtree 2008). We respond to the choices offered to us by corporations and marketers through selecting our preferred way of engaging with the internet, given our specific circumstances. In western countries we choose our Internet Service Provider from a range of possible companies; then we opt for dial-up or broadband access. Our browser choice also says something about us. Do you choose Internet Explorer, the Microsoft megalith, or the increasingly prevalent Mozilla Firefox, an open source application and thus a product of 'the Bazaar', rather than 'the Cathedral' (Raymond 2001)?

In the West, internet users tend to think in terms of Google or Yahoo, or equivalents, when they want to search the web. In China, however, three-quarters of the online population use Baidu (Chmielewski 2007). Baidu is a locally developed Chinese search engine, and is also the first Chinese company listed on the US-based NASDAQ-100. Founder Robin Li has a Computer Science degree from the State University of New York, Buffalo, and he worked at InfoSeek in 1997 before returning to China to set up Baidu in 2000. By 2007, Baidu had 74 per cent of Chinese online searches against Google's 18 per cent, even though the time a Google search takes a Chinese-speaking enquirer is significantly shorter: '30 seconds versus 55 seconds through Baidu' (Chmielewski 2007). It may be that consumers are motivated by Baidu's patriotic slogan 'We know Chinese best'; or it may be that they are offended by the Google approach to the Chinese censorship regime which flags to users whenever they try to access a prohibited site that cannot be displayed because of local laws. According to Chmielewski (2007), who cites an anonymous Chinese source, 'The Chinese people were quite indignant ... That's like coming here and saying, "I'm in your house, I'll eat your food, but let me tell you upfront that I don't particularly like it"'. In China, choosing to use Google as your preferred search engine would be a very specific statement.

Alongside these service and software choices, and our consumer decisions about which computer we use and why, stands our relationship with the internet itself. We respond to the internet by prioritising different activities which reflect our interests and our experience. Do we predominantly use the internet to connect to others via email or chat, to research information, to post to blogs or contribute to wikis, or to engage with others through social network sites or in online game play? Each person has a different pattern of engagement.

Herbert Schiller, who was an influential critic of US media, often wrote from a perspective that constructs capitalism as a form of control. In his reflection upon the global pervasiveness of US culture, he decided it demonstrated that western lifestyles have a hold on the imaginations and energy of majority, poorer, countries. 'Our technology – computerized weapons systems, medical scanners, the Internet – sets the standard to which developing countries aspire' (Schiller 2000: 149).

Even prior to the widespread take-up of the internet, Schiller had argued that the old colonial imperialism has been replaced by a 'soft' cultural and commercial imperialism which included:

the English language itself, shopping in American-styled malls ... the music of internationally publicised performers, following newsagency reports or watching the Cable News Network in scores of foreign locales, reading translations of commercial best-sellers, and eating in franchised fast food restaurants around the world ... The domination that exists today, though still bearing a marked American imprint, is better understood as transnational corporate cultural domination. (Schiller 1991: 15)

The implications of Schiller's construction of a pervasive soft imperialism are particularly serious for smaller nations trying to preserve their language and culture. English operates as a global lingua franca; a default language spoken by people who do not share a mother tongue. Magnifying the power of the language, the US is the dominant exporter of global popular culture and these media products have significant influence on people around the world (e.g. Miller 1994). In line with UNESCO's 2002 'Universal Declaration on Cultural Diversity', a number of nations are working to balance this influence by using the web to communicate alternative priorities and languages. For the Irish, the ubiquity of the web has spurred calls for the greater development of Irish Gaelic content to support the maintenance and advance of a language rescued from extinction. For the French, the Google Books project became the catalyst for an international campaign. We will consider both of these examples of cultural self-defence before turning to the construction of social and cultural capital through Web 2.0 technologies, particularly as these relate to social networks such as Facebook; and the micro-blogging practices of Twitter.

Reflection: Do you agree with the idea of 'soft imperialism'?

Does US culture have a big impact on the way other countries do things?
Is this a problem?

EXPLORING NEW MEDIA USE IN RELATION TO IRISH GAELIC

Irish Gaelic ('Old Irish'), one of the Celtic tongues, had been in decline for some centuries following the English colonisation of Ireland. After huge loss of life and forced migration during the Great Famine of 1845–49, at the time of the first census to include a language question in 1851, the proportion of the population claiming to speak Irish as their only language was 5 per cent. The Gaelic League was set up in 1893 to halt the decline but remained so marginal that 'even the 1916 Declaration of Independence was written in English' (Walsh 2001: 2). By the 1920s, the proportion of the population claiming any competency with Irish at all had fallen to 18 per cent (O'Rourke 2005: 274). The 'Gaeltacht', or Irish-speaking areas of The Republic of Ireland are in previously isolated regions to the north, south and west of the country, and account for 2.4 per cent of the population (Fleming and Debski 2007: 85). Historically these rural areas have been extremely poor and generally peripheral to the national economy. As the twentieth century progressed and economic conditions improved, people began to predict the death of the Irish language (Hindley 1990).

Since the formation of the Gaelic League, a number of other strategies have been employed to help revive Irish. These include the launching of an Irish-language television station TG4 (Kenny 2005), and bilingualism in the Irish school system with considerable growth in the number of schools outside the Gaeltacht in which Irish is the medium of education. The rise in the number of Irish-medium schools from sixteen in 1972 to 176 in 2000 indicates the symbolic importance of the language to the country, and a keenness among non-Irish speakers to see their children educated in a specifically Irish context (Walsh 2001: 2). Additionally the Irish sought, successfully, to have the language adopted as one of the official working languages of the European Union. Recent census data indicates that 43 per cent of Ireland's residents claim competency in Irish; and linguistic research indicates that 5–10 per cent use the language daily (O'Rourke 2007: 275). Given that 'as the level of exposure to the language decreases, so too does the level of communicative usage', internet use in Irish has been recognised as a critical element in language maintenance and development (Fleming and Debski 2007).

Fleming and Debski (2007) examined the internet and SMS texting habits of Irish children in three different educational contexts. They constructed internet use, including searching, chat and email, along with mobile phone texting, as being 'networked communications'. Some of the research participants attended an Irish language school in an Irish-speaking area where about a third of the students spoke Irish at home and English was a taught subject (Irish dominant). Others were from an English background attending a school where Irish is the medium of instruction (Mixed language). The third group comprised children from an English background, attending an English language school in which Irish was taught as a subject (English dominant).

Two separate classes from each of these three linguistic contexts took part in the research; one at primary level (10–12 years old) and one at upper secondary (16–18 years old). Students from theses six classes were involved in completing a self-report survey that involved some open-question responses, gathering qualitative as well as quantitative data, with a total of 125 children participating. All the participating secondary students, and two-thirds of the primary students, had their own mobile phone. Fleming and Debski's hypothesis, which is to say the idea they were exploring through their research, was that if Irish was being used for communication in new media contexts then it might reveal 'itself as a modern language and a living language of communication' (Fleming and Debski 2007: 88).

The two new media questions that Fleming and Debski wished their research to address were: 'What are the patterns in [schoolchildren's] use of Irish through networked communications?' and 'How can these patterns be useful in making recommendations for the use of modern technology in language maintenance?'. Most children reported that they almost never logged onto Irish websites. This was true for 97.5 per cent (English dominant), 90.5 per cent (Mixed language), and 85 per cent (Irish dominant) of respondents. 'The main reason [given] for children not accessing sites through Irish was that they did not know of any. English was generally seen by them to be the language of the Internet' (Fleming and Debski 2007: 94).

English-dominant children never, or rarely, used Irish for sending emails, whereas 5 per cent of Mixed language and 12 per cent of Irish dominant children reported sometimes or often using Irish in email communication. In their responses the children indicated that they 'sent emails in Irish to friends and family with whom they would speak Irish in face-to-face situations' (Fleming and Debski 2007: 94). More Irish was used in online chat by all three groups. 'While not being especially high, respondents reported using it for words and phrases that sound better in Irish, for salutations [and ...] [u]sers tend to use Irish in international chat rooms, both to show off and to communicate with Irish people without being understood by others' (Fleming and Debski 2007: 94).

Even in text messaging, where at least some children from all three contexts 'sometimes' used Irish to text, their usage appears to be specifically related to those times when they communicate with people with whom they speak Irish face-to-face, including at school. When the two groups of children from Irish language schools were asked why they texted school friends in Irish, they tended to answer along the lines of 'I'd send them in Irish because it might be something to do with school'. Fleming and Debski consider that this response demonstrates 'the children consider Irish their school language' (2007: 95). A 'fair to moderate' statistical correlation was established between participants' texting behaviour in Irish and the amount they spoke Irish outside school. That is to say, there is a correlation between the amount of Irish that is spoken in voluntary contexts and the likelihood of using it as the language of a text communication.

Only one in eight of the children who lived in English-speaking areas had ever tried to use the internet to learn or improve their Irish, while the Gaeltacht respondents had almost never done so (one in 39). The children reported several barriers to the use of new media in supporting their Irish language communications. These barriers included the lack of text prediction on mobile phones, and the absence of spell checkers for Irish in word processing. Additionally, Irish diacritical marks – the little signs like French accents that help distinguish one word from another, and which can alter the sound spoken, and which differentiate between words – are generally not available on mobile phones and are comparatively inaccessible on computers. In summarising the findings, Fleming and Debski noted that children from schools where Irish is the medium of instruction were more likely to change between using English and Irish, whereas those from the English language schools had 'higher tendencies to interject Irish constructions into their everyday speech' (Fleming and Debski 2007: 96), rather than fully use the language.

Classifying the reported usage patterns of the Irish language as generally 'tokenistic', Fleming and Debski comment that these patterns demonstrate that the Irish language used is often simplified, or takes a 'small interjections' form. Even so, this informal use would suit it to new media communications if the established disadvantages of diacritical marks, spell checkers and text prediction could be overcome. Fleming and Debski express concern that in the schools they studied there are no Irish language computer-based networks connecting children with other Irish speakers. Such larger digital networks can encourage the children to use the language in their online communications. Similarly, there is a comparative dearth of Irish language content on the internet.

Fleming and Debski's concern is that the lack of everyday opportunities to use Irish outside school means that school students' language abilities will diminish over time. 'They need more services, media and documentation to be made available in Irish, so they see it as still being relevant to their lives after they leave the school domain' (Fleming and Debski 2007: 99). This case study establishes one aspect of the perceived threat to a minority language posed by the widespread use of English on the internet. It calls for the creation of better Irish language resources on the web, and specific Irish language networks to link Irish speakers and encourage language use in new media contexts. As we see in Chapter 8, resource development is rarely a simple matter of 'if you build it, they will come' (Bonniface et al. 2005, 2006a). Given the widespread community support for the revitalisation of Irish Gaelic, however, better web resources coupled with an appropriate policy environment may help build bilingual competencies and further integrate the minority language into everyday life.

The next case study concerns attempts to resist the power of the English language medium to determine the resources available online. It argues that the fact that most of the big internet companies are English-language based (as Google is) has the potential to magnify comparative differences in language usage.

LA FRANCOPHONIE, EUROPEAN CULTURE AND THE GOOGLE BOOKS PROJECT

In 2004 Google announced its ambition to digitise the world's books. Working originally with five libraries – four in the US and one in the UK – Google's stated aim was to digitise and make available on the web every book which is no longer in copyright. The initial target was 15 million volumes in six years, becoming 30 million volumes in ten years. Google's plan for copyright books was to digitise them to make them searchable at the level of full text contents, including unique strings of words, with limited portions of the whole available for viewing (Google Books n.d.). Depending upon Google's agreement with the copyright holder, the person making the search would be able to access 'snippets' (no agreement with holder) or whole pages (if so agreed) of the copyright book. At each point, the page or the snippet displayed would be determined by the word or word-string searched for. In effect, Google was suggesting that they would create a digital archive of the printed word.

According to Ron Rotunda (n.d.), Professor of Law, the project would 'narrow the educational divide by giving every child with web access the ability to search the collection of the greatest library online'. Even so, there was an outcry from publishers over possible copyright infringement. The publishing industry went on to initiate legal action (*McGraw Hill* v. *Google*). In 2005 Google announced an opt-out provision whereby copyright holders could withdraw their books from the project. This failed to placate complainants who argued that it presumes consent whereas 'the burden should be on a potential infringer to respect the rights of copyright holders' (Jordan 2007: 33).

In addition to the action from publishers, McGraw-Hill having been joined by others, including Penguin, Pearson, Simon and Schuster and John Wiley, Google faced legal action from the Authors Guild in the US, and from other groups internationally, who believed that Google's activities breached their copyright. Most of these cases are still pending (Justia.com n.d.) although Google had a win in 2006 when German publisher WBG dropped their action after being advised that it was unlikely to be successful. At the same time, the idea of a 'web library' electrified librarians' discussions worldwide. Blake (2004), a US Librarian blogger, comments: 'If the web is a library, why do we need a building full of books? Why do we need librarians? That's an easy question for us to answer, but I don't think it is for much of the population, and that should scare us'.

Jean-Nöel Jeanneney, President of the Bibliothèque Nationale de France (the National Library of France), while recognising 'the dream that a treasure trove of knowledge, accumulated for centuries, would be opened up to the benefit of all' (Jeanneney 2006: 5), had different concerns. These started with Google's perceived Anglo-centric bias, which is always an issue for *La Francophonie*: the French-speaking world, and extended from there. Specifically, Jeanneney's argument developed into five key points, as indicated in Figure 5.1.

(i) that the selection of books to be digitised is overwhelmingly English-language based;

(ii) the presentation of snippets and pages entirely driven by key-word searches of (iii) Google-digitised books is culturally, contextually and organisationally questionable;

(iii) the ranking of results has a strong English bias and does not take into account factors outside the Google algorithm, such as scholars' judgements of importance;

(iv) agreements between Google and source libraries leave the digitised texts in the hands of Google, a private company, when it is in the public interest to have these more accessible; and

(v) the US provision for 'fair use' under copyright laws differs significantly from equivalent laws which operate in Europe. (Bearman 2006)

Source: Adapted from Jeanneney (2006)

Figure 5.1: An outline of Jeanneney's argument against the Google Books project

Jeanneney's first concern, about the primacy of the English language, led him to say that there is a need to defend 'at all costs ... the other European languages bearing diverse and complementary cultures' (2006: 7). He goes on to assert that Google's choices will amount to a prioritisation of ideas and arguments that fit into the US view of the world. Choices and priorities are inevitable since the initial goal of 15 million books represented a fraction of the printed works of the globe, with

Jeanneney's estimation of published books in the West alone running to over 100 million. Commenting that non-English speaking European scholarship includes much work translated from English, he expressed concern that there was little balance in English-speaking scholars' evaluations of non-English speaking scholarly contributions. Indeed, only 3 per cent of the annual published output of the US is in translation from other languages. 'The weight of American publishers may be overwhelming ... the dominance of work from the United States may become even greater than it is today' (Jeanneney 2006: 6).

Second, the issue of context caused Jeanneney significant concern. Addressing the matter as if it were a scientific endeavour, where the sample to be searched is representative of the whole, Jeanneney commented (2006: 68) that Google's value as a search tool 'is hard to judge since the service is accompanied by no precise information about the limits of the search or the representativeness of the corpus in which it is carried out'. Within a week of Google's announcement, Michael Gorman (2004), who was to become President of the American Library Association (2005–6), underlined concerns about unrepresentative extracts, this time at the level of the book. '[T]he books in great libraries are much more than the sum of their parts', he said. Gorman went on to distinguish between 'information' and 'knowledge': 'When it comes to information, a snippet from Page 142 might be useful. When it comes to recorded knowledge, a snippet from Page 142 must be understood in the context of pages 1 through 141 or the text was not worth writing and publishing in the first place' (Gorman 2004).

Third, it seemed possible that Google's AdWords auction system, a major income stream for the company which determines top dollar for key advertising placements on relevant web pages, might introduce commercial elements that have a further distorting effect upon Google's ranking system. Google's PageRank algorithm, discussed in Chapter 2, is a patented and commercially secret property. It operates according to assumptions and instructions that may introduce unacknowledged distortions and biases. PageRank values websites according to the number of websites linking to each of them, not by any particular indication of quality. It's likely that a search about vampires, depending upon the terms used, would prioritise Stephenie Mayer's website well above the site of a world authority on vampire mythology. This would be because Stephenie Meyer is author of the best-selling *Twilight* series and would have many fan links. Even though a recognised world authority might have written as many books, and would have academic credentials, they will inevitably be less popular. (See Chapter 7 for more about the public sphere.)

According to Jeanneney, his early 2006 searches for Cervantes (the author of *Don Quixote* [1605]), used the Spanish Google site. The search 'curiously first brought up five works in French, followed by three works in English, before, in the ninth and final position, there appeared a collection of excepts of Don Quixote in the author's own language [Spanish]' (2006: 12). Up to the point of digitisation, noted Jeanneney (2006: 30), books had been the only commercial medium not to carry advertising, but the Google Books project would frank results to favour Google's advertisers. Google asserted that their service was not distorted by their advertising. They suggested Google Books provided readers with the benefit of putting them directly in touch with booksellers and with libraries able to supply the book in which they were interested, and added there were no plans to charge libraries or booksellers for these introductions. Google's reassurances did not placate their critics.

Fourth, given that Google is a commercial enterprise, and citing the example of Netscape which had been very successful and then was suddenly no more, Jeanneney questioned what would happen to the digitised collection of the Google Book's collaborating libraries were Google to cease trading. The implication here is that the online resource is too important to leave solely in the hands of a private corporation, to be disposed if at its own discretion. Further, Bearman (2006) comments that 'None of the contracts with Google made public thus far permit value-added reuse of scans made for Google in products and services offered by others'. This is important because for old and rare books the act of scanning implies possible risk and degradation, and thus the results should be available for as many uses as possible so that further scanning is not required.

Fifth, and finally, Jeanneney points to the critical importance of liaison between digitisers, publishers, authors and translators. 'No success in this field is imaginable without the agreement of publishers [. . . and] the protection of the material and the moral and intellectual rights of the author (the latter rights, insufficiently defended in America, are critical in Europe)' (2006: 79). This remains an issue in Europe. In the USA, Google reached a settlement with the Authors Guild and the Association of American Publishers towards the end of 2008, subject to US court approval. Objectors to this settlement, which include Microsoft and Amazon, had until September 2009 to lodge their grounds (Singel 2009). Although any court-approved settlement would only be valid in the US, a number of governments, including Germany, Canada and New Zealand, also registered objections (Albanese 2009). Raising the stakes, there are indications that US government lawyers are scrutinising these Google Book developments with a view to possible future antitrust actions (Schonfeld 2009).

Jeanneney's response to the threat from Google Book was not simply to repudiate the Google vision, but to help foster a Europe-wide response by an appeal to 'the sensibilities and the civic-mindedness of European citizens'. His suggestion of a digital archive of European print material was swiftly endorsed when 'twenty-two of the twenty-four national libraries in the European Union signed the motion' he had proposed (Jeanneney 2006: 10). The European Digital Library (BNE Bibliothèque Numérique Européenne) was conceived as a corrective to the apparent excesses and exclusions of the Google project, and has similarities with initiatives from Yahoo and Microsoft, and Amazon's 'Search Inside' feature. The European Digital Library project, as finally funded, integrated the 'catalogues and the digital collections of the National Libraries of [nine European nations] into the European Library: thanks to the project, all EU countries are now members of the European Library service' (EDL Project n.d.). This response underlines the importance nations place upon the social and cultural content of the internet, and the value they see in providing resources from a wide range of languages.

Having discussed two attempts to rein in some aspects of internet development, while promoting others, this chapter considers developers' attempts to rewrite the internet to make it 'semantic'. It is to this project of customisation that we turn now.

WEB 2.0, WEB 3.0 AND THE SEMANTIC WEB

What is Web 2.0? What do people mean when they talk about Web 3.0 or 'the Semantic Web'? Definitions of these terms are extraordinarily diverse, and heavily dependent upon whether they are offered from a technological, or social sciences, or a humanities perspective. Even so, with some caveats relating to the Japanese iMode service discussed below, Web 2.0 is generally positioned as comprising the web-based and user-based innovations that followed on from the crash in hi-tech stocks after the 2000 'Tech Wreck' (BBC News 2000). Web 2.0 initiatives include collaborative endeavours such as Wikipedia and peer-to-peer file-sharing protocols such as BitTorrent, as well as social networks such as those created through Flickr and Facebook.

Addressing the nature of Web 2.0, Hendler and Golbeck (2008: 15) suggest that 'The fact that the sharing of content can be enhanced by personal connections, rather than primarily via search or other query techniques, has emerged as a major, and perhaps defining, aspect of successful Web 2.0 applications'. Hendler and Golbeck support this argument using the example of YouTube. Videos on YouTube (see Chapter 9) do not become popular as a result of users one by one tagging their content following on from millions of individual, disconnected searches. Instead, YouTube videos are made prominent through sharing popular posts via emails, blogs, social network sites and other recommendations made by key individuals, who often act as opinion leaders (see Chapter 8). Where these communication practices are harnessed to commercial ends and promote products to consumers, they are often called 'viral marketing' or word-of-mouth promotion.

In the context of Web 2.0, such linking mechanisms constitute social activity which builds personal relationships and develops or strengthens networks and 'taste cultures': people who share similar views about videos they enjoy. Japanese-style anime might be an example of one taste culture.

> Once a video has 'made it', getting many thousands of views, it can become a popular node in the network of videos, which are linked by a number of metadata features (who they are by, what the main subject is, where the content originated, etc.). Search in YouTube is primarily enhanced by the social context, not by the 'semantic content' of what is in the videos (Marcus and Perez, 2007). While automated technologies to create indexes of these videos are being sought, the primary indexing comes through the social overlay of the site. (Hendler and Golbeck 2008: 15)

The web before Web 2.0 was not called Web 1.0 at the time, it was just 'the Web'. In retrospect this web, as it was created by Tim Berners-Lee and as it developed over its first decade, can be considered to be Web 1.0. The first web was defined by the creation of web pages that linked through to accessible content, and by the development of effective search and index strategies to uncover and use that content. Much of the growth of Web 1.0 can be attributed to user-created content, consequently work done by users in creating digital content is not a new feature of Web 2.0. Instead, Web 2.0 is defined by new levels of sociality and collaboration, where users build upon the activities of previous users.

In Web 1.0, a surfer might have accessed a great site and then emailed their friends about it. The friends might also access the site, perhaps by copying and pasting the address into their browser. Possibly the site had a counter to indicate the number of visitors, but a user could not generally gauge its popularity before clicking through. In Web 2.0, an email would include the link so someone could click through seamlessly. At the same time, the promo image for site, video, book, etc. often presents star ratings from other users, along with the number of views, and these tools help someone decide whether or not to access the material. Through accessing a site, and then linking it to a personal blog or social network page, the user contributes to a network dynamic. The online activity produces links between the user's social network and the site that affect the likelihood of other people also finding, accessing and valuing the same material. Given the importance of these background linkages to the development of social networks, users produce value through accessing sites, as well as through crafting, tagging and uploading specific content onto them.

It is fortunate that what Hendler and Golbeck term the 'social overlay' of a site has inherent value, since users' tagging practices are inconsistent. Tags are not an effective organising tool for most social network sites. In Flickr, the social network centred upon sharing photos and videos which was bought by Yahoo in 2005, the millions of content-providing members can organise their 3 billion photos and videos (as at November 2008) around such themes as 'photographer, tag, time, text, and group, and ... place' (Flickr 2009). It is the 'tag' function that allows the content-provider/photographer to categorise an image or video, to enhance its searchability and allow the file to be organised alongside millions of others.

Tags categorise the visual content of all files posted. Information about a photo is itself part of the content, and is called 'metadata': data about data. Once an image has been posted, depending upon its access parameters, other users of the site can also add tags. This continuing expansion of metadata is sometimes said to create a 'cloud' of information around the core data, providing a context for it (Bruns 2008a: 173). It is through searching the metadata including time, place and photographer, as well as content, that much non-verbal material, such as videos and photos, can be organised. Other parameters that can be included in searches, and in the metadata about the content posted, include information about the links to and from different items and the activity of browsing itself.

Flickr's tagging criteria uses a 'folksonomy', defined by Tapscott and Williams (2006: 42), as 'essentially a bottom-up, organic taxonomy that organises content on the web'. Whereas 'taxonomy' was the term originally applied to the categorisation of biological specimens and living species, folksonomy is an ad hoc process 'relying on generic practices of tagging existing content using randomly, manually chosen keywords' (Bruns 2008a: 173). Most established taxonomies use an internal hier-archical organisation. As an example, humans are a species (*homo sapiens*) and part of the order of primates. The primate order also includes the chimpanzee species, and that of the ring-tailed lemur, along with many others. The classification hierarchy makes it evident that, while all humans are primates, not all primates are human since the order 'primate' includes a number of species. Folksonomies are non-hierarchical; they are flat, and no term has any predefined relationship with any other. This makes it much harder to organise information and relationships other than via the 'social overlay' of the social network, informed by folksonomy tags.

Even though 'people who use similar tags are likely to have overlapping interests' (Tapscott and Williams 2006: 42), problems arise in terms of the lack of specificity of the tags used. Ambiguity can prevent powerful links at the content level. For example, Hendler and Golbeck note that 'many common tags on Flickr include terms like 'dad' (80,000+ photos), 'Fred' (90,000+ photos), and 'My (something)' (over 80,000,000 photos). Clearly these terms are not very useful outside specific contexts' (2008: 16). With Web 2.0, where the tag-terms leave off the social network takes over.

It is notoriously difficult to look into the technological future, but every era tries to do so and the visions say as much about the people who share them as they do about technology or the future. The vision for the Semantic Web, or Web 3.0, is that it may eventually be able to address Web 2.0's lack of connectivity at the content level. According to some ways of looking at the web, Web 2.0 builds rich, deep networks at the level of social actors. Web 3.0 aims to develop equivalent rich, deep linkages for content, which can be processed in a meaningful way by machines (Vossen and Hagemann 2007: 282). The idea is that Web 3.0 adds a machine-processing activity to the power already provided through social networks. Web 3.0 is Web 2.0 plus the Semantic Web. These visions have a good pedigree, but are yet to become reality. They have been developed by the web's inventor, Tim Berners-Lee, and explained in *The Semantic Web – A new form of Web content that is meaningful to computers will unleash a revolution of new possibilities* (Berners-Lee et al. 2001).

The use of the term 'semantic' relates to the communication of meaning. It requires data to be 'machine-*processable*, where the semantics determine what a machine can do with the data beyond simply reading it' (Vossen and Hagemann 2007: 289). Berners-Lee et al. (2001) address this requirement for meaning by suggesting that semantic content will be built into new web pages at the time of their creation as appropriate languages and protocols are developed and become more generally available. The aim is to make semantic tools easy to use for non-specialists. '[T]hese developments will usher in significant new functionality as machines become much better able to process and "understand" the data that they merely display at present' (2001: 31).

In contrast to the flat organisational structure, the 'heterarchy' of folksonomies, the aim of the semantic information is to create hierarchical taxonomies of information. Acknowledging that it is impossible to create a flexible taxonomical model that also provides a rigid structure, Berners-Lee et al. argue that developers should 'accept that paradoxes and unanswerable questions are a price that must be paid to achieve versatility. We make the language for the rules as expressive as needed to allow the Web to reason as widely as desired' (2001: 32). The example given of the kind of paradox that the Semantic Web would need to be able to handle is the status of the paradoxical sentence 'This sentence is false'.

Although Berners-Lee's 2001 vision of the Semantic Web is still under construction, some of its component parts already exist. For example, Internationalized Resource Identifiers (IRIs) will provide 'unique, global identification' which can be used to structure information in the Semantic Web (Vossen and Hagemann 2007: 292). These IRIs can be built upon existing URLs (Uniform Resource Locators), which often start with http:// to indicate that they take the form of a hypertext transfer protocol. One application of the IRI approach is the proprietary Digital

Object Identifier or DOI system. This allows the web to link, not to a location as accessed via a URL, but to a specific object, document, image or entity. The DOI system works regardless of broken web links and the object's actual location. It is like the difference between dialling a mobile phone number compared with a landline that requires an area code and a number string which indicates the telephone exchange centre. The developing schema for the Semantic Web would ensure that each element of meaning would have its own IRI which would be understandable to the machines that process it. Hendler and Golbeck (2008: 19) sum up the potential thus:

> For the Semantic Web, the [... IRIs] provide a set of semantic linkages that applications are starting to take advantage of ... [F]inding ways to combine (link) the social structures of the Web 2.0 applications with the semantic structures of the Semantic Web is a compelling way to bring together two different networking spaces, allowing the total value to increase enormously.

The plan is for the heterarchy, the same-level linkages of Web 2.0 social and collaborative networks, to be balanced and made powerful by the hierarchy of Semantic Web applications. In theory, this combination of heterarchy and hierarchy will create a Web 3.0 experience that is much greater than the sum of its parts. Although this is an interesting idea, new visions of the future are constantly evolving and we can be certain that accurate predictions are achieved as much through luck as through knowledge.

SOCIAL NETWORKING, WEB 2.0 AND MOBILITY

Along with definitions of Web 2.0 that foreground the sharing of content, as argued by Hendler and Golbeck (2008: 15); or definitions that privilege metadata tags (Pesce 2006), some attention should also be paid to the increasing social and cultural implications of mobility of access to the internet. For most western consumers, this development was spearheaded by the BlackBerry, which was introduced in 2002 to provide mobile phone services, web browsing, email, and other wireless applications. Developed by Canadian company Research In Motion (RIM), their BlackBerry Connect software is also sometimes used to enable other companies' mobile products to connect to the internet. Mobility of internet access in North America and Europe thus coincided with the development of a range of Web 2.0 companies, including collaborative endeavours like Wikipedia and BitTorrent protocols (both started in 2001) and early social network sites, such as Friendster (founded in 2002).

Globally, however, the mobile-access concept had already been proven in Japan where iMode launched in 1999. Within two years, iMode's parent company NTT DoCoMo (Nippon Telegraph and Telephone '*do co*mmunications over the *mo*bile network') had developed a '[US]\$187 billion market capitalization, the highest of any company in Japan' (Mullins 2007: 29). Internet-enabled mobile phones dramatically impacted upon Japanese connectivity rates. At the point of iMode's launch '12.2 per cent of the population had internet access, compared with 39 per cent of the US population, 21 per cent of the British population and 23 per cent of the Korean population' (Mullins 2007: 30). By 2001, two years later, internet subscribers accounted for 44 per cent of the Japanese population (Aizu 2003: 120). As well as allowing text-based communication and camera-phone mobile users to email images and post them to the net, the mobile phone has the potential to 'gather and transmit its location, and make available services in the vicinity, says Goggin (2006: 197) adding:

> Weather forecasts, tourist attractions, landmarks, restaurants, gas stations, repair shops, ATM locations, theatres, public transportation options (including schedules) are some examples of the information provision filtered to the user location. (Fraunholz et al. 2005: 144–5; cited in Goggin 2006: 197)

Such services are increasingly provided via new generation mobiles such as the iPhone. These applications require 3G technologies (third generation, see Chapter 4), while the information sources discussed are generally internet-based. Opportunistic access to in-the-minute information is increasingly able to enrich everyday activities with cultural and social information, such as using a 3G phone for map directions. Mobile phone access to the internet is associated with greater sociability, according to Castells et al. citing Ishii (2004: 56), in contrast with 'high-intensity users of the PC Internet … , heavy users of the mobile Internet are actually more active in interpersonal communications and socializing' (2007: 92). Even so, it is only recently that mobile technology has generally supported members of social networking sites such as MySpace, Bebo and Facebook who wish to use their phones to interact with their online profiles, and those of their friends, while in transit.

Nicola Green discusses 'interactional aspects introduced by mobility (collectively viewing texts and images on a mobile phone while on the move as well as sending them to other mobile devices, or the posting of an account of everyday travels through a city while conducting them)' (2009: 274). Among the multitudes of possible applications for these services, mobile internet access helps recruit 'citizen scientists' to report bird sightings to ornithologists' websites (www.birdguides. com). All these aspects of interactivity indicate the value of internet-enabled mobile phones for those participating in online social network sites, on-the-move blogging, field reporting and citizen journalism (see Chapter 7).

Twitter is a cross-over social network/micro-blogging service, founded in 2006, that is reminiscent of SMS (Short Message Service) texting practices of 2G phones. Permitting messages of up to 140 characters, the constraints upon a 'tweet' (a Twitter message) are similar to those placed upon SMS texts in the early days of mobiles when the upper limit was 160 characters. The aim of Twitter is to write in the moment of 'everyday actions, habits, experiences—everyday trivia—[since] this forges connections between individuals who are physically remote from each other' (Crawford 2009: 250). Sometimes these micro-moment posts are also used to provide up-to-the-minute information about chaotic and breaking news, as was evident in the Mumbai attacks of November 2008 where Twitter users offered some of the on-the-ground citizen-journalism reporting.

People connected into a Twitter network can choose to access their incoming tweets through a variety of digital media and applications, including email, SMS, instant messaging clients and the Twitter website. Crawford discusses the 'dispersed sense of intimacy generated by regular contact with a wider circle [... of] friends, acquaintances, colleagues' fostered by the sharing of the everyday (2009: 251–2). Indeed, Crawford cites Moyal (1989 [reprinted 1995]) and Rakow (1992) as evidence that sharing the banalities of the everyday is a form of care-giving. Although Twitter can be very personal and intimate, it is also possible to read global exchanges across the continents and in multiple languages via the internet (Twittervision n.d.). Viewed in this way Twitter makes a surprisingly moving conversational collage, showcasing both diversity and specificity. 'Lev Grossman in *Time* magazine describes Twitter as the "cocaine of blogging or e-mail but refined into crack"' (Crawford 2009: 255).

Given that Twitter is a relative newcomer, as well as being a hybrid between a micro-message blog and a social network site, the major mid-2000s Web 2.0 social networks were Facebook and MySpace. The services offered by Facebook are outlined as allowing: '[U]sers to create profiles and articulate connections with other users, who are then listed as "friends"'. Certain other features, like testimonials, the ability to join groups of shared interest, and the ability to post pictures are also increasingly incorporated into online social networking software' (Lampe et al. 2006: 167).

Social network members were also critical of the take-up of a number of other Web 2.0 offerings, with such activities as photo and video sharing occurring both within tools provided in the site's architecture and via specialist sites. MySpace users were so heavily committed to posting and reviewing YouTube content, for example, that 17.5 per cent of the video-sharing traffic was linked back to MySpace social network members at the time of YouTube's sale to Google in 2006 (Tancer 2007).

In terms of the social and cultural implications of Web 2.0 social networks, these are clearly significant, if hard to quantify. There is some disagreement, for example, as to whether social networks are primarily used to stay in touch online with people already known in offline contexts, or vice versa, or whether these dynamics change over time and reflect specific circumstances (Lampe et al. 2006). danah boyd (who eschews capital letters in her name) differentiates between the social network notion of friending, partly attributable as a verb to the activities of the first established social network site Friendster, and the actual processes of making and being friends:

> While some participants believe that people should only indicate meaningful relationships, it is primarily non-participants who perpetuate the expectation that Friending is the same as listing one's closest buddies ... Friendship helps people write community into being in social network sites. Through these imagined egocentric communities, participants are able to express who they are and locate themselves culturally. In turn, this provides individuals with a contextual frame through which they can properly socialize with other participants. (boyd 2006)

boyd is making oblique reference here to the idea of 'social capital'.

Social capital is much talked about, and defined in a number of ways. The notion of capital constructs these social processes within a notionally economic framework whereby people 'invest' in their social networks with the expectation that they will be able to 'draw upon' these networks in difficult times. Adler and Kwon offer a recent definition (2002): 'Social capital is the goodwill available to individuals and groups. Its source lies in the structure and content of the actor's social relations. Its effects flow from the information, influence, and solidarity it makes available to the actor' (2002: 23).

boyd's comments also indicate how activity on social networking sites has implications for the cultural project of differentiating 'the self' through our individual consumption of goods and services, as explained by the theory of consumption (Miller 1987). The goods and services consumed include those implied both by the social network site and the networks of friends and acquaintances. These activities of self-exploration, community-building and relationship-contexting, carried out while on the move or in comparatively stationary environments, are central to the cultural work necessarily performed as part of our engagement in social networks; as part of our activity in building social capital. Notions of community, and especially web-based community, are explored further in Chapter 8.

Summary

- This chapter discusses how each of us has an individual experience on the web. We construct our own online environment through a range of deliberate choices that are also affected by where we live, the services that are available and affordable, and the regulatory environment.
- It includes two examples of where the internet has been constructed as a possible benefit for, or a possible threat to, the development of national culture. The examples chosen were the support of the Irish Gaelic language in Ireland, and a French librarian's response to Google Books.
- Differentiating between 'the web' (by default, Web 1.0), Web 2.0 and the 'Semantic Web', the discussion addresses deliberate attempts to create new web functionality. One example is the way in which new media technologies, such as the iPhone, are being used to access the internet while on the move. Twitter, and social networking sites such as Facebook, particularly benefit from in-the-minute access.

Chapter 6 introduces some problematic uses of the internet which can act as triggers for legislation and regulation. Pornography and online defamation will be considered in this context.

6 REGULATION AND LEGISLATION: PORNOGRAPHY AND CYBER STALKING

INTRODUCTION

What meanings do you associate with 'the internet'? Even acknowledging our discussion about how everyone configures their own experience of a technology, that may seem like a funny question. Given the time spent in previous chapters investigating the internet's beginnings, it is tempting to answer in a technological or historical or policy framework. Yet these explanations may not quite capture the meaning that the internet has for you. Your experience is likely to relate to what has strongly influenced you in your activities on the internet. You might feel passionate about game play, for example, or connecting with family and friends through Facebook; or you may feel fearful having been traumatised by a cyber stalker or identity thief. Whatever the case, we can assume the meanings you've constructed for your narrative of 'the internet' differ in significant ways from other people's.

While our ideas of the internet may differ, the chances are that the concepts we hold overlap sufficiently for us to have a sensible conversation about it. The essential details of the internet are agreed; it is the discourse around those details that differs from person to person. If we agree to differ about the meanings we have made in relation to the internet, what do we mean by 'discourse'? Jonathan Culler's (2002 [1981]: 189, 190) definition offers a useful starting point:

> [T]he theory of narrative requires a distinction between what I shall call 'story'—a sequence of actions and events, conceived as independent of their manifestation in discourse—and what I shall call 'discourse', the discursive presentation or narration of events [... The story is] an invariant core, a constant against which the variables of narrative presentation can be measured.

Another way of saying this is that people can look at the same series of events and choose to explain them in different ways. Going back to our differing notions of the internet, the details of what we believe the internet to be will be the core, or the story; the way we think and explain the core to ourselves and others is the discourse, and it is the narrative that determines the kinds of discourse we use. One person's internet narrative might focus on exploration; another's on community; a third on being swamped by an avalanche of information. The recognition that discourses differ leads to the relevance of discourse analysis as a way of exploring and exposing the principles underlying the use of a specific narrative or a range of narratives. Discourse analysis is one research tool used by social constructionists to explain the complex dynamics of social and cultural meaning-making. This is examined further in a first section below.

This chapter investigates the internet as if it were a risky place requiring regulation, legislation and care. For some people, some of the time and in some circumstances, internet use can lead to a number of risky and unpleasant outcomes. Laws and regulations are in place to limit exposure to significant risks. Some of these risks were a focus of EU Kids Online, a multi-country research network led by Professor Sonia Livingstone and Dr Leslie Haddon at the LSE and co-sponsored by the LSE and the European Community Safer Internet Plus Programme.

Between 2006 and 2009 researchers from twenty-one European Union countries collaborated to examine the findings of national and international studies of children and young people's use of the internet. The EU Kids Online project conceptualised risk according to three main categories (Hasebrink et al. 2009: 8): 'Content', in which the user is the recipient of a mass communication; 'Contact', in which the user participates in risky interpersonal communication; and 'Conduct' in which the user does things which might have risk, such as revealing personal contact details, posting compromising images, meeting up with strangers, infringing copyright or hacking into a network. These issues are further examined in Chapter 9 in relation to children in the family home.

To illustrate different ways in which the internet is portrayed, Haddon and Stald (2008), both part of the EU Kids Online project, conducted a 14-country review of press coverage concerning the internet for the months of October and November 2007. Their research demonstrated that press coverage of internet risks was much higher than press coverage of internet opportunities and benefits. With the exception of Denmark, where 81 per cent of press coverage concerned leisure/play/entertainment stories, and Bulgaria, where it was judged there were too few stories to categorise, the remaining twelve countries – Austria, Belgium, Estonia, Germany, Greece, Ireland, Italy, Norway, Portugal, Slovenia, Spain and UK – had the largest proportion of their press stories in the category concerning legal/crime/

police content. No country had the largest share of their press coverage relating the internet to education.

Although the press may generally focus their internet coverage on legal/crime/police stories, domestic perceptions of the internet are often presented as a competition between its educational value and its potential for fun and entertainment. Back in 1997, David Marshall had noted that parents consider 'computer literacy is the passage to a comfortable future [. . . but] The arcade game dimension of the computer shifts its value from information source to entertainment site' (Marshall 1997: 71). Parents bought computers because they saw them as educational, while children wanted computers because they saw them as fun. These different perspectives on computers and the internet reflect different ways of conceptualising the internet.

This chapter looks at two examples of risk as these affect adults, and for which there are regulatory and legislative remedies where the risks become substantial. Pornography is an example of a content risk where a judgement of legal or illegal content can depend on the participants' birth dates, upon the informed consent of the parties involved in the making of pornography and upon the age of the viewer. Further, there is some indication of commercial risk (see the discussion of Prodigy below) in that restricting and regulating online interaction to exclude the possibility of sexual content can be a risk for the service provider. Consumers may head towards more liberal and less regulated environments. In contrast, cyber stalking is an example of a contact risk. Even though there may be no physical danger, it may be difficult to ensure that an individual's right to protect their reputation, and to communicate in open and respectful ways, is upheld.

These case studies on pornography and cyber stalking are preceded by a discussion of discourse analysis, developing the theme introduced above, because it is in constructing and discussing the internet as a place of risk rather than a place of creativity, education and fun that we open up a number of debates, while closing down others. This consideration of narrative theory and discourse analysis will help make that process clearer.

Reflection: What's your biggest risk?

Are you aware of taking risks in your online behaviours?
Would these be content, contact or conduct risks?
What might be the consequences of the risks you run?

DISCOURSE ANALYSIS

When we look at the ways in which people see the same thing differently it can help us to understand the complexity of experiences and associations. Parents might see the computer as an educational tool, children might see it as a games machine or a way of chatting with friends. The media might see computer use as a risky activity and discuss it predominantly in terms of legal, crime and police stories. Howard Rheingold rationalised his early experiences of a mid-1980s internet community, the WELL (or 'Whole Earth 'Lectronic Link'), in terms of a 'groupmind'. He used the notion of the brain to explain the synergies in knowledge and experience resulting from internet users getting together in cyberspace and 'tapping into this multibrained organism of collective expertise' (Rheingold 2000: 109). Here the terms mind, brain and organism are being used as metaphors. Metaphors can be useful for communicating meaning through discourse.

One important feature of metaphors is that they don't have to be either/or, they can be and/also. Multiple metaphors can indicate a range of appropriate and interesting discourses. Gareth Morgan (2006) developed a series of metaphors to help people understand complex organisations. He argues that we can use a range of metaphors to help construct our understandings of organisations, as indicated in Figure 6.1.

(i)   machines, with different parts functioning together as an efficient whole;

(ii)   organisms, growing and evolving;

(iii)   brains, with self-organising and interconnecting properties;

(iv)   cultures, with their own social realities;

(v)   political systems, with conflict, competition and regulation;

(vi)   psychic prisons, controlling the ways that 'inmates' talk, think and act;

(vii)   continuously changing and constantly in states of flux and transition, and finally

(viii) instruments of domination, whereby the organisation becomes a tool of suppression.

Source: Based on Morgan (2006) Contents Table

Figure 6.1: Morgan's metaphors for organisations

Morgan suggests that not only is it possible to construct meanings concerning a single organisation according to a number of these metaphors, but also that there is value in so doing. Multiple metaphors reveal multiple aspects of the organisation that might otherwise be hidden and not addressed. A willingness to see a range of possibilities also protects against a belief in certainty: '[T]here can be no single theory or metaphor that gives an all-purpose point of view. There can be no "correct theory" for structuring everything we do' (Morgan 2006: 338). Discourse analysis helps us to see the role played by metaphors in a text. Discourses can also frame a range of viewpoints: for example race, class, gender and culture all provide different perspectives for examining and analysing texts. The use of discourse analysis acknowledges that people make sense of information using different strategies, perspectives and experiences.

When we talk about a range of possible discourses, we talk about different 'discursive' approaches. Discursively, the 'history of the internet' might be seen as entirely a project of the US Armed Forces given, as is the case, that ARPA/DARPA is an agency within the Department of Defense, and the first beginnings of the internet were as a result of work commissioned by people who were employed and funded by the Pentagon. It would have been entirely consistent with 'the facts' if the narrative in this book had strongly emphasised the militaristic aspects of this development, especially in view of the Chapter 1 A to E mnemonic of the five power groupings behind the development of technology, which places the armed forces first. The narrative presented in Chapter 2, however, was far more centred on the passion that early internet developers felt for their work, and the ways in which they collaborated across military, university and business lines.

This discursive approach to narrating the story/core of the beginning of the internet is somewhat distanced from a construction of the internet as a repressive outcome of a militaristic plan. Instead, the narrative history of the internet offered in Chapter 2 concentrates upon what technology tells us about ourselves and each other in terms of people's behaviour and practices with it. This is also the function of the case studies to follow.

PORNOGRAPHY

In terms of a product or service that drives uptake of the internet, spawns new business models and prompts service and technology upgrades, pornography has sometimes been called 'the killer app'. This indicates its role in single-handedly driving consumer demand for an increased range of delivery mechanisms including new and emerging technologies. Even in a post-feminist world pornography is generally acknowledged to be a product predominantly aimed at males, and in some circumstances this constructs porn consumers as a desirable advertising demographic. For many pornography users, the internet is simply a more convenient and accessible way to obtain material that might otherwise be procured via magazines, videos and DVDs. The benefits of internet-delivered pornography can include round-the-clock access, some free products paid for via advertising, and privacy of consumption (Fisher and Barak 2001; Albury 2003).

Online pornography use is sometimes an activity that complicates the everyday life of the 'adult entertainment' user, especially when pornography is accessed through work-based resources, by under-age youth, or in jurisdictions where it is illegal. Constructing the internet as a pornographic delivery system might seem to position the technology predominantly as a means of accessing media content in private space. The digital trails that link pornography with the consumer have the capacity to make the private very public, however, sometimes at significant social and legal cost. The reverberations of accessing online pornography thus do not always end with the consumption of the pornography itself. Sometimes porn consumers experience secondary effects of their construction of the internet when they are traced via digital trails and called upon to account for their use of work time or employer's technology, or their affiliations with certain legal or illegal taste cultures in pornography.

The adult entertainment industry, as the pornography business prefers to be known, generally suffers from a bad press. It has been constructed as exploiting and degrading the women who work in porn, demeaning those men that use it, and making satisfying relationships harder to achieve in 'real life' (RL). Recent research with pornography users (McKee et al. 2008) indicates a more positive picture. Over 1,000 pornography users completed a survey that showed 57 per cent of respondents thought it had a positive effect on their lives, with a further 35 per cent saying that it had no effect on their lives (McKee et al. 2008: 83). (One per cent said it had a large negative effect, and 6 per cent that it had a small negative effect.) The kinds of positive effects attributed to pornography use by these respondents included making users 'more relaxed and comfortable about sex', making them 'more open-minded and willing to experiment', and making users 'more tolerant of other people's sexual pleasures' (2008: 85).

McKee and his co-authors suggest that negative perceptions of porn continue to circulate because 'many porn consumers are relatively closeted, if not actually ashamed, when it comes to their porn consumption' (2008: 178), and this might explain why such a large consumer group – about one-third of all adults in western countries, according to Roy Morgan and similar commercial research organisations (McKee et al. 2008: 25) – is comparatively silent. Research also indicates that about 10 to 20 per cent of porn users are women, often consuming porn with their partners as part of their private sex lives (2008: 27). Such figures suggest that over half of adult males in western countries may consume pornography, conforming with a social stereotype that: 'Every ordinary man likes porn. We know this because of magazines like *Ralph* and *Loaded*, semi-pornographic men's magazines that are all about "booze, babes and balls"' (McKee et al. 2008: 25).

Voss attributes the stigma associated with the adult entertainment industry to 'the heightened and paradoxical reactions surrounding the non-normativity of sexuality and commerce' (Voss 2007: 6). This perception refers to a general public construction of sexuality as private, and not appropriately commercialised, even if significant numbers of people use online interactions and resources to foster their private sex lives. Three-quarters (76 per cent) of the people surveyed by McKee et al. (2008: 34) spent less than three hours per week using pornography, with 41 per cent of all respondents accessing porn for less than one hour per week. The researchers note that most of their respondents were recruited to their study via a mail-out to customers by an adult entertainment DVD/video company. Smaller numbers responded to McKee's online survey, so these figures may not fully represent the experience of people who use the internet to access porn.

As well as noting the paradoxical elements of the hidden market in porn, which seems to be much larger than public discussion and self-identification would indicate, this chapter considers porn as a major driver for the uptake and adoption of new technologies. Several studies have indicated the central role pornography plays in driving the development and uptake of new technologies (Coopersmith 2006; Voss 2007). There are four main reasons for this.

First, consumers of pornography are often young adult males: the *Ralph* and *Loaded* reader stereotype. This is also the demographic for people most likely to be early adopters of new technology and can indicate comparatively high levels of uncommitted income (Coopersmith 2006: 3). There appears to be a mutually-reinforcing linkage between a willingness to use new technology, a capacity to pay for it, and a desire to access pornographic content that creates an incentive to adopt.

Second, pornography use sometimes involves a social stigma (Voss 2007). This means that users have an incentive to access pornography discreetly and to consume it in private. Both discretion and privacy of use can be supported in many domestic online environments. It should be noted here – underlining the perception of stigma, and encouraging the 'closeted' use of porn – that some employers have successfully sacked workers for accessing legal pornography using work computers (McKee et al. 2008: 49). Although it is arguable as to whether access to pornography would count as a civil liberty; in a number of countries pornography is heavily censored or illegal. These are often countries where take-up of the internet is less pervasive or comparatively public, with high use of cybercafes, for example. Such countries include China, Iran and Saudi Arabia.

Third, new technologies ideally require a stable income stream to keep the sector growing while a more varied suite of content products is developed and marketed. This means that people who make and market pornography typically experiment with technological innovations and are allied with early developers of products and services. This is in contrast with many other media markets. For example, as the large music producers were trying to rein in the peer-to-peer networks such as Napster, so the pornography industry was developing its wares. 'Instead of fighting file sharing, some in [the porn] industry—estimated to be generating $750 million to $1 billion per year in revenue—are quietly finding new ways to profit from it', commented *San Francisco Chronicle* writer Benny Evangelista (2003), quoting Grokster President Wayne Rosso as saying 'The porn guys are smart, they've figured out how to use the technology'.

Finally, porn consumers are motivated to upgrade equipment, services and their technical skills to take advantage of new services and products such as high-speed downloads and portable mobile phone content. They also choose to engage with technology in a comparatively anonymous way, preferring to access online sex-related forums using pseudonyms. Commenting on the mid-1990s competition between online services Prodigy, CompuServe and AOL, Kara Swisher argues (2003: 40–1) that it was the policy of allowing users to develop their own online spaces in private that allowed AOL to dominate the emerging online market: 'AOL's anonymous screen names, unmonitored chat rooms and easy attachment of graphical files [...] set it apart from the other online services'. She adds that a 'Prodigy executive told me in 1996, that AOL's privacy policy in chat rooms was "[the reason] why AOL has eight million members and Prodigy had faded to a shadow of its former self"' (ibid.: 41).

Unsurprisingly, given the prevalence of pornography on the web, and the enthusiasm of some internet users to access it, sex-related terms are amongst the words most frequently searched for. Indeed, most search engines offer two separate reports for purchasers of information about search word frequency: with adult filter on (which excludes sex-related terms) and without the filter. Frequency of word search has commercial currency since the use of appropriate search terms can increase relevant traffic to commercial websites, and thus increase click-through rates and profitability. Coopersmith (2006) comments that, when all search terms are included, 'Wordtracker found that the first 6 of the top 10 and 10 of the top 20 search terms on several web metacrawlers over a four-month period in late 2005 were pornographic' (2006: 5).

In an earlier report, a 2003 study of peer-to-peer network Gnutella indicated that 42 per cent of the 22 million searches during the 18-day period investigated were for pornography, compared with 38 per cent for music (Evangelista 2003). The predominantly teenage male LANing communities, where members set up self-contained Local Area Networks (see Chapter 8), generally have game play as their primary purpose. Additionally, members often use BitTorrent sites to access porn and then swap it from hard drives to hard drive in face-to-face (F2F) LANfests, while taking part in gaming marathons (Green and Guinery 2006). Peer-to-peer porn sharing offers dual benefits to users. It normalises porn access and use, since the material downloaded is also being used by people known to the downloader: peers in similar circumstances. Further, it by-passes some of the negative associations of accessing porn using commercial websites, such as explicit pop-up porn and '"mouse-trapping" (opening multiple porn sites that viewers are unable to click out of)' (McKee 2008: 186).

Voss argues that the stigma associated with the adult entertainment industry has affected innovation, including technological innovation, in a number of ways. It affects the recruitment of people into the industry, with people concerned about the effect of a period of employment in the porn business upon their future career prospects and their social and emotional relationships (Voss 2007: 9). At a business-to-business level, 'even firms which did not directly deal in adult content but provided third-party services, such as billing and marketing' could suffer from an association with porn companies, with managers describing how people from mainstream companies might respond by *backing away slowly* and *making the sign of the cross*' (Voss 2007: 10, italics in original). Within the industry itself, however, there is significant interaction and sharing. This occurs both on 'industry-specific online message boards' (ibid.: 11), where managers and employees get themselves known and promote their own companies and expertise both publicly and using private instant messaging, and at regular trade shows. One implication of this is that, since the porn industry is a relatively stigmatised one, people working in it are likely to get their next promotion, or their next job, with a competitor so the public and private links are generally kept positive.

The cross-industry networks work vertically (following the company hierarchy of ICT employees, managers, CEO, etc.) and horizontally, with links between people working in equivalent roles or positions. '[N]ews about which new types of billing programmes, content presentation technology (e.g. high-definition streaming) and other tools being used by competing firms across the sector is quickly disseminated across the industry' (Voss 2007: 12). Voss comments, however, that employees working on new technology development are generally absent from such exchanges in an attempt to keep leading-edge development secret. She attributes this relative exclusion both to the importance of new technology, products and services to the porn industry, and to the 'long hours and overwork' of many technology developers in the industry. '[K]nowledge about technology development, and the individuals who generate and embody such knowledge, is kept firmly away from the network' (ibid.: 13).

Although the porn industry is prone to 'copycat' new ways of delivering products, the secrecy allows some competitive advantage since the details of how to make the innovation work are not always evident from the end product. Voss suggests that there is an inadequate understanding of intellectual property (IP) law and practice in the porn industry, possibly as a result of people with this expertise choosing to work in other sectors. 'The lack of knowledge in the industry about legal protection of products of innovation inadvertently leads to widespread appropriation (which ironically acts as a further driver towards secrecy)' (Voss 2007: 17). This suggests that the rapid adoption and creation of technological advances by porn producers and distributors may be as much due to market pull and disregard of IP as it is to factors intrinsic to the adult entertainment industry.

Coopersmith comments that the '[m]ost innovative' use of the new online tech-nology 'was the referral or pass-through ring, which swapped [porn site] visitors with competitors' (2006: 8). The funding model was a micro-fee for the referring organisation, or a commission if the referral made a purchase. This approach has parallels with the Amazon model where associated websites pay Amazon a small fee for customers who access their sites through the Amazon.com link, or vice versa. Benefits include customer access to a wider range of products, prices and producers and the benefit to businesses that their products are more likely to be seen by more consumers.

The porn industry had early success with linked web sites. Journalist Gareth Branwyn commented in 1999 that 'The most trafficked Web rings are found in the amateur e-porn and adult Webcam communities'. A web ring connects a necklace of linked sites with each site sharing common navigation features. In theory, consistently clicking 'previous' or 'next' will bring the user back to the site from which they started. This is made more likely by having a host site that connects with all the other sites and stands in for any of them where a site may have gone offline or been discontinued. Some hosts charge for providing web services; others provide a free service as a marketing strategy. Branwyn documents almost 58 million unique visitors visiting free host *Porn City* in January 1999. Porn City provided free server space for adult content in return for guaranteed advertising rights in prime locations on the web pages. Server space is a particularly valuable commodity in the porn industry since hosts have to be able to 'handle the special hardware, bandwidth and security requirements of adult content' (Branwyn 1999).

XXX websites also attract the usual income streams, including advertising and subscriptions. Model subscription packages began as a basic monthly fee, or a cost per download from a single site, but period subscriptions to a ring of sites became increasingly popular once a credit card payment combined with the AVS (Adult Verification System) allowed access to a wide range of free and commercial products from multiple companies without further charge per view. Participating commercial sites found that it made better financial sense to share subscriptions from many consumers signing up for a large variety of services rather than fighting other providers to gather up small numbers of individual customers who were entitled to access only a few sites.

Echoing concerns about stigma, many online payment options specifically exclude services which may possibly include pornography. Early webcam pioneer Jennifer Ringley broadcast continuous images of her life in her flat 24/7 from 1996, including her relocation from Pennsylvania to Washington DC, and then from Washington DC to California. Her motivation, credited with seeding the idea for *Big Brother* and other reality shows was simply to allow others an insight into 'a virtual human zoo ... I keep JenniCam alive not because I want or need to be watched, but because I simply don't mind being watched' (Burkeman 2004). She also amassed a fortune from her annual US$15 subscriptions. Eventually, the internationally famous JenniCam closed in January 2004: 'Visitors with nothing better to do than watch her cameras for hours on end occasionally caught sight of her naked, contravening PayPal's regulations and forcing closure of the site' (Burkeman 2004).

Although the payment channels may be restricted, adult entertainment subscription fees tend to increase with interactivity options and the suite of services available (Coopersmith 2006: 8). This mimics what AOL had discovered in the mid-1990s, to their benefit (Swisher 2003: 40–1). The move towards persuading users to pay more for an increased range of premium services is an example of 'upselling'. Cross-selling persuades a consumer to buy what they had originally intended, plus an additional item, whereas upselling persuades the consumer to buy a more expensive product than the one originally planned. In order to achieve advertising cut-through with the multiplicity of adult sites available, successful hosts have to be prepared to spend big on their publicity. Even in the early days, as Branwyn noted (1999), it was expensive to buy online advertising space linked to premium search terms. The kind of desirable internet real estate came into play when consumers typed certain words into the bigger search engines. This meant that when a specific word was typed, it would trigger an advertisement, presumably for an adult entertainment service: 'Words like sex, anal and blowjob can sell for six figures' (Branwyn 1999).

Not all pornography on the web is commercial. McKee et al. identify 'two main strands: glossy, expensive couples porn and boy/girl-next-door amateurs porn' (2008: 182). Domestic porn production has blossomed since accessible and affordable technologies were developed which allowed images to be recorded and edited, then posted on the web.

> This democratization of pornography is part of a larger trend of innovation from below by users (as opposed to innovation from above by manufacturers) and the rise of technical hobbies and do-it-yourself projects among American males of all classes ... Now anyone can—and many do—create and distribute their own pornography because barriers to entry and transaction costs have been greatly reduced. (Coopersmith 2006: 10)

McKee et al. argue (2008: 131) that amateur porn, as a comparatively new phenomenon, allows its creators and users to straddle the boundaries of paired dualities: celebrities–ordinary people; porn stars–everyday sexuality; kink–domesticity; and public–private sexuality. They cite Barcan's (2002) research on 'Keith', a domestic porn producer, as indicating that 'amateurs are performing their ordinariness, rather than their stardom' and suggest it is this which helps their audiences relate to them and which 'makes them attractive' (McKee et al. 2008: 132). Barcan comments that 'This style brings with it a powerful trio of viewer associations and expectations— the expectation of truth, the sense of intimacy, and the mobilisation of voyeurism'. The absence of a commercial superstructure to this interaction with everyday porn makes the development of online taste communities and interactive chat much more straightforward and affordable.

Addressing the ways in which sexuality is 'lived in everyday life', Rival, Slater and Miller (1998) compared ethnographic work on sexuality 'in Amazonian societies, Trinidad, and on the Internet'. Their paper includes Don Slater's accounts of fieldwork on early cybersex sites that feature the swapping of 'sexpics' and synchronous IRC (Internet Relay Chat), where people use the internet to exchange lines of text, in public or private contexts, similar to instant messaging conversations. Sexpics IRC is introduced in terms of its 'unreality': 'no material cares or dangers ... no enduring commitments; performance is unproblematic; desire is inexhaustible, as is desirability' (Rival et al. 1998: 301).

Nonetheless, this disjuncture between the unproblematic online and the invisible offline is more apparent than real. Slater talks about the cross-over between online and RL as being about far more than sexuality, since participants often venture into IRC discussions of their RL. The everyday tends to be characterised as 'boring, a drudgery of maintaining self and family ... a lonely place, a place where one is aware of one's separation from others including one's partner and family' (ibid.: 304). The purposes of the juxtaposition of online and offline by those who take part in sexpics

IRC seem to take one of three main forms: escapist fantasy play, an exit strategy which might one day actually be used in RL; or an 'aphrodisiac for real life' (ibid.: 304) to stimulate and enliven the daily reality of domesticity.

Even constructed neutrally and, primarily, as a trigger for online engagement, there is no doubt that some pornography and some uses of pornography are problematic for society and for individuals. Pornography made without consent, or with those unable to give consent – involving children, for example, or bestiality – is illegal in almost all global jurisdictions. Violent pornography, where participants are or appear to be emotionally or physically abused, is likewise illegal in many countries. For these and other reasons, access to pornography and the content of pornography is extensively regulated and policed. McKee et al. offer a *Manifesto for Ethical Porn* (2008: 186–7) which includes sex education for young people and internet filters to reduce the chances of under-age access; regulation of access and content, ethical production practices including safe sex and commitments to performers' positive physical and mental health, and ethical marketing and distribution. They also comment that 'No one should ever be exposed to porn (or any kind of sexual interaction) against their will' (ibid.: 186).

For those porn consumer who may feel their pornography use has become problematic, and who wish to alter the ways in which they relate to pornography, McKee et al. have a range of suggested responses to ethical dilemmas arising from these perceptions (ibid.: 179–181). These are not limited to (but do not absolutely discount) the suggestions of the anti-porn lobby 'to stop consuming porn entirely' (ibid.: 178). Another source of information on this area is the Center for Internet Addiction Recovery's (2006) resources on Cybersex/Cyberporn Addiction. Definitions of cybersex and cyberporn differ, but cyberporn consumption might be constructed as a subset of cybersex activities. Cybersex would also include consensual erotic interactions between sexual partners using texting, webcam and other digital technologies. Such interactions would take account of those between people who are partners in long-term sexual relationships, as well as between people who have yet to meet F2F. As we have seen here, discussions of pornography, as with discussions of sexuality itself, raise important issues quite apart from those of the technical delivery of content.

Reflection: Worrying content

Some people worry more about hate sites and violent images than they do about pornography. Which do you see as most concerning? Why?

CYBER STALKING AND DEFAMATION

Cyber stalking, cyber harassment, and cyber bullying all refer to the behaviour of an aggressor to a victim using digital technology. The terms are generally interchangeable in everyday life, while the notion of defamation – whereby someone has their reputation attacked – has a specific legal meaning. This case study examines a real-world case of cyber stalking and harassment that partly took the form of defamation. It is drawn from life to demonstrate the comparative unpredictability and the wide-ranging affects of this form of attack.

While few people have the time and energy to be dedicated cyber stalkers over the long term, as reported here, victims who are persecuted in this way find it an immense challenge to continue their daily life unaffected. Cyber harassment raises vital issues about the pervasiveness and unity of the internet in comparison with the piecemeal nature of legal and regulatory responses. It also touches upon the relative importance of the right of free speech, sometimes in direct opposition to the right of individuals to be protected from unwarranted attack. This case study examines these issues in terms of a specific stalker, Mr Bill White, a US citizen, and his attacks upon his one-time colleague and Australian academic, Associate Professor Trevor Cullen. It addresses some of the remedies attempted by Cullen, a professional journalist and communications academic, and their relative ineffectiveness up to (and beyond) White's eventual death in 2004. This case study is based on work carried out by Ms Julie Dare for her Honours thesis (2005), and her resulting publications. Both Cullen and Dare have given their permission for their experiences and their work to be detailed here.

An internet search for 'Dr Trevor Cullen' produces a series of complex, and as it happens ironic, results as well as some hundreds of hits. The first site listed is a MAKO site (Movement Against Kindred Offenders), an Australian organisation dedicated to publicising sex offenders, their crimes, sentences and known whereabouts. The MAKO site identifies child sex offender Trevor Cullen, a one-time Brisbane dentist. Dentist Cullen was convicted in 2004, having first come to the attention of the police in 2000. The irony of this circumstance is that since the late 1990s, White had been making similar and unfounded allegations about a different Trevor Cullen, a priest and academic. White's harassment began through the use of fax machines, and progressed to the internet as that became more accessible. (Hereafter, all references to Cullen are to the innocent victim of cyber stalker White.)

Many of the posts on the first pages of the 'Trevor Cullen' search results chart the attempts of Cullen to defend himself against untrue and defamatory allegations of paedophilia, at a time when Cullen was still serving in holy orders as a Catholic priest as well as teaching in a tertiary journalism program in a small Roman Catholic university in Papua New Guinea (PNG). White and Cullen had worked together briefly at the Divine Word University (DWU) in Mandang PNG in 1996. One semester into his three-year contract, White was sacked for spreading untrue and malicious rumours about other members of staff. After his dismissal, and with time on his hands as a result of persistent unemployment, White carried out his harassment of current and past DWU staffers, and upon any people (like Professor John Henningham, Cullen's highly respected PhD supervisor) who defended them. White registered hundreds of websites in the names of his victims and opened numerous email accounts.

Sir Peter Barter, a former Acting Governor-General of PNG, and a member of the Governing Council of DWU, was one such victim. He commented: 'Mr White has at least 80 email names addresses registered, he has sent countless messages to influential people, the media and even messages in my own name to myself' (Barter 2002). Indeed, White often stole the email identities of his targets in order to further embarrass and harass them. The saga linking White to Cullen seems to have begun when Cullen responded to a series of troubling posts by White on the Pacific Forum website a year or so after White's sacking. In July 1998 Cullen wrote to the web maestro (a non-gendered reference to people who might otherwise be termed 'webmasters') asking that action be taken against White's abusive and defamatory postings. 'Instead, his [Cullen's] letter was posted on the website, and within two days White had created a web page in Dr Cullen's name alleging he was a paedophile and had committed academic fraud' (Dare 2005). Since Cullen was at that point in the middle of his PhD research at the University of Queensland, examining the impact of HIV/AIDS reporting upon the growing South Pacific epidemic, such allegations were calculated to have a devastating effect upon Cullen's developing academic career.

Cyber stalking is not a rare occurrence, but it is difficult to counter effectively. CyberAngels (2009) was launched in 1995 by volunteer citizen support group, the red-beret Guardian Angels, to help promote internet safety. They run mainly US-based workshops on handling cyber harassment and cyber bullying. WiredSafety (n.d.) is larger than CyberAngels and has less of a vigilante image. It offers, among other services, free internationally accessible web-based training programs to promote safety on the internet for educators, families, law enforcers and other citizen and community groups. Along with organisations such as Google and Microsoft, WiredSafety is a member of the Harvard University-based, Berkman Center for Internet and Society-supported, Internet Safety Technical Task Force (ISTTF), whose report on *Enhancing Child Safety and Online Technologies* was set up specifically to address the challenges posed by social networking sites and released early in 2009 (SNS Safety 2008). Their final report on safeguarding young people from online risks addresses the development and promotion of technologies and techniques that aim to create a safer environment for young people using the internet.

WiredSafety offers a range of resources for victims of cyber stalking and cyber harassment, including individualised help, a self-paced interactive guide and online tutorial materials. Their advice to people suffering the kinds of attacks perpetrated by White upon his victims is that 'Ignoring the communications sent to you is the best first step to stopping most cyberstalking/harassment. Unless your situation involves a truly obsessed or depraved harasser, most will lose interest quickly if they don't get the reaction they seek' (WiredSafety n.d.). Unfortunately, White was such a depraved harasser. So how did Cullen handle the situation, and with what effect?

White was so obsessional that, in addition to Cullen himself, everyone who worked with Cullen and whom White judged to be supporting him was also subjected to his attacks. This list included colleagues, employers, student guilds, journalists, lawyers and research partners. The scale of these attacks enabled the development of an informal 'victim support' group whereby the people that White attacked banded together to support each other. Even so, the attacks continued growing in pace and scale, to the extent that White at one stage had Cullen linked to sixty-four defamatory sites. Cullen and his co-victims decided to retaliate, initially in a low-key way and in measured terms for public consumption, along the lines of exercising a right of reply. This was the role played by many of the publicly posted documents, some of which are still found on the web. As a result of the harassment, Cullen and his co-attacked found themselves spending significant time and money learning about the internet and the intricacies of web site construction and legal redress. In addition to this drain on his resources, Cullen was asked embarrassing questions by his students and others who did not know the story, and he was concerned about the impact of the defamatory attacks upon his quest to find an academic position.

In both 2001 and 2003, Cullen went to the Australian police who advised him that they were powerless to act unless there was a credible likelihood of White physically attacking him in Australia in person. This was not foreseeable since White lived in the US, had limited financial resources, and was unlikely to travel internationally. At about this time, Cullen, who had recently gained a position at Edith Cowan University, was spending significant sums of money researching his legal options. His new colleagues had begun to attract White's fire, and a new set of students were asking questions. In April 2002, having successfully gained permission to serve White with legal documents at his Californian home, Cullen sued him for defamation through the Western Australian Supreme Court, seeking to stop the attacks, remove the defamatory materials and gain financial redress for the harm done by his comments. The situation was complicated by the fact that defamation at that time was a state matter in Australia and the law consequently varied across Australia's different legal jurisdictions. Court costs in the region of Aus$8,000 were kept as low as possible by a supportive lawyer who donated significant time to the ground-breaking case.

'White did not appear at the proceedings, nor did he raise any defence to the defamatory statements. Dr Cullen was awarded $70,000 in compensatory damages and a further $25,000 in exemplary damages, in recognition of the deliberate nature of White's attacks' (Dare 2004: 11). Indeed, the judge commented that the damages should 'be sufficient to signal to the public the vindication of his [Cullen's] reputation' (Newnes J cited in Dare 2004: 17). There was considerable publicity for this outcome: at the point that the judgment was delivered it was the largest internet defamation award ever handed down in Australia. Newspaper articles appeared in *The West Australian* (O'Leary 2003: 13), *The Sunday Times* (of Perth) (Hellard 2003) and *The Los Angeles Times* (Hyman 2003). There was also broadcasting coverage, including an item on Australia's ABC *7.30 Report* (O'Donnell 2003).

Even with an Australian judgment in Cullen's favour, however, approaches to White's ISP site hosts, to US domain-name suppliers and to search engines such as Google resulted in no positive action. Given that freedom of speech is vigorously defended in the US as the First Amendment cornerstone of the Constitution, it seems that the right of a US citizen to defame took precedence over the right of a non-US citizen to protection from defamation. Cullen was advised that only a US Court Order would authorise the removal of the defamatory material. This would have been an extraordinarily expensive and drawn-out process since the Australian judgment would not have been accepted in a US court, but would have been subject to an essential re-hearing of the case under US law. White meanwhile had linked together many of his sites attacking Cullen and his related victims. This ring of sites often has the effect of maximising search engine visibility, moving a site or collection of sites higher in the order in which they are displayed after a search.

Subsequently, and the genesis is uncertain although it is not Cullen's work, one of White's victims developed *Bill White Exposed* (n.d.). This website may seem somewhat offensive in itself, but that is to a lesser degree and with different intent from the web sites through which White attacked his victims. The content becomes serious half-way down, after the animated image of the smiling toad, and begins to outline some of the substantive issues as well as identifying White and his actual address. The *Bill White Exposed* site is the remedy often promoted as an appropriate 'right of reply' to defamatory material: an equivalent attack in similar terms. This right of reply redress is sometimes suggested as the best possible response to cyber stalking since it preserves the notion of the internet as a locale for free speech.

Dare comments (2005) that: 'Many critics accuse plaintiffs of using the legal system to stifle freedom of expression, effectively 'chilling' robust debate, and situate the debate within a 'David and Goliath' context, wherein wealthy individuals and corporations use defamation laws to stifle opposition'. The term 'chilling' here is widely used – as in www.chillingeffects.org – to refer to inhibiting forces that influence what is posted. The effect of this chill is to make online comments more conservative. It also leads to self-censoring and the withholding of views. Chillingeffects.org has a special section on defamation and offers university 'Law Clinic'-based advice on how to avoid viewpoints being frozen out of internet debates. Often, defamation actions are interpreted as an attack on free speech, rather than a right to defend one's reputation against baseless lies.

Most discussions of defamation start from the premise that the action is brought as a way to chill debate or end it altogether. Dare argues differently in this case. She suggests that defending White's 'right to defame' on free speech grounds fails to acknowledge the impact of White's postings in suppressing free speech, and in disrupting interaction on public discussion sites, such as the Pacific Forum. Further, as victim Henningham argues, to the extent that White's defamatory statements about corruption and illegality were believed, it is possible that White's Cullen-related attacks on missionaries, medical doctors, aid workers and charitable organisations had harmful impacts upon thousands of people who might otherwise have received assistance (cited in Dare 2005).

The impact of White's activities in inhibiting free speech also affected the press. When the media began to take an interest in Cullen's forthcoming court case, a number of journalists contacted White for his side of the story. They and their editors were subsequently subject to their own abusive websites once White realised they did not see matters as he did. The hard copy of *The West Australian* story (O'Leary 2003) was not posted in the online version of the paper, even though this would have been expected. Dare (2005) comments that 'according to the journalist who covered the story, the newspaper's proprietors decided the risk of attracting Bill White's attention was too great'.

Concluding that White's defamatory postings by themselves created a de facto restriction of free speech on the internet, Dare's view (2005) is that:

> whereas defamation laws operate within a transparent system of laws and regulations, and are open to debate and review, White's form of 'regulation' is completely arbitrary ... the insidious nature of the threat posed by individuals such as White – a threat that often escapes the notice of the broader public and the media – represents a greater risk to an active and engaged public sphere than traditional defamation suits.

Dare's contribution to this debate was such that The Honorable Jim McGinty, Western Australian Attorney-General at the time, asked her permission to circulate a copy of her Honours thesis to the Standing Committee of [Australian] Attorneys-General (SCAG) Defamation Working Group.

There is no doubt that White, and stalkers like him, have direct effects upon the lives of those they harass, even where the risk of physical harm is minimal. It is also clear that conventional remedies, such as a resort to law, further punish the victim through extracting costs, fees and stress in circumstances that rarely allow a realistic prospect of recovering those expenses. Victims with a professional reputation to protect may also find themselves under considerable pressure from employers and social institutions to sue the defamer, since this is one of the few effective ways to demonstrate to third parties that the defamatory allegations are without substance. All these circumstances are made more complex where the harasser and the victim are located in separate legal jurisdictions. The alternative remedy, which is using the internet as a vehicle for a right of reply, is also an impost upon the victim who is required to continually monitor the attacks and develop the skills and knowledge to respond to them appropriately. In this case, however, White's death eventually led to the cessation of most of his websites – but only once the contracts he had agreed with the ISPs hosting them ran out.

Reflection: Free Speech on the Internet

Do you think it's more important that internet-communicated speech is 'free' or 'fair'?
Who gets to decide what constitutes 'free' or 'fair' speech?

Summary

- Chapter 6 considers constructions of the internet as a risky place, with a specific focus upon content risk (pornography) and contact risk (cyber harassment).
- Discussions about the internet as a risky place raise issues about narrative theory, discourse analysis and metaphor. These are briefly addressed before examining the major case studies of the chapter.
- The internet is considered as a major conduit for accessing pornography and this is constructed as a risky activity in some circumstances. Pornography is acknowledged as one of the internet's 'killer applications',

and as a major driver of technical advance. It can be commercially risky for an organisation to regulate so heavily that pornography is not accessible via the internet.

- The case study on cyber harassment is based around the experiences of a real person, Associate Professor Trevor Cullen, whose fight to clear his name involved a range of strategies in response to the attacks of his persecutor, the late Mr Bill White.

- This chapter has raised issues concerning the public sphere: in terms of media coverage of children's use of the internet; in terms of narrative and discourse analysis; and in terms of the importance of free speech relative to the right not to be defamed.

Chapter 7 focuses upon the relationship between the internet and the public sphere.

7 THE PUBLIC SPHERE

INTRODUCTION

Chapter 6 considered claims that the internet should be a space for free information exchange, but also a place that might need to be regulated to protect people from risks, harassment and lies. This chapter continues that discussion by examining the notion of the public sphere as:

> a realm of our social life in which something approaching public opinion can be formed. Access is guaranteed to all citizens. A portion of the public sphere comes into being in every conversation in which private individuals assemble to form a public body. ... Citizens behave as a public body when they confer in an unrestricted fashion – that is with the guarantee of freedom of assembly and association and the freedom to express and publish their opinions – about matters of general interest. ... The public sphere as a sphere that mediates between society and state, in which the public organises itself as the bearer of public opinion, accords with the principle of the public sphere – that principle of public information which once had to be fought for against the arcane policies of monarchies and which since that time has made possible the democratic control of state activities. (Habermas 1989a: 73–4)

At the time that Habermas was developing his theory, 'the media of the public sphere [... were] newspapers and magazines, radio and television' (1989a: 73). Today, this list would include the internet. Habermas was careful to distinguish between 'mere opinions (cultural assumptions, normative attitudes, collective prejudices and values) [that] seem to persist unchanged in their natural form as a kind of sediment of history' and public opinion which 'can by definition come into existence only when a reasoning public is supposed' (1989a: 74). These aspects of Habermas's theory have triggered huge debate. The idea of a 'reasoning public' implies that some publics are less reasonable than others, and that judgements can and need to be made about where reasoning starts and ends in order to accord legitimacy to public opinion. Indeed, Habermas defines public opinion as 'the tasks of criticism and control which a public body of citizens informally – and, in periodic elections, formally as well – practices vis-à-vis the ruling structure organized in the form of a state' (1989a: 73). Public opinion formation in Habermas's mind is a grave and serious responsibility.

Habermas positions the public sphere as growing out of 'a specific phase of bourgeois society' in the second half of the eighteenth century, starting more or less with the revolutionary movements in America (1775–1783) and in France (1789–1799). The 'bourgeois' in this sense can be loosely defined as wealthy, educated men, usually merchants and writers, who were not part of the 'ruling class' and consequently not involved in parliament. These men were also not caught up in day-to-day fighting or working and had the luxury of being able to participate in protracted debate. They met in the coffee houses of London to read the newspapers and political pamphlets and discuss the implications for commerce and politics of the day's events, and of revolutionary ideals. At that point, 'society' was 'a private realm occupying a position in opposition to the state' (Habermas 1989a: 75), but it was clearly no longer a 'private domestic authority' since it came into existence through the formation of public opinion.

Habermas argues that the proper functioning of the public sphere was lost when it became 'a field for the competition of interests … Laws which obviously have come about under the "pressure of the street" can scarcely still be understood as arising from the consensus of private individuals engaged in public discussion' (ibid.: 77). In particular, when the public sphere expanded beyond the bourgeoisie, it lost not only its 'social exclusivity' but also 'the coherence created by bourgeois social institutions and a relatively high standard of education' (ibid.: 77). Many commentators accept the notion of a public sphere but object to Habermas's reservations and qualifications about the contemporary public sphere. Some particularly highlight concerns that the original coffee house culture excluded women and people who had to work for their income, and was mainly financed by wealth generated from the slave trade. It's a big debate which is summarised, synthesised and developed by McKee (2004), among others.

Alan McKee (2004) particularly disagrees with claims that the concept of a 'coherent' public sphere has been compromised by its expansion beyond the bourgeoisie, and the inclusion of popular culture and the mass media. He argues that accusations of the contemporary public sphere becoming trivialised, commercialised, turned into a spectacle, fragmented and creative of political apathy are evidence of the public sphere becoming more inclusive and moving away from a cultural space dominated by white, Anglo, middle-class, serious, educated, masculine values.

Trivialisation, according to McKee, is simply conservative speak for 'women's perspectives', some of which are emotional as well as political. Commercialisation relates to middle-class-based judgements about what interests working-class audiences, and is sometimes implied in discussions about the 'dumbing down' of media content. McKee (citing Aaronovitch 2003: 23) comments that programs such as *Big Brother* and *Wife Swap* remind '"you of that most easily forgotten thing of all; the possibility of something else. The chance that there is, after all, an explanation" for the behaviour of people from backgrounds different from your own' (McKee 2004: 102). Such diversity of perspectives effectively enriches culture.

A complaint against spectacle, in McKee's mind, is a complaint against the *way* in which matters are addressed in popular culture, as well as the topics discussed and the content presented. Discussing the political communication purposes of Black rap music, specifically the Public Enemy video of *By the time I get to Arizona*, McKee comments that the 'visual, aural and bodily' communication of the message is as critical to the Black public sphere as 'written rational modes of communication are to traditional western philosophers' (ibid.: 107). Similarly, the complaint against fragmentation is constructed as a serious, educated regret that not all people engage with the same material in the same middle-class orderly way at the same time; and that different taste cultures – McKee's focus is on Queer communities – choose to embrace 'diversity rather than uniformity' (ibid.: 146). The value of this embracing of diversity is evident in the legitimising of a range of 'publics': each entitled to their own overlapping, or competing, or diametrically opposed, public sphere.

McKee's final defence of the contemporary public sphere is to argue that popular culture does not produce political apathy. Using youth culture as his example, McKee suggests that the problem is one of definition: political action has been redefined but the status quo has failed to notice. Whereas political action might once have meant campaigning for legislation to distribute resources more equitably, it now 'aims to change culture rather than legislation, and hopes for recognition rather than redistribution' (ibid.: 174). The citizen-produced information, knowledge and cultural products available on the internet are evidence of a huge surge of creative and culture-changing energy unleashed over the past decade. Overall, McKee suggests that the public sphere in contemporary culture has moved on from Habermas's restricted ideas concerning the bourgeoisie. These days it is multi-class; emotional; inclusive of genders, sexual orientations, and educational in/experience; diverse and fragmented. This is one way to see the internet and the kinds of information, knowledge and culture on display.

Moving on from discussing the concept of public sphere, this chapter considers three case studies. These are the Electronic Frontier Foundation (EFF), which campaigns for freedom of speech and other civil liberties in the digital domain; Wikipedia and YouTube. But first we will look at the comparatively new phenomenon of blogging and citizen-journalism as a way of investigating the identification of quality information accessible via the web. The sheer diversity of information available raises a critical question: how do we know which information to pay attention to, and which to discard? The web is a repository for scholarly knowledge, and academic researchers use it to gather reputable information on subjects as diverse as Anglo-Saxon culture through to the use of zoological parks to support endangered species. The web is also chaotic, misleading, fragmented and includes a range of opinions and superstitions which no commercial publisher would ever consider dignifying in print. Given the immense amount of information on the internet, we will shortly consider how to decide which information is reliable, following on from some further thoughts concerning the public sphere.

Reflection: The public sphere

Habermas thought that the public sphere was important for democracy, facilitating participation in society.

One argument supporting internet use might be that it enhances democracy by allowing more voices to be heard.

What do you think about this argument?

ONLINE RESEARCH AND ASSESSING THE VALIDITY OF INFORMATION ON THE INTERNET: THE EXAMPLE OF CITIZEN-JOURNALISM

Given the opportunities for free speech on the internet, it becomes important to recognise that not all information is equally valid or equally relevant for any given purpose. Indeed, much of the information on the internet is incomplete or wrong and some is actively dangerous and misleading. Selecting appropriate information for any given purpose requires critical assessment of the uses to which it is to be put. Using the internet to carry out research is a continuous exercise in critical analysis.

People who search for information do so with a variety of agendas. For example, someone with a serious illness who has been told by their medical team that there is nothing more to be done using conventional medicine might deliberately seek out the details of alternative remedies and support groups which most medical authorities would suggest that patients avoid. Similarly, people trying to find out the on-the-ground implications of the Iraq War, which started on 20 March 2003, soon learned about a citizen-journalist Iraqi blogger writing in English, known as Salam Pax. This was not an official source of record, as the well-established 'quality' newspapers see themselves to be: papers such as *The Times* of London, the *New York Times* and the *Washington Post*. Pax's blog was alternative news. He wrote about his daily life in Iraq and offered a very different perspective from the western media and from Al-Jazeera, the Arabic-language news network. What was more, he 'juxtaposed what he and relatives witnessed with what was reported in mainstream Western and Arab news media' (Haas 2005: 388).

The model for establishing validity in the blogosphere is a very different process from that which applies to the western mass media. Bruns (2008a: 69–80) discusses how the conventional media adopt a gatekeeper approach, where newspapers' editorial teams select the staff and the stories that appear in the paper. Written material is filtered and sub-edited to check quality first, and then published. This hierarchical and controlled process is contrasted with the approach of blogging and community-based media production, which is characterised as being 'publish first' and then the reader checks the quality afterwards (ibid.: 74). It is a kind of *caveat emptor* – buyer beware. If this seems like an archaic term, Google gives 1,180,000 web references for its use.

Bruns's view is that news blogging works because stories produced by citizen-journalists set out to achieve different ends from those produced by the mass media. 'The story itself is not the final product, it's just the starting point, because ultimately the goal of every story is to start discussion, to start a lot of people saying what they think about it' (Foster, quoted in Bruns 2008a: 81). News blogger Salam Pax provided a personal and credible view of the war as it was experienced in daily life on the streets of Baghdad, but it was clear that 'Salam Pax' was a pseudonym. Both words mean 'peace': the first in Arabic, the second in Latin; and there was a clear question of the authenticity of the person behind the name. This issue was sufficiently important for *The Guardian* newspaper to track Pax down at the end of May 2003 to establish that there was a person (Salam al-Janabi) behind Salam Pax's alias (McCarthy 2003).

Like Pax's blogs, McCarthy's newspaper story is vivid with the detail of an eye-witness encounter. Unlike Pax's accounts, it also has the brand of an authoritative media source, the UK's *Guardian* newspaper. McCarthy's story provided evidence that Pax existed and that his contribution was important, but it was not an analysis of his relevance or a discussion of why he became a phenomenon on the internet and a much-quoted personal perspective on the Iraq War, used by the western mass media. For analytical and critical information of that kind it is appropriate to refer to more reflective works such as Hamilton and Jenner (2003), or the scholarly contribution of Haas (2005), or the Literary Criticism account of the importance of the first person 'I' autobiographical statement in Gillian Whitlock's (2007) book *Soft Weapons: Autobiography In Transit*.

Over the past three paragraphs, this chapter has critiqued the relative validity of Salam Pax's blog according to a range of parameters and purposes, while demonstrating some of the processes by which it is possible to gauge the acceptability of source material. The first purpose in this critique was to introduce the notion of the citizen-journalist blog, which is an important internet-related innovation not extensively discussed elsewhere in this book. As with the various IMC (Independent Media Center, Indymedia) sites (Indymedia n.d.), whose slogan is 'don't hate the media, be the media', the internet has made Pax's contribution to the public sphere much more relevant and accessible. There will have been many diaries kept by articulate, English-speaking Iraqis, but Pax's is particularly important because it impacted upon the events as they were unfolding. It provided an on-the-ground view during the second Gulf War which was read by soldiers and military strategists, as well as by middle-class intellectuals, schoolchildren and pacifists. For many people, Pax's blog was a useful additional source for framing opinions and informing discussion while the war was in process. This was also the case with citizen-journalist coverage of the Mumbai attacks in November 2008, and is likely to be a recurring pattern in future incidents of unfolding public trauma.

Allucquère Rosanne Stone's (1991) classic case study of the mature-aged disabled online confidante 'Julie', who was in fact a persona created by a middle-aged male psychiatrist, demonstrates how easy it is to be deceived about important matters of fact when the only evidence for the existence of someone is their internet-based communication (see Chapter 8). Consequently, in 2003 when Pax first became important, and in 2009 when evidence was being collected to develop the example used here, it became critical to seek proof of authenticity. A first step was accessing Wikipedia. This was only a first step since the purpose of the preliminary search is purely to define the kinds of authoritative materials that might be available. A search engine like Google might also have been a starting point had Wikipedia not produced valuable information.

In fact, it was Wikipedia which contained the useful information that 'In May 2003, *The Guardian* newspaper tracked the man down and printed a story indicating that he did indeed live in Iraq, with the given name Salam' (Wikipedia 'Salam Pax' n.d.). The Wikipedia entry linked to *The Guardian*, giving access to their website (2009). This enabled a search for 'Salam Pax' using the guardian.co.uk search function. A careful scrutiny of stories referring to Salam Pax published in May 2003 revealed the article by Rory McCarthy cited earlier. It's worth noting here that Wikipedia made a credible starting point, but not an end point. In academic research it is rarely appropriate to cite Wikipedia articles when the evidence supporting the entries, the primary sources, can be accessed simply by following relevant links or hunting further afield or with different search terms.

McCarthy, as a journalist working for a respectable, globally-recognisable newspaper, is an authoritative source for most purposes. Unfortunately, a single newspaper article is generally not sufficient for a piece of academic writing. Since this information search was being carried out as part of an academic writing process, the McCarthy article required further back-up before it could be used with confidence. Newspaper editors commission and then vet journalists' stories and there is no reason to disbelieve McCarthy's contribution, but the article was not produced according to the 'gold standard' of academic writing, which is via informed/'expert' peer review. When scholarly articles are subject to double-blind peer review this means that all information that might identify the author is removed, and the article is sent out for assessment by at least two 'readers' or reviewers. Readers are selected by the journal's editor on the basis of their expertise in the field to which the article contributes. The author has no say in which readers will be asked to read the article, and the readers are not told who the author is. The idea of the double-blind review is that the article is judged on the basis of merit, rather than the reputation of the author. For most academic purposes, scholarly articles from well-known academic journals are the best possible sources to inform a persuasive, well-founded argument.

Libraries at schools, colleges and universities have a range of databases which make it possible to search for references to 'Salam Pax' in scholarly journal articles. These databases are available to students and university staff and use various key terms to help identify relevant information published about Pax in academic journals, and when. Further, many academic institutions make it possible for library members to use Google Scholar to access a range of materials online. Google Scholar, like Google and Google Books, is a full-text database. It can be accessed by clicking on the 'more' tab on the Google homepage, which releases a drop down menu including both the 'Scholar' link and an entry point to Google 'Books'. The full-text database means that every word in every article or book is stored separately and can be searched for individually, or as one or more of a string of words in specific order. By using the advanced search function, in particular the 'with the exact phrase' field, it is possible to ensure that the Google Scholar database is searched for the term 'Salam+Pax' rather than one word or both separately. At the point when this search was carried out, Google Scholar identified 391 separate articles or sources with the term 'Salam Pax' held on the database. The same end would have been achieved in the normal Scholar search by enclosing the term 'Salam Pax' in inverted commas: that's one way to bypass the need to click through to the 'exact phrase' field.

Academic libraries often hold online subscriptions to scholarly journals, as well as collecting and offering hard-copy print versions of articles. Among the references offered by Google Scholar to the search term 'Salam Pax' were several articles held on secure databases that could be accessed immediately via a researcher's personal password, which authenticates the inquirer as a member of an institution with a valid subscription to the journals. Given this choice, it was possible to select between available references in the knowledge that a subsection was easily accessible to online. Google Scholar, based as it is on the same kinds of principles as Larry Page's PageRank innovation, which underpins the Google search engine itself (Chapter 2), not only references the full text of articles but also includes all the references that each of those articles cite. Thus, as it displays information about the articles on its database which refer to Salam Pax, so Google Scholar also displays information about articles that have referenced the article featured. Indeed, the order in which the 391 database items were offered in response to the Salam+Pax search term privileged articles that had been multiply cited. Among the first three articles (most of the highest ranked sources were books based on his blog written by Salam Pax himself) were two with International/Policy Studies titles (*Foreign Affairs*, *Foreign Policy*). This field of study is somewhat removed from the expertise in new media, cultural studies and communications that had prompted the search, so the status of those journals is not immediately clear to a researcher with a new media background. Given this, it makes more sense to look further. Ultimately it was decided to refer to Hamilton and Jenner (2003) for the three paragraphs that introduced this section, implicitly comparing their account with 'the scholarly contribution of Haas (2005)'.

For new media research, the Hamilton and Jenner article might not appear fully authoritative for academic purposes since the journal *Foreign Affairs* is published by the Council on Foreign Relations and is described as both 'a journal' and 'a magazine'. A magazine implies commissioned work and a lack of arm's length peer review. Together with the fact that the paper at 2,702 words is short for a peer-reviewed scholarly article, raises the possibility that the Hamilton and Jenner piece might not itself be peer-reviewed even though the authors' biographies certainly positioned them as academics. Further, since the Council on Foreign Relations has been in existence since 1921 and is 'a nonpartisan and independent membership organisation' (CFR 2009), it seemed likely that there was no direct university affiliation. A university sponsorship might have made it seem more scholarly to a university researcher, somewhat ignorant of the International and Policy Studies field. Finally, Hamilton and Jenner had commented (2003: 131) that Salam Pax's 'authenticity has since been validated by an American newsperson'. This non-specific statement seemed hard to prove or disprove, whereas a number of sources (Wikipedia, *The Guardian* and Haas 2005) had provided verifiable information that Pax's identity had been confirmed by a *Guardian* reporter (who might also be 'an American newsperson'). Where possible, when accuracy is particularly important, the rule of thumb that a piece of information should be checked across three or more separate sources offers some defence against hearsay and woolliness.

Having noted those details about the Hamilton and Jenner (2003) piece, it is prudent to pay comparatively closer attention to the Haas article (2005). Haas had been published in *Journalism Studies*, published by Routledge, and was an appropriate source for a communications and cultural studies scholarly reference. Had the research required been more wide-ranging, perhaps informing an in-depth article on blogging, with particular reference to Salam Pax, more references would have been required, and more ideas considered for incorporation. A first step here might have been to examine other references offered in response to the Salam+Pax search, coupled with clicking-through on the Google Scholar link from the Haas article to the 23 articles that had cited it. Usefully, by using citation links, and the citations linked to the citations, a researcher can check the updated arguments in the field as well as reassuring themselves that the debates around the topic are still current.

A different strategy that might have been followed to prepare the first three paragraphs of this section would have been to use the Advanced Scholar Search function to identify articles by specific authors, such as Axel Bruns, who is a specialist on blogging and the author of a recent book in the area (2008a). A quick search indicates that Bruns has had an article published mentioning Pax: referenced in this book as Bruns 2008b. Further, it would have also been useful to check how current it is to write about Salam Pax by stipulating that Google Scholar list relevant Salam+Pax articles from 2008 onwards. This is achieved by inserting 2008 into the first box on the line marked 'Date: Return articles published between …' According to the Google Scholar website, there were 16 articles referring to Salam Pax published in 2008, and 25 published in 2007.

For the purposes of the section published here, however, the single Haas (2005) reference is sufficient. Even so, it was still worth making a separate query via Google Books. 'Books' is accessed via the same drop down menu as 'Scholar'; triggered via the 'more' button on the Google homepage. 'Advanced Books Search' again allows the option of 'with the exact phrase' for Salam+Pax. Google Books provided 302 links to materials in the database referring to Salam Pax, some of which provided 'snippet view'. Snippet view shows the reader four or five lines with the sought-for term in the centre of the snippet. Conroy and Hanson's book (2007) was the most highly ranked reference apart from the books written by Pax himself. It offers snippet view and had three snippets visible plus the information that 'Salam Pax' appears on four pages. There are snippets from pages 20, 21 and 22. It is quite possible that the fourth snippet-view page is the index.

The next book in the Salam+Pax Google Books list was Whitlock (2007). It offers a 'limited view', which is more extensive than a snippet view. The page offered, 27, had five references to Salam Pax in a scanned-in text of the full page. Limited view also has a 'Search in this book' facility. Entering 'Salam Pax' (with inverted commas) yielded a number of page references (without a summary of the total number on offer) from which it was clear that Whitlock's (2007) study of *Soft Weapons: Autobiography In Transit*, although a 'literary criticism' text, takes a specific interest in the eye-witness, first person account which had particularly recommended Salam Pax to his readership, and which had been also remarked upon when discussing the McCarthy (2003) account of Pax's identification. On the basis of the information provided, it could have been worth requesting the book via the library as something that is likely to be relevant to a larger study of Salam Pax's contribution.

At this point the basic facts had been established, and a reasonable amount of theory covered. On the basis of information gleaned it was possible to sketch out a writing plan. To check that the search strategies had been reasonably comprehensive, however, it was also worth googling 'Salam Pax'. Google's information is less processed than Wikipedia's; it is mainly raw web materials and relatively hard to validate, except through reference to other entries followed by a step-by-step verification trail to arrive at authorities that can be accepted as trustworthy for a given specific purpose. The short-cuts to determining quality in the results of a Google search mainly rely on the authority of the site indicated, or the author of the material, or both. There were 84,300 Google hits for 'Salam Pax'. The first was a piece by Pax, the second was the Wikipedia entry which had already been used, and the third was the McCarthy piece from *The Guardian*, 30 May 2003, about how Salam Pax had been sought and found. This indicated that Google's ranking system was working in line with the priorities already followed, even though Google results differ with country and with language.

It was not until the second page (screen) of Google's 84,300 references that substantially different material was offered. Here, there was a BBC story. The BBC *Newsnight* (2008) account allowed Salam Pax to update his readers, revealing that he and his family had left Iraq and were living in the UK. Some measure of quality is offered by the BBC website, as would also be the case with a recognised newspaper or a report from an organisation affiliated with a university, with a national government, or with a major library. Also on the second screen was a transcript of an ABC (Australian public broadcasting) in-depth interview program called *Enough Rope* (2004). This provided a very personal insight into Salam Pax's life, and revealed that he was gay and his mother was Shia Muslim while his father was a Sunni. However, it was clear that the Wikipedia, Google Scholar and Google Books searches had already revealed the really valuable kinds of scholarly information required by an academic research task.

Clearly this account of how someone might seek quality information on the internet relies on a range of research tools which might at any stage need revisiting:

for example, if Google's Scholar site were closed down, or if it stopped being free or was no longer linked to a library's offerings. There are also a number of books about using the web to find good information which offer a more extensive and rounded set of options. These include Alan November's (2008), *Web Literacy For Educators*, which is as valid for general students as it is for the educators of the title. The important thing to remember when using the internet to carry out research is the standard required for the task in hand. Scholarly work should draw upon scholarly work, rather than upon Google or Wikipedia. Academic books and journals are retained and accessible in reliable and permanent ways, whereas Wikipedia is subject to continuous change (see below), and material accessed via Google can be deleted at any point. Fortunately the web is an effective doorway to much scholarly work, although not all of it, which is the point made by Jeanneny (2006: ch. 5).

Reflection: What makes an information source trustworthy?

What evidence do you look for before deciding to trust information from the internet?

THE ELECTRONIC FRONTIER FOUNDATION

Some members of the online community construct the internet as the ultimate place for free speech and open access to information. In choosing the name 'Electronic Frontier Foundation' at its foundation in 1990, EFF created a sense of affinity between the internet as it was emerging in the last decade of the twentieth century and the mythological frontier freedoms of early pioneers. In the first half of the nineteenth century, communities such as the Mormons were motivated to move west to land that eventually became the State of Utah, to establish their own territories where they could live as they chose under their own rules. Effectively, these pioneers set up a new frontier in the search for freedom.

The implication of the EFF title was that people in search of freedoms that were now circumscribed by everyday life might find what they were looking for in the electronic frontiers of the internet. The EFF was set up specifically to protect freedom of speech on the internet; to promote people's civil liberties, and to defend them (EFF 2009). One of the co-founders of EFF was *Grateful Dead* lyricist John Perry Barlow who, along with his co-founders, was a member of the WELL online community.

The early euphoria about the potential freedoms of the internet was challenged by the reality and the power of government regulation, especially as these were exercised in attempts to control web-communicated images of pornography. On 8 February 1996 the hugely controversial US *Communications Decency Act* (CDA), a sub-section of the *Telecommunications Act* 1996, was signed into law by President Clinton, prior to subsequently being declared unconstitutional by the US Supreme Court in 1997. On the same day, and explicitly linking the action to the CDA legislation, Barlow wrote *A Declaration of the Independence of Cyberspace* (Barlow 1996). The title of this statement concerning the principles of internet autonomy tapped into the emotive history of the US *Declaration of Independence* and its association with the struggle for freedom from colonial oppression. It reads as a liberationist manifesto:

> We are creating a world that all may enter without privilege or prejudice accorded by race, economic power, military force, or station of birth. We are creating a world where anyone, anywhere may express his or her beliefs, no matter how singular, without fear of being coerced into silence or conformity. Your legal concepts of property, expression, identity, movement, and context do not apply to us. They are all based on matter, and there is no matter here. (Barlow 1996)

Material or not, the digital world has proven susceptible to government regulation, as indicated by the discussions on China's controls over the internet (see Chapter 3). Further, experience has taught that one person's free speech can translate into the unacceptable persecution of another through cyber-harassment and defamatory comment, as discussed in Chapter 6. Even so, EFF is an effective champion for the rights of people on the internet, and it has links with equivalent country-based campaigns in most of the world's democracies. Its relevance here is to remind us that information on the internet includes many 'singular' beliefs, and this needs to be taken into account when deciding what to trust. It is also a reminder that in some jurisdictions, such as Myanmar (Burma), Vietnam and Iran, even widely-held beliefs cannot be safely communicated using the internet.

Reflection: A declaration of the independence of cyberspace

How realistic is Barlow's declaration?
How independent is the internet from the politics and governments of the countries in which it is accessed?

WIKIPEDIA

Wikipedia is the best known and most successful agenda setter in the wiki-based prosumer-driven category of web content. Wikipedia is also 'social in the sense that it gets better if more people use it, since more people can contribute more knowledge, or can correct details in existing knowledge for which they are experts' (Vossen and Hagemann 2007: 57). Axel Bruns sees both blogs and wikis as key drivers of Web 2.0 development (see Chapter 5). If citizen journalism such as that practised by Salam Pax is an example of a blog, and blogging is a foundational Web 2.0 application, wikis are another. Bruns also sees key differences between wikis and blogs:

> Where blogs are founded in the first place on a temporal organization and classification of their contents (customarily listing the most recently created articles in the most prominent position), and therefore proceed from a time-based logic, wikis instead implement a space-based structure. Wikis enable their users to create a network of knowledge that is structured ad hoc through multiple interlinkages between individual pieces of information in the knowledge base; they represent, in short, a rapidly changing microcosm of the structures of the wider Web beyond their own technological boundaries. (Bruns 2008a: 102)

Wikis also include mechanisms to see the changes made to pages over time, features to notify key people when a page is changed, and discussion pages which are tied into entries where issues can be addressed: 'as well as other pages for setting policy and norms (and their associated history and discussion pages)' (Stvilia et al. 2008: 986). These features are central to the Wikipedia quest for information quality.

Wikipedia arose from the ashes of Nupedia, a project which intended to harness the skills of volunteer experts but involved professional paid checkers of the content. Jimmy Wales, founder of Nupedia in 2000, and the later Wikipedia in 2001, was intrigued by the emerging open source movement and unsure whether the principles would work in areas other than software, so he set up an online encyclopaedia 'to see if it could be done' (Pink 2005). This was achieved using a seven-step validation process of article assignment, fact checking, review, copy-editing and approval. Two of these processes involved back-up open collaboration: open review and open copy-editing; in both cases the review and copy-editing was offered to the public only after professionals had taken the lead. 'After 18+ months and $250,000', Wales says, 'we had 12 articles' (Pink 2005).

Soon afterwards, Wales found out about wikis. These allow 'anybody with Web access to go to a site and edit, delete, or add to what's there'. Wales started a wiki version of the encyclopaedia. 'Within a month, they had 200 articles. In a year, they had 18,000. And on 20 September 2004, when the Hebrew edition added an article on Kazakhstan's flag, Wikipedia had its one millionth article' (Pink 2005). Wales had demonstrated that open-source principles could work for encyclopedias if the software and the organising principles were right. There is significant administrative work, but it's almost all done by volunteers. There are duties such as 'administering pages, developing software, finding copyright-free photos, moderating conflicts, and patrolling for vandalism. With only five paid staffers, volunteers perform most of it' (Tapscott and Williams 2006: 72). Wales has noted, however, that 'Wikipedia is not primarily a technological innovation, but a social and design innovation' (Wales cited by Hendler and Golbeck 2008: 15).

Bruns, who uses the term 'produser' where some might use 'prosumer', argues that the success of the Wikipedia project indicates four preconditions for effectiveness, as outlined in Figure 7.1.

1. Trust in the potential capacity of the contributors to meet the demands of the project in a non-hierarchical way, with barriers to engagement set as low as possible to include as many produsers as possible;
2. Solve problems through enabling contributors to work on challenges that interest them, in ways that interest them, rather than directing people to work on tasks that someone else has decided are critical;
3. Set up 'granular' content-creation practices; small, separate tasks 'requiring a limited set of skills and a limited degree of user investment'. If the consequences of task failure are low and reversible then produsers can learn on the job and administrative direction is minimised;
4. share ownership of processes, tasks and outcomes with equal access to information, and reject inflexible production models.

Source: Based on Bruns 2008a: 19–20)

Figure 7.1: Bruns's preconditions for the creation of an effective wiki

Additionally, there are general principles that Wikipedians should adhere to. They should be unbiased in what they write, and act in good faith to improve the encyclopedia. The guidelines are sometimes summed up as 'Neutral Point of View', 'Verifiability' and 'No Original Research' (Bruns 2008a: 113). Just in case not everyone follows the rules, a number of 'semi-protected' articles have watch-lists: people who are notified when the entry is changed. Watched entries include the biographies of political figures and religious faiths and movements. The watchers are vigilant. A study by MIT and IBM 'found that cases of mass deletions, a common form of vandalism, were corrected in a median time of 2.8 minutes. When an obscenity accompanied the mass deletion, the median time dropped to 1.7 minutes' (Pink 2005). The Wikipedia process has produced a self-correcting, continually updated site. Further, in 2005 it had over 500,000 articles in English compared with the 80,000 on offer in Encyclopedia Britannica. By 2007, the number of articles in English had risen to two million (Bruns 2008a:107), while some commentators estimate that an average of almost 2,000 new articles in English is posted every day (Tapscott and Williams 2006: 76).

So why is Wikipedia generally unacceptable as a stand-alone, academic-quality reference for research papers and essays? *Wired* journalist Daniel Pink provides an answer: 'Encyclopedias aspire to be infallible. But Wikipedia requires that the perfect never be the enemy of the good. Citizen editors don't need to make an entry flawless. They just need to make it better. As a result, even many Wikipedians believe the site is not as good as traditional encyclopedias' (Pink 2005). A study by *Nature* magazine of 42 science entries revealed that Wikipedia was less reliable than *Britannica*, but neither was perfect. *Britannica* had three errors per article, Wikipedia four (Tapscott and Williams 2006: 75). Wikipedia swiftly corrected the errors identified.

As a compensation for always being a work in progress, Wikipedia content is constantly growing, changing and responding. During the days in which the 2008 Mumbai attacks were in progress, 26–29 November, Wikipedia provided a record of the unfolding events. This was less a critique of the mass media, which tends to be the focus of citizen-journalist blogs, but was instead a 'chronicling of history as it happens' (Bruns 2008a: 104). For many people who watched the three-day horror unfold, including professional journalists, the new pages on Wikipedia, the tweets on Twitter, and images on Flickr and YouTube, offered an organic multi-dimensionality missing from the polished, packaged, professional news services. According to Wales, wikis 'let people who share a passion also share a project' (Pink 2005). A revitalised prosumer-driven public sphere is emerging from that passionate participation.

YOUTUBE

Google bought YouTube in a $1.65 billion share deal in October 2006, valuing the smaller company at approximately 3 per cent of Google. When the deal was announced, Eric Schmidt, Google CEO, stated that YouTube 'complements Google's mission to organize the world's information and make it universally accessible and useful' (Google 2006). Implicitly, the information Schmidt referred to in terms of YouTube was digital video: both prosumer-made and paid-professional. In improving the searchability of the YouTube archive, and offering YouTube video sources as relevant items of information alongside websites, pdfs and other language-based documents, Google was arguably adding value to what was already a vibrant and growing video community, and improving the services Google offered to its core search clients. Since that time searches on Google increasingly offer relevant YouTube content, and there has been significant integration of written and visual data sources within the Google databases. At the point where it was acquired, the YouTube service was growing exponentially with 'more than 100 million video views every day with 65,000 new videos uploaded daily' (Google 2006). It had come a long way for an idea which was not yet two years old.

YouTube was started in February 2005 by Chad Hurley, a graphic designer and user interface expert, Steve Chen a Taiwanese-born engineer, and Jawed Karim a computer scientist who had migrated from Germany to the US in his early teens. They had all previously worked for PayPal, and had become millionaires when that company was bought by eBay in 2002. Their idea was to set up a site that allowed registered users to upload short digital videos, of less than ten minutes, typically from cell phones, cameras and camcorders, for other people to access. Anyone could access the open content, but only community members could post. Indicating that the YouTube community was an important element in the deal, Google announced that the YouTube management team would continue to operate the company independently. By April 2008, there were over 80 million YouTube videos (Burgess 2008: 102).

When Google bought his company, Hurley claimed that 'Our community has played a vital role in changing the way that people consume media, creating a new clip culture' (Google 2006). Like Wikipedia, YouTube had dramatically rewritten the possibilities for interactive participation in the public sphere. Building upon the social networking potential, leveraged to a significant extent by the social networking site MySpace, which was providing 17.5 per cent of all YouTube traffic at the point of sale (Tancer 2006), YouTube registers the total number of times each video has been viewed and offers users the opportunity to rate and comment on videos they watch. Given the huge audience accessing the service, and the tens of thousands of videos uploaded daily, YouTube's community members were readily able to find content of interest and share it with friends while still gaining a sense of an overall YouTube brand and service.

YouTube was not a file-sharing service in the ways in which Kazaa and Napster had been, however. When YouTube users access the material that interests them, the video is not downloaded onto viewers' computers, thus avoiding some of the legal issues associated with peer-to-peer systems. Instead, images are streamed from the

YouTube site but the links to access specific video content can be easily embedded in blogs, websites and emails and forwarded virally from one person to another. Because YouTube controls the videos posted on its site, they are in a position to remove pornography and other material banned by the site's rules. They can also respond to 'cease and desist' notices from copyright holders. Even so, one strategy adopted by YouTube to minimize friction with old media such as film and television companies is a range of forward-looking agreements under which some copyright material is allowed on the site. As BBC News business editor Tim Weber indicated:

> According to the theory of the long tail – where niche content can attract relatively large audiences by being findable and available on demand – it could create a win-win situation. Old media conglomerates can finally reach the audiences that have abandoned them for the on-demand world of the internet. (Weber 2006)

Writing about 'Viral video, YouTube and the dynamics of participatory culture', Jean Burgess (2008: 101) defines viral marketing as 'the attempt to exploit the network effects of word-of-mouth and internet communication in order to induce a massive number of users to pass on marketing 'messages' and brand information "voluntarily"'. YouTube offers examples of 'viral video' and internet 'memes' (a meme is the smallest possible element of culture, analogous to the gene in biology), artistic fragments and ideas that are adopted by large communities of users and then employed as part of the indicators of community membership. Burgess notes that internet memes 'spread and mutate via distributed networks in ways that the original producers cannot determine and control' (2008: 101). Indeed, according to Burgess, these memes sometimes become 'the mechanisms via which cultural *practices* are originated, adopted and (sometimes) retained *within* social networks', and cultural value can be attributed 'to the extent that it [the meme] acts as a hub for further creative activity by a wide range of participants in this social network [YouTube]' (2008: 102, italics in original).

Burgess's example, 'All your chocolate rain are belong to us' builds upon a turn of the century viral Flash animation of the opening sequence of the European version of the Japanese game *Zero Wing*, where the plot of the game is explained in a poorly translated context scene in which the beleaguered captain of a battleship is told 'All your base are belong to us'. Like the LAN clan Big Dikk Pimpz's (BDP) 'REPRESENT!!1' graffiti (Green and Guinery 2006), the in-joke comes from enjoying a claim to authority which includes a display of inadequacy (see Chapter 8). In the case of 'REPRESENT!!1', the failing is that, in demanding the audience's respect (as do the Nas lyrics for the song of the same name), the author has let slip the Shift key so that the final exclamation mark has become 1. In the case of 'All

your base are belong to us', the fun lies in appreciating the poor translation within the claim.

In a site of over 80 million videos, and rising, very few can reach a level of prominence equivalent to, say, *Harry Potter* in the world of publishing. The YouTube equivalent to the fan fiction communities (Chapter 8) are those which take a popular text and rework it to create something new that speaks in a different way to the fan community. This is the case with Tay Zonday's user-created music video 'Chocolate rain' (Zonday n.d.), an anti-racist 'self-penned' song which had been viewed over 47 million times as at February 2010. According to Burgess it was 'the combination of oddness and earnest amateurism' that caught the attention of an internet community 4chan.org whose 'members swarmed YouTube to push 'Chocolate Rain' up the rankings initially, motivated ... around absurdist and sometimes cruel frathouse culture' (2008: 104).

Once the song had achieved some salience, a number of parodies, remixes and mash-ups followed. These include a Star Wars/Vader spoof drawing attention to the fact that Zonday turns away from his microphone to breathe; Vanilla Snow, which is a 'white' response to the chocolate 'black'; and 'All your Chocolate Rain are belong to us' (*All your ...* n.d.) a mash-up of the original song. The term 'mash-up' here borrows from the notion of a major traffic pile-up, indicating that images from two or more sources have been combined together to create the revised, or re-imagined, work. In this case, the mash-up edits Chocolate Rain with the flash sequence from *Zero Wing*, while the resulting melange advertises itself on YouTube as 'The world's most nonsensical mistranslation in the style of the world's most nonsensical anti-racism song'.

Starting out as a small element of a larger study of 4,300 highly popular YouTube videos, undertaken with Joshua Green (Burgess and Green 2009), Burgess's analysis of the Chocolate Rain meme argues that the 'textual hooks' and 'key signifiers' that catch the attention of the audience cannot be identified in advance of community take-up. Once they have been widely celebrated, however, the hooks and signifiers are 'available for plugging into other forms, texts and intertexts—they become part of the available cultural repertoire of vernacular video ... even apparently pointless, nihilistic and playful forms of creativity are contributions to knowledge' (Burgess 2008: 106). The point that Burgess makes here is that the success of these prosumer videos lies not in their professionalism, or necessarily their inherent qualities of production or performance, but in their capacity to offer cultural material, a meme, that can be appropriated and circulated by the audience/community. Sometimes, the audience/community is recognised by a professional performer taking a popular internet meme and making a song from it. This reverse experience was the case with the Numa-Numa meme, remixed by Rihanna (Milian 2008).

The community is not a passive recipient of the user-created viral video. Instead, community members do necessary and additional work by essentialising elements of the video in a manner which allows the cultural fragments to acquire specific meanings in new contexts. Such circulation typically takes the form of an in-joke, as with the BDP 'REPRESENT!!1' image (Green and Guinery 2009). This would be a meaningless text to people other than gamers. The value of the joke lies in the fact that the only people the BDP LAN clan are interested in impressing are other gamers. In creating and sharing new popular culture meanings from older materials, communities and social networks are also creating new ties between members and setting boundaries of practice that distinguish them from 'outsiders'.

Reflection: User-led culture

How does your use of YouTube, Twitter, Facebook and other social network-based sites differ from conventional information-driven internet searches?

Summary

- This chapter introduces and critiques Habermas's notion of the public sphere before considering how we can be confident in the usefulness of information we find on the internet. The work of the Electronic Frontier Foundation is used to underline the variety of 'singular views' accessible through the internet, as well as reminding us that some people are unable to use the internet to circulate even mainstream views because of repressive governments.
- Blogging and wikis are identified as particularly representing the new dynamism of Web 2.0. Blogging is addressed in the case study on Salam Pax, which also examines how to evaluate web-based information, while the history and operation of Wikipedia is discussed separately.
- The case study on YouTube introduces the notion of the internet meme through a consideration of Burgess's work (2008) on the 'chocolate rain' meme.

Chapter 8 builds on web-based social networks to look at online communities.

8 COMMUNITY

INTRODUCTION

What is your view of community? How does it interrelate with your view of the internet? Do you use the internet and its various elements of social media: 'IM [instant messaging], chat rooms, social network sites, email, blogging' (SNS Safety 2008: 21), as ways in which to build and maintain community? For most readers of this book, the internet is a key element in the development and maintenance of community. Clearly, there are any number of internet-related case studies that could have been considered in this chapter. Many organisations use websites and email lists to build communities around a shared passion: some succeed. One of the most influential and extraordinary examples of the building of an internet-based community of interest is the US MoveOn organisation.

Set up in 1998 by internet start-up millionaires Wes Boyd and Joan Blades, MoveOn.org originally arose out of their desire for the Clinton administration to move on from the scandal surrounding President Clinton's affair with Monica Lewinsky and return to a left-wing political agenda. The movement attracted the attention of seriously wealthy George Soros and also gained support from other left-inclined citizens. By 2003, claims Wolf (2004), MoveOn's email list had reached 2.3 million subscribers. Although this momentum did not unseat President George W. Bush's bid in the 2004 Presidential elections for a second term, it may have been part of the dynamic that tipped the balance in favour of a more radical agenda with the election of President Barack Obama in 2008. At that point, MoveOn claimed 4.2 million members (Move On 2008).

Obama's presidential campaign has been celebrated as the moment when the internet came of age in mobilising everyday citizens across the US, both to work for the eventual Democratic win and to contribute huge numbers of small donations to fund the costs of the campaign (Miller 2008). MoveOn.org was only one part of that dynamic, but it is an important indicator of the potential for bringing together communities of like-minded individuals. Indeed, there were over 1,000 election parties in towns and other geographical communities across the US facilitated by

MoveOn in the wake of Obama's success. The MoveOn.org phenomenon has also spawned equivalent organisations in other countries. One example is GetUp.org.au in Australia (Get Up 2009), while Avaaz.org (Avaaz 2009) operates in 14 languages and has a mission to raise international awareness about global issues and matters of social justice around the world. In the UK the TheyWorkForYou.com organisation is another way in which the internet is being used to enable voters to scrutinise and influence the democratic process by making the actions of members of parliament more visible, and making elected representatives more accountable (They Work For You 2009).

But are these coalitions of interests and political agendas really communities? Are they 'movements', but not 'communities'? The answer to these questions depends in part upon how people define the terms they use, how they feel about the communication they experience and how emotionally invested they are in the groups concerned. Certainly, one person's online group can be another person's community.

In the first half of the twentieth century, research on community often started with, and overlapped, research on family. Thus Arensberg and Kimball's (1940) Harvard-sponsored study of *Family and Community in Ireland* and Young and Willmott's study of *Family and Kinship in East London* (1957) examined working-class communities in rural and urban settings, respectively, underlining the importance of family within community. In contrast, Talcott Parsons' (1943) essay 'The kinship system of the contemporary United States', theorised that the dominant feature of American society was that of the 'isolated nuclear family', and triggered extensive research for several decades to determine whether or not the nuclear family was isolated from their extended kinship network (Sussman 1965), or whether support and care continued through mechanisms such as a sense of mutual obligation and a desire to get together (Anderson 1971).

To some extent research in these decades examined community either as an adjunct to co-located family, or as a local replacement for distant family. In particular, the offering of 'small services', such as child-minding required proximity. Where family were distant or unavailable such services tended to be exchanged within the community on a reciprocal basis, building social networks and communal obligations. Over time it was recognised that many functions of community are also carried out at a distance, using technologies including ICTs and the car, and that the focus on locality may have been overemphasised (Litwark and Szelenyi 1969). In particular, family would travel to care for a distant family member in times of illness, stress or turmoil (Baldassar 2007).

In the early days of the internet there was substantial discussion about whether online communities could ever have the richness and depth of physical, geographical communities (Green 1999). People talked about their experiences online in terms of the quality of connection. Howard Rheingold's definition that 'virtual communities are social aggregations that emerge from the Net when enough people carry on those public discussions long enough, with sufficient human feeling, to form webs of personal relationships in cyberspace' (Rheingold 2000: xx), suggests that community is brought into being through affective investment. Shawn Wilbur also sees emotional engagement as central: 'for those who doubt the possibility of online intimacy, I can only speak of … hours sitting at my keyboard with tears streaming down my face, or convulsed with laughter' (Wilbur 1997: 18).

A complementary opinion, that community is related to perception rather than grounded in location can be drawn from the work of Benedict Anderson (1991 [1983]), who comments in *Imagined Communities* that every community, including those located in geographical space, 'is imagined because the members of even the smallest nation will never know most of their fellow members, meet them, or even hear of them, yet in the minds of each lives the image of their communion'. He goes on to comment that 'all communities larger than primordial villages of face-to-face contact (and perhaps even these) are imagined' (Anderson 1991: 6).

Finally, Daniel Miller and Don Slater carried out ethnographic fieldwork in Trinidad, in the West Indies, to examine Trinidadian uses of the internet. They concluded that online community was not a shadowy placeless substitution for real community, but a way in which Trinidadians could engage with an existing community differently. In particular, online community allowed deeper (more 'spiritual') engagement, with greater opportunity to absorb the impact of a communication and to craft a reply, without slowing down the exchange as a letter does (Miller and Slater 2000: 182–3). Trinidadians also found it easy to integrate internet use into every day family and community life. The implication of Miller and Slater's work (ibid.) is that the internet is part of real life: there's nothing virtual about it; and the communities found on the internet are similarly authentic communities operating in a different context from face-to-face communities. Often the two contexts complemented each other, as with the use of the internet to unite members of the global Trinidadian diaspora with their friends and family still living on the island.

There is continuing research attention being paid to how online communities function and organise themselves and the benefits they deliver offline to their online members. Three case studies are used here to explore different aspects of online community and how these relate to face-to-face communities. Korean LANing takes the (generally masculine) culture of interactive gaming and examines how this has been celebrated and made into an event phenomenon in South Korea, and what this says both about cultural specificity of online communities and about the public investments made by Koreans in their internet infrastructure. The generally masculine case study of online games is contrasted with that of fan fiction writers and readers, who are typically young women and teenage girls. The final case study, HeartNet, has been chosen to interrogate the notion of whether online communities can offer support for older internet users that are beyond the everyday capacity of most offline communities. Is there a particular advantage to building up social capital in an online community?

Reflection: What makes a community?

Do you see yourself as belonging to one or more communities?
What is it that makes 'a community', rather than 'a neighbourhood' or 'online group'?

LAN CULTURE

The Republic of Korea (South Korea) has adopted computer gaming in a way unlike elsewhere. For example, compared with other game-invested countries, like the US (36 per cent) and Japan (39 per cent), 65.9 per cent of Korean women play online games (Carr et al. 2006: 163). In a country with a population of around 50 million, but with a popular culture reach well beyond its borders, *Lineage II* is Korea's answer to the American title *World of Warcraft*, and second in global reach (Beavis 2007: 54–5). These Massively Multiplayer Online Role-Playing Games (MMORPGs) attract millions of subscribers (Carr et al. 2006: 27). 'In 2005, the Korean online game market was worth US$1.4 billion, accounting for 56% of the entire Asia Pacific market share' (Jin and Chee 2008: 38); by March 2007 this amounted to '32% of the world's online gaming market' (ibid.: 42).

Korean citizens' commitment to online interactivity in domestic contexts and at PC bangs (Korean internet cafés) mirrors an over-arching national commitment to digital technology. According to Hwang and Park (2009: 234), in 2007 the South Korean 'IT industry's share in total GDP exceeded 16.9 per cent and its contribution to GDP growth was 30 per cent'. While there were only 100 PC bangs in 1997, at the time of the 1990s Asian economic crisis, the flight to small entrepreneurial businesses as a way of avoiding unemployment has been credited with fuelling the growth in PC bang numbers to 25,000 by May 2002. At this point, the market peaked before stabilising at 20,000 in 2005 'because of market saturation and the growing access to broadband services in the home' (Jin and Chee 2008: 48). Approximately 90 per cent of Korean households were connected to broadband services by 2007 (MIC 2007).

The research, development and national priority given to a fast broadband infrastructure make online connection easily accessible and comparatively cheap, driving high participation rates. The average Korean citizen enjoys fast, affordable access and download speeds unparalleled elsewhere apart from Japan (BuddeComm 2009). Another element of the dynamic which supports online game-play is attributed to historical and socio-cultural factors in that Korea was colonised by Japan in the early years of the twentieth century, and many console games are produced in Japan. Although the ban on Japanese cultural products, including 'console games, films and music' was lifted in 1998, 'the historic tension between the two countries has proven persistent and difficult to surmount', especially since such global console game companies as Sony, Nintendo and Sega are Japanese (Jin and Chee 2008: 47). This avoidance of Japanese cultural products has helped to promote the growth of online gaming in Korea, which is part of a burgeoning global market for video games that seems to withstand economic crises, even while other entertainment sectors falter.

Tracey Jennings, a Canadian partner in consultancy giant Price Waterhouse Coopers, comments that the global video games market 'still shows significant growth: 18 per cent in 2008 is quite remarkable when you contrast that to the number of [entertainment] segments that have been contracting'. She attributes this resilience to: video games not being dependent on advertising revenue; the continuing popularity of newer platforms such as the Wii, Nintendo DS, XBox 360 and PS3; broadband adoption since this enables better engagement with MMORPGs; and the take-up of wireless which facilitates 'smart phone' gaming, as with the iPhone (Jennings 2009).

Just as not all computer games involve internet access, not all players play the same kinds of games. For instance, many Korean women 'play online puzzle and card games, rather than the mainstream titles advertised on television or lining the shelves of computer game retailers' (Carr et al. 2006: 2), while their sons might play militaristic FPS (first person shooter) titles. Differentiation in the games market means that not all gamers have the same potential attraction to marketers. Commercial games developers tend to invest in 'high profile games with massive production budgets. Such games ... continue to be aggressively marketed at youthful, male consumers' (Carr et al. 2006: 2).

In Korea, the Ministry of Culture and Tourism (MCT 2004) has identified online games as being 'the central industry that will complete the IT revolution due to the combination of content and high technologies' (ibid.: 6). Seoul held the first ever World Cyber Games in 2000, attracting a field of 174 competitors representing 17 countries, and continued hosting the games for the next three years, with the number of countries increasing to the point where 74 nations were represented in the 2007 competition in Seattle, Washington (Hutchins 2008: 855, 856). E-game skills and competencies are honed in Korea's local PC bangs through engagement with 'LAN culture', typically involving groups of adolescent boys and young men.

'In the early days of the internet, LANs were Local Area Networks (usually housed in a set of connected spaces, such as a school, or the floor of an office block)' (Green and Guinery 2006), although LANs and their Wide Area equivalents, WANs, are now subsumed into generic networks, '[t]he LAN title has now been appropriated by LANers, and recognises their reinvented skills which allow them to setup a temporary, portable network in a specific locality' (ibid.). Such activities require extensive collaboration both in terms of technological skills and game-playing. 'The assembled computers are all connected and powered up so that they are both interlinked and online. LANers also wear headsets to keep their aural feed localised so that they can still hear each other when shouting out comments, instructions and witticisms during a game' (ibid.). Jin and Chee (2008) credit the engagement in games and similar activities with assisting Korean youth to construct 'tight-knit communities ... [they have] become another channel of human relationships, in other words, part of people's actual lives' (ibid.: 39).

Writing about Malaysia, Nichols et al. (2006: 1–3) record the testosterone-fuelled dynamic of players engaged in the 'LAN arena':

> This huge dimly-lit cavern is filled with more than a thousand PCs, each with a trendily-dressed young gamer, all with headphones clamped to their heads, hunched over keyboard and mouse, frantically clicking and tapping. Some have small groups of friends behind them, egging them on; others are playing solo. ... What is happening here is not immediately obvious to the uninitiated. It might appear that these gamers are wrapped up in their own little fantasy worlds, oblivious to everyone around them. In fact, they're not. Most of them are playing games as part of teams composed of several others in the room. The LAN – or local area network – means that all the computers you see are linked together ... there are a great many games being played back and forth across the network [and the internet] all at the same time, each with its own rhythm of triumph and defeat, exhilaration and disappointment.

Along with acknowledging that much online gaming is an important communal and community-building activity (Morris 2004), recent writing has as often focused on the positive social impacts of gaming as any perceived negative ones. The out-dated perceptions of 'Nintendo (no-friend-o)' (Marshall 1997) have been countered by researchers as diverse as journalist Steven Johnson (2005) and psychology professor Kevin Durkin (Durkin and Barber 2002). These commentators argue that online games can be highly interactive and educational, and that games players are likely to be sociable, with strong friendships and positive parental relationships. This perception has been underlined by Jin and Chee's (2008) ethnographic study of PC bangs.

Noting that the PC bang is a de facto community centre to which young people are drawn during their journey from school to home, or to one of the after-hours cramming colleges, Jin and Chee comment that 'almost all youth interviewed talked about their online activities in relation to obligation and duty, whether it was to their friends and promised times for logging on or [whether it was] to their guild, clan or band of blood brothers' (2008: 50). Costs are reasonable, at US$1 per hour playing, but the sociability access means that not all participants would be playing all the time, as with players who are watched by friends.

Carl, a gamer, explained why he chooses to play at PC bangs, even though he has his own computer at home: 'The difference is that home is alone and the PC bang is with people. ... PC bang can be more together, and you know, Koreans like to be together ... so that makes PC bang culture. When we play the [same] game at home we feel something empty' (Jin and Chee 2008: 51). There is also an online micro-economy in building virtual game items for sale on Korean gamer site Itembay.com and its equivalents. This can lead to incomes of US$100 per week for dedicated players. In a community with 93 per cent unemployment in the 15–19 age group, and a job market distorted by compulsory male service in the armed forces, this makes online competency a credible skill for young people who are out of work, and possibly an act of celebrating civilian life, since, according to Carl, 'there is no Internet during army service' (Jin and Chee 2008: 51–2). Games are therefore implicated in issues of autonomy, self-esteem and social status, as well as offering intrinsic rewards in terms of skill development and incremental achievement.

These insights are reinforced by participant-observer work with a teenage male Australian LANing clan BDP which operates in domestic rather than internet café contexts (see Chapter 7). In a more privileged environment, albeit with slower internet speeds, middle-class LANers gain effective online access as part of a family broadband and telecom subscription, and set about persuading their parent(s) to increase the download quota. At this point the gamer has

> access to any other non-filtered communication channels available – from MSN, chats, blogs through to porn and engagement in the copyright infringing download communities accessing music, films, TV programming and alternative digital media. Such 'investments' in online materials become a status point for the young person concerned – the person in a given peer circle with the greatest internet access, and the largest capacity for storing downloaded materials, is in a good position to develop key-guest status for the evolving LANparty culture ... Alongside the playing of the game, the interconnected gamers set up a peer-to-peer file sharing network allowing the accumulation of desired 'wares' (TV, films, games, music, photos and other digital media) from each other's hard drives. (Green and Guinery 2006)

While gaming skills are often honed in known friendship circles, real recognition is offered by impressing strangers. This can either happen at LANfests, weekend-long community LAN parties which resonate Nichols et al.'s description of the Malaysian LAN arena (2006: 1–3), cited earlier, or online. The trick online is to use the games programs to identify servers with active games in progress that are not located so far away as to slow the play down, as indicated by the ping rate. Desirable games also have enough players to make the game interesting, but do not have so many gamers online that individual game-play techniques are lost. 'One of the biggest compliments that can be paid to a teenage gamer is for a clan leader to ask the LANer if they are interested in becoming a clan member' (Green and Guinery 2006). Among the reciprocal community commitments incumbent upon joining a clan of strangers is the undertaking on the part of a new member to be available at certain times and for given hours, and to upskill, developing an under-standing of clan strengths and strategies. In return there is an implied undertaking that the senior clan members will mentor the newbies (n00bs). 'LANing culture – as with hacker culture, open source, blogging and wikipedia culture – valorises excess and builds in tests of commitment' (Green and Guinery 2006). It also builds community.

In the same way that different clan members will have differentiated skills and separate roles as part of the online clan, so they also have complementary areas of technical expertise. It becomes important for each clan to have access to a LANer who has the skills to 'pimp' their machines, modifying them to the highest possible gaming specifications (specs) by improving, for example, the graphics resolution. Judging between fast, powerful, fit-for-purpose machines is one of the tests of strength often trialled at LANfests. It is the equivalent of a shoot out. Speccing a machine 'involves increasing the hard drive capacity to allow for the storage of an ever-greater downloaded 'library' of material and priming the machine to make it operate faster than specifications would usually allow – thereby increasing frame rate' (Green and Guinery 2006). These modifications might run the risk of overheating the CPU, central processor unit, which consequently requires a range of cooling solutions from fans through to heat sinks.

At the ultimate, gamers aspire to water-cooled computers, 'to flat screen non-reflective monitors and enhanced video graphics cards to optimise the game aes-thetics (and the blood splatter patterns) … with sound-surround audio and neon illuminated working computer innards'. It is at LANfests, surrounded by local gamers with all their hardware, files and games on display, that participants are introduced to new games, technology and downloads. 'The community-based LANs become a clan of clans (or a group of groups). Red Flag LAN (RFLAN) is one such LAN community, immortalised – as many are – in a *YouTube* documentary (RFLAN 2006)' (Green and Guinery 2006).

This gaming case study refers to the construction of game communities online and offline by gamers who make appointments in real-time contexts to go online to serve a specific role in shared enterprises with established collaborators. Often these engagements start out involving friends and acquaintances already known offline at home, at school, and from PC bang environments. Gaming clan members tend to develop a range of complementary online 'specialisations'; in a FPS context one might be a radio operator, another could be an armaments specialist. When playing online, good gamers might be spotted and recruited by clan leaders not personally known to the gamer, and inducted into a new online clan: a community with a range of rights, responsibilities and obligations.

Gamers' activities also have implications for the community development of their technology skills. While FPS gaming culture is often pervasive among young male players in the western world, RTS (real-time strategy) culture is particularly marked in Korea where the most effective gamers are national celebrities. Boxer, the gamer alter-ego of Lim Yo Hwan, has a fan club of more than half a million members, and professional gamers act like any other celebrities, 'marrying supermodels, making vast amounts of money, and engaging in other such activities deemed worthy of spectacle and intrigue' (Jin and Chee 2008: 49).

Reflection: The value of online video games

Even though many games are criticised for their violent content, and for being 'a waste of time', do you see any value in developing skills in online game-play?

FAN FICTION COMMUNITIES

With their beginnings in original 1930s fan communities dating back to the early days of Hollywood, and to science fiction fanzines (Thomas 2006: 226), fan fiction communities do more than get together online to talk about their passion: they produce and consume materials which reinforce aspects of their fan identities, allowing them to enjoy richer, prosumer fan experiences.

Henry Jenkins, writing about *Convergence Culture* (2006), uses the stand-out *Harry Potter* (HP) fan community to discuss fan fiction. One reason why the HP community is so huge is the power of the brand itself, based on the books by J.K. Rowling, and the fact that the fans include millions of teenage readers willing to experiment with innovative ways of communicating using new media. Green and

Guinery (2004), in a participant-observer account of a fan fiction community, noted that the phenomenal growth of the HP fandom can be directly related to take-up of the internet, and to middle-class readers' internet access. Harry Potter first made an appearance in 1997, in *The Philosopher's* or *The Sorcerer's Stone*, depending upon the publishers' market. At that time, the character of Harry was eleven, and much of his audience was of a similar age. They were about to discover the internet. In many western countries, a majority of two-parent families with school-aged children were online by 2000 (e.g. ABS 2001). From the parents' point of view, this may have been to support the kids' education: from the children's points of view, this new connectivity opened many possibilities to explore aspects of culture that they had already found interesting. One area of engagement for HP fans was the online fan fiction communities.

Communities depend on individuals engaging with the general exchanges, projecting themselves and their identity in an ongoing conversation. This dynamic was aided by the unfolding HP narrative, which did not conclude until the publication of the seventh and final book, *Harry Potter and the Deathly Hallows*, in 2007. In an earlier era, Nancy Baym analysed the importance of the space between episodes of soap operas to the Usenet fan groups who discussed them:

> The viewers' relationship with characters, the viewers' understanding of socio-emotional experience, and soap opera's narrative structure, in which moments of maximal suspense are always followed by temporal gaps, work together to ensure that fans will use the gaps during and between shows to discuss with one another possible outcomes and possible interpretations of what has been seen. (Baym 1995: 143)

The HP universe comprised an increasing number of books and films, but there were spaces between these – long spaces, as far as the fans were concerned. Speculation, analysis and fantasy in these spaces fuelled the rampant growth of many fan fiction sites, and a proliferation of stories. For example, between 16 August and 4 October 2004, HP fan fiction writers posted an additional 9,196 stories on one general fan fiction site, fanfiction.net, at a time when the HP node had 147,067 stories, compared with its nearest 'rival', *Lord of the Rings*, with 33,189 stories (Green and Guinery 2004). Fanfiction.net writers form only one of a number of HP communities, as the discussion of the *Sugar Quill* site indicates below.

There are critical differences between many of these groups in terms of whether the HP focus is a specialist node in a general fan fiction site (as with fanfiction.net) or whether it caters only and specifically for HP fans (as *Sugar Quill* does). Other dimensions include whether anyone can post anything, or whether all stores are read and polished prior to acceptance: do they need to go through a beta-reading process? 'Beta reading takes its name from beta testing in computer programming: fans seek out advice on the rough drafts of their nearly completed stories so that they can smooth out 'bugs' and take them to the next level' (Jenkins 2006: 179). This mentoring and support improves the writing of both the mentor and the mentee. Some sites only take narratives entirely consistent with J.K. Rowling's vision, indicating a fully moderated site in which assessors make informed judgement. Others accept related stories, or stories that accept part of the 'canon', for example, popular author Midnight Blue gives the setting of her evolving fan fiction *The Mirror of Maybe* as 'after *Harry Potter and the Goblet of Fire* and as an alternative to the events detailed in *Harry Potter and the Order of the Phoenix*, [this] is a Slash story involving Harry Potter and Severus Snape' (cited in Green and Guinery 2004).

A further difference between sites is whether the stories posted are suitable for all ages, or whether they are categorised as suited for adults only (no matter the age of the author). Unlike the Adult Verification System that goes hand in hand with credit card use for porn sites, however, fans can access 18-plus sites such as restrictedsection.org through declaring themselves to be adult. Authors are asked to indicate what makes each story adult-only: for example, 'Please put a warning if your story contains content that may be offensive to some authors [*sic*], such as m/m [male-on-male] sex, graphic sex or violence, violent sex, character death, major angst, BDSM [Bondage, Dominance and Sadomasochism], non-con (rape) etc' (cited in Green and Guinery 2004). Adult-content HP fan fiction includes a range of specialist pairings such as Twincest: incest between one of the sets of HP twins; or Weasleycest: incest within the Weasley family. Tosenberger comments that the sheer size of the fandom means it is a collection of subgroups, 'and each subgroup can churn out its own stories for its own audience with impunity' (2008: 191).

Through their construction of the HP narrative, and their conjectures about motives and consequences, fans present themselves as identities with whom others might agree (positive affirmation), or disagree (offering the chance for engagement through exchange). Even now that the over-arching narrative of the Harry Potter canon is concluded, fans can still explore 'pretty little tree-lined side streets' ancillary to the accepted story. As Sweeney Agonistes, editor of *Sugar Quill*, (n.d.) put it in an interview, fan fiction writers are not correcting J.K. Rowling's text but delighting in it: 'I don't write to fanfic to "fix" things, I write it to ... speculate on what *might* have led up to something, or what *could* result from some other thing. A story that leaves these wonderful corners isn't a story that needs fixing, it's a story that invites exploration' (Jenkins 2006: 181–2). That exploration is most enticingly carried out in a community context.

Many HP communities have been started and run by teenage fans. One such, central to Jenkins's account of the HP Fandom, was *The Daily Prophet*, www.

dprophet.com, a newspaper circulating at Hogwarts School of Witchcraft and Wizardry and part of the HP canon. Heather Lawver, the site's founder, was home-schooled so lacked an everyday exposure to school newsletters but had a clear idea about what her paper should look like and how to coordinate her hundreds of HP fan-contributors around the world. She also knew how to market the scheme to journalists' parents. As she explained it in her open letter *To the adults*, *The Daily Prophet* brings 'the world of literature to life ... exploring books, diving into the characters and analysing great literature ... By creating this faux world we are learning, creating, and enjoying ourselves in a friendly utopian society'. The site has experienced many down times, partly because of Lawver's health problems and possibly because of Warner Bros professionalization of the *Daily Prophet* title, but the fan newspaper is only one of the contributions Lawver made to HP fandom. The other involved her contribution to cross-site community action against Warner Bros when they instituted what came to be known as The *Potter* War.

The *Potter* War began in 2000 after Warner Bros bought the merchandising rights to everything apart from J.K. Rowling's books. 'Its legal department followed standard operating procedure. Threatening letters were automatically sent to site owners who [had] registered Web domain names that included trademarked words from the *Potter* universe', wrote Weise in *USA Today* (Weise 2001), adding 'But most of these were fan sites set up by children and teens. They were terrified by official letters demanding that the domain be handed over lest the matter be referred to company lawyers'. In the UK, a Warner Bros letter to British teenager Claire Field informed her that her site 'The boy who lived' was "likely to cause consumer confusion or dilution of intellectual property rights'. Field and her father hired lawyers to negotiate with Warner Bros and went public, circulating negative publicity about the action in the mass media (Bringers n.d.). Alistair Alexander, a seasoned web campaigner, set up potterwar.org.uk (now defunct) to support a number of teenagers in the UK and internationally who had received Warner Bros 'cease and desist' notices.

In the US, Lawver set up her own Defense Against the Dark Arts campaign (dprophet.com/dada) 'Protecting Fans From the Real You-Know-Who' and led a fan boycott of all HP merchandise. Lawver commented that Warner Bros 'under-estimated how interconnected out fandom was. They underestimated the fact that we knew those kids in Poland [an example she'd given Jenkins] and we knew the rinky dink sites and we cared about them' (Jenkins 2006: 186). The HP community had developed links across the various 'subgroups'; including language, culture and national affiliations, with a particularly effective trans-Atlantic axis. Eventually even Warner Bros got the message: 'We didn't know what we had on our hands early on in dealing with *Harry Potter* ... as soon as we realized we were causing consternation to children or their parents, we stopped it' (Warner spokeswoman and brand manager Diane Nelson, quoted in Jenkins 2006: 187). In fact, the action against Claire Field lasted over three months before Warner Bros dropped the demand for the transference of the domain name.

Through her involvement with *The Daily Prophet*, Lawver, the home-schooled Potter fan, had learned about: coordinating an international online community; writing and editing a digital newspaper; educational and pedagogical arguments for prosumer involvement; organising and running public relations campaigns; and copyright law. Outside the fan communities, educators began to argue about whether prosumer activity was a threat to a child's learning (it distracted them from their studies: the displacement argument), or whether it was an almost ideal collaborative learning milieu. Spurred on by Jenkins's (2004) remark that 'some of the best writing instruction takes place outside the classroom in online communities', teacher-educator Angela Thomas investigated online community *Middle Earth Insanity* to explore the social processes of fan fiction engagement. She comments that 'the range of practices within the community is quite astonishing: collaborative writing of fan fiction, the teaching of each other about the intricate details and specialised knowledge of the field ..., and dealing with management issues related to a 200-member community', adding that 'For a group of predominantly 13–17 year-olds the level of writing, discussion and negotiation involved in these practices is remarkably sophisticated' (2006: 229).

Notwithstanding *Sugar Quill* Sweeney Agonistes' view that fan fiction does not set out to 'fix' the canon, Thomas notes (2006: 234) that *Middle Earth Insanity*, which is partly based on *Star Wars*, includes a number of female Jedi knights which is at odds with Lucas's original epics. Similarly, she comments that 'slash fiction ... in which same-sex relationships are explored' can, for some young prosumers, provide 'a medium for exploring these issues and for seeing themselves reflected in texts that might otherwise marginalise them' (Thomas 2006: 236). Naturally, for predominantly teenage and young adult prosumer communities, romantic attraction, desire, love and sex are major themes.

Once stories deviate dramatically from the accepted canon, with a romantic pairing of Harry Potter with Draco Malfoy, for example, the oeuvre is referred to as 'fanon' – the non-canon world according to fans' creative, minority or subversive engagements with the text. Given that many members of fan communities engage with other members in face-to-face contexts such as schools, as well as online, what people are prepared to write or not write; or read or not read; becomes part of their public persona. 'The range of identities that can be constructed using the many online HP FF [fan fiction] genres, however, permits wide scope for FF members to identify with dissident constructions of the HP narrative and helps to add to the momentum with which his fame increases' (Green and Guinery 2004). At the same time, fanon dissenters occasionally feel embraced by the mainstream canon. One such moment is linked to the scene in the film of *Harry Potter and the Prisoner of Azkaban* where Draco blows Harry an origami bird in a Defence Against the Dark Arts class. It looks like a blown kiss, and the Harry/Draco slash prosumers certainly read it that way. Another instance is Rowling's indication 'that Dumbledore was gay and had loved Grindelwald ... Slash fans are often accused of "distorting" or "misreading" texts, so this public validation of their method of reading is a somewhat rare pleasure' (Tosenberger 2008: 187).

Linking back to Chapter 6 and discussions of the mainly male audience for visual pornography, Tosenberger notes that most writers of slash fan fiction – indeed, most writers of all fan fiction – are female. 'The existence of slash complicate[s] conventional notions about women's interests in erotica in general and the types of erotica women were supposed to be interested in (i.e. heterosexual romance novels) ... PWPs ("Plot? What plot?" or "Porn without plot") abound' (2008: 189, 194). Tosenberger also argues that the large slash communities allow safe space for the exploration of queerness and non-hetero sexuality in the company of supportive prosumer communities in a way that celebrates the exuberant bliss (*'jouissance'*: 201) of young adult sex:

> In an era when representations of adolescent sexuality are both exploited and policed, Potter fandom is an arena in which fans of all ages, genders and sexual orientations can tell stories to satisfy their own desires; this freedom is especially valuable for younger fans, whose self-expressions are heavily monitored in institutional settings ... Potter fandom is a lively, intellectually stimulating, and tolerant interpretive community. (Tosenberger 2008: 202)

Reflection: Nurturing the fans

Do you agree that organisations which buy popular culture products need to protect their investments? Should fans be exempt from the usual constraints of Intellectual Property law?

HEARTNET AND SOME ONLINE RESEARCH ISSUES

Many avid gamers and fan fiction writers have grown up alongside the internet and have integrated online connection into their communication repertoires, relating digitally with their F2F friends, as well as forming communities with people they are unlikely to meet in person. Different communication issues impact upon community membership for those who come to the internet as mature adults. HeartNet Australia, heartnet.com.au, was set up as an online research community to investigate these communication dynamics. Jointly funded by the ARC, Australian Research Council and the NHFA, National Heart Foundation of Australia (WA division), HeartNet was designed to help people recovering from heart disease to support each other in adopting heart-healthy attitudes and behaviours in a semi-moderated environment, where the lay (not medically-trained) moderator checked in every few hours.

The concept of moderation is critical to most well-run communities. It implies that there is a group of people with administrator rights: able to remove objectionable posts, or exclude people who repeatedly contravene the rules from further participation in the community. Moderators are usually volunteers drawn from a pool of keen community members. They may be paid, but the necessity to secure an income stream or raise enough money to fund salaries means that the website tends not to be controlled by members, which can affect the sense of community that develops there. Volunteer moderators are likely to take on roles in addition to the 'disciplining' of participants and the control of content. Many moderators in fan fiction communities, for example, will also be beta readers and prosumers in their own right. In HeartNet, the key moderator and administrator has been the PhD student working on the project. There have been two; Leesa Bonniface (now Leesa Costello) and Lynsey Uridge. Supporting the research students are the project's Chief Investigators and a number of specialist web administrators.

At one point, when the community had grown to ten times the size originally anticipated, four members were invited to become moderators. This case study particularly concerns two of these, Rich and Francis (not their real names). In addition to members who act as moderators, most sites have rules and recommended operating procedures. In a community such as HeartNet there is a combination of warnings and 'terms and conditions'. Warnings include the instruction to participants not to act upon health or medical information posted on the site without first consulting their physician. Terms and conditions include the informed consent provisions required by a research project: letting participants know that they can leave at any time, and that the site is for research and posts may be published provided the community member is not identifiable.

In the past, most research into online communities was carried out on sites which were not designed as research projects. This raised a number of ethical issues such as: is it all right for a researcher to quote from a public discussion board even if none of the people involved in the discussion have agreed to be quoted? If a site's moderator and administrator have agreed to the research, does everyone else involved have to agree too? For university-based research most of these issues are discussed between the researchers and the Faculty or University Human Research Ethics Committee. These precautions are taken in part to prevent the sense of betrayal recorded by Stone (1991), when an early group of internet-users discovered that the online friend they thought was a disabled older woman 'Julie' was, in fact, a male psychiatrist. When Julie's confidantes learned abut the deception, their reactions 'varied from humorous resignation to blind rage' (Stone 1992: 82), and some felt totally betrayed. Full disclosure of the research process at the outset of the online relationship is deemed to protect against such distress.

The fact that the internet is accessible round the clock, assuming technology and connectivity, means that online support is more accessible and available than via other avenues. Given that this is not a 'medicalised' community, in that moderation is by the community and not by medical workers, HeartNet members know and share the reality of the daily challenges of living with heart disease, rather than promoting an idealised medical model of care and rehabilitation. Phase 2 attracted many positive comments, reassuring to the researchers and to HeartNet members:

> (Jane): 'I discovered this site while surfing the net. I haven't really sought much support since my heart attack which was nearly a year ago, but wish I had since it would have made those darker days a lot easier to get through'. An American heart patient ... joined the community (Sam): 'I have a lot to be positive about and feel grateful to have found this site full of caring people'. Further, some returnees, who had experienced the first iteration of the site, were warm with acknowledgement (Betty): 'the site is taking off in leeps [*sic*] and bounds. You should all be so proud'. (Bonniface et al. 2005)

In line with Rheingold's views (cited earlier), human feeling would appear to be a touchstone of community. That feeling may be intense, and is not always positive. For example, in the second year of the site's successful operation, it became all too clear to the research team that the fostered community had indeed become organic: it split over 'a high-stakes dispute, over some six to eight months, between two groups of community 'members' which led to official proceedings, social welfare investigations, psychological assessments, indications of a suicide risk and, unsurprisingly, extensive Ethics Committee involvement' (Green and Costello 2009: 462). The split represented the fracture in the previously strong friendship between Rich and Francis.

The word 'members', above, is put into inverted commas because several of the affected parties resigned from HeartNet. This may have been because they were unhappy at the researchers' and moderators' attempts to defuse the situation, or possibly so that moderators would no longer be able to intervene in the continuing incendiary exchanges via private message. (In online community terms, these protracted altercations are often called 'flame wars'.) Additionally, there were issues with authenticity. Upon joining, members had been advised to use only nicknames and the internal private messaging system to communicate with other people, and to protect their privacy in the public domain of the discussion board. This worked well in theory, but had soon given way to authentic communications including face-to-face meetings and community walks, which are clearly of benefit to heart patients. Indeed, such authenticity had also been seen as indicative of community-creation (Bonniface et al. 2006b).

So, what had caused the fracture? In brief, Rich was a keen sportsperson and a positive competitor, while Francis had excellent IT skills. Rich, looking for some benefit side-effects to patients' medication regimes, to counter the many negatives, posted a comment about one of his drugs:

> It is little wonder that this medication [specified earlier] is a BANNED SUBSTANCE by the IOC [International Olympic Committee]. It helps to stop tremors. I recently completed the semi automatic mini 14 assault rifle course as a sniper with the [... Service]. I managed to secure 29 kill shots out of 30. ... I can only put this level of accuracy down to the fact that I didn't develop the shakes as most shooters do. (Green and Costello 2009: 466)

Gavin, a friend of Francis, replied to this post, suggesting that Rich needed to be retrained when he came off the medication in case someone was killed as a result of inexpert sniper fire. Although Francis was not involved in this exchange, Gavin had identified himself as Francis's friend. He was later removed from the community when he failed to provide any means of contact other than a free web-based email. Gavin's phone and address details both had errors in them, and he was not prepared to communicate with any of the research group. Since his bona fides were impossible to determine at a time of rising tension, this led to exclusion. In the meantime, the situation continued to escalate with Leanne, a friend of Rich's, responding to Gavin that 'Rich had shot well before his heart attack and continues to shoot well following his heart attack and suggesting that if Gavin was worried about Rich killing someone then he had better stay out of the way' (Green and Costello 2009: 467). This was interpreted by Gavin and Francis's group as a 'death threat' and the research team were asked to exclude Leanne, which they declined to do, arguing that her statement might be ill-advised, but it was not a threat.

Given the strong bonds of friendship that had existed between the parties, Rich's up-front personality, and the regime of regular but intermittent moderating, there had been occasions when Rich has posted to the discussion boards and signed off with his own photo and his real name instead of his avatar. It was very simple for any well-established member of the community to have enough information on Rich to contact his employers. Someone did this anonymously and in guaranteed confidence, reporting to Rich's employers that he had been talking about his 'sniper training', his work and his professional life inappropriately on the site. This had devastating consequences. Rich's gun licence was removed pending an internal investigation and psychological reports. Rather than, as he saw it, let down his team by being unavailable for armed duty, Rich took leave while the investigation proceeded. The site exploded with accusations and retaliations. Gavin, Francis and their supporters were criticised by other community members who suspected that they had been involved in 'shopping Rich', even though Francis obtained a letter from Rich's employers warranting that the person who had contacted them was not Francis.

Table 8.1: Lines of conflict in the HeartNet case study

Rich, a sportsman.	*Francis, an IT expert.*
Leanne, a friend of Rich.	Gavin, a friend of Francis (excluded when his identity could not be established and he refused to respond to administrators except via a free email service). Jackie, a friend of Francis.
Other of Rich's friends resign when an anonymous tip-off, apparently from a HeartNet member, leads to Rich's employers investigating Rich's posts on the site.	Some of Francis's friends tell researchers that conflict on the site is affecting their health. Researchers exclude them on these grounds, although non-members are still able to visit as guests.

It was about this time that some members of the disputing parties informed the research team that the stress of the situation was making them ill. Their view was that some of the 'attackers' should be expelled. Instead, the team took the view that if the stress was affecting members' health, then the research injunction to 'first do no harm' had to apply and the members who felt unwell should be excluded on medical grounds. Although one member was subsequently reinstated with a doctor's letter, this person experienced the tension as starting again, felt physically affected and was again excluded. This person immediately set up a competitor site and invited their supporters to split HeartNet and join them. At this point Francis and his supporters had left the site; while a number of Rich supporters also resigned at what they saw as a breach of privacy and integrity, with the content of Rich's posts having been first made public to his employers, by the anonymous complainant, and then subject to discussions between the employers' investigation committee and the research team.

Ultimately, Rich was reinstated in his professional work role although reprimanded. The strain had clearly taken a toll and his posts were far less personal thereafter. It seemed as though things had calmed down until a dynamic of 'negative reciprocity' came into play. One of the benefits of a functional online community is the development of reciprocal 'gifting' whereby members give each other time, regard, concern and support. Such gift economies (Cheal 1988) entail emotional investment and build social capital. The opposite dynamic also works, sucking regard, concern and support from a social system. This was the spiral in which HeartNet was unravelling.

Past-members, who had resigned or been asked to leave on health grounds, nonetheless kept returning, either to the site, or in communications with the research team. In particular, Francis was continuing to receive 'hate mail' from people who had resigned from HeartNet. He wanted to see them expelled, but the research team explained this was impossible since the named perpetrators were not currently members. Administrators gave an undertaking not to readmit the offending ex-members to membership, but this was deemed unsatisfactory. Jackie, one of Francis's friends, and at that point still a member, started to contact senior figures in the Heart charity, the university and the research funding organisations demanding that 'justice be done' and Rich supporters be expelled. Francis joined in some of these communications. The situation escalated to the point that some senior leaders of organisations associated with the research received literally dozens of emails from Jackie, some of which stated that her own health was under threat. Reluctantly, and with support from ethics advisors, the team decided to terminate Jackie's membership on the grounds of her burgeoning health stresses.

Francis posted to a blog that he knew was read by site members that he was so unwell as a result of the stress that he was unable to work and was living on disability benefits. Jackie was also known to be living on single-parent benefits:

> Both were thrown into turmoil when the social welfare agencies responsible for administering their payments launched an investigation as a result of a tip-off alleging that they were an undeclared couple living together, which had direct implications for their level of social support and the rules of their income streams. Further, Francis's landlord was contacted by social welfare investigators and – averse to 'trouble' – the landlord gave Francis notice, telling him that his lease would not be renewed at the end of its term. (Green and Costello 2009: 470)

Francis and Jackie assumed that the source of the tip-off, which the social services accepted as justified, had been one of the Rich supporters. Jackie felt that she needed to move towns to establish her status as a single person, while Francis argued that HeartNet had 'made him homeless'. There were also a number of other developments that continued to reverberate for another year. However, a partially successful attempt at conciliation, involving the University Ethics Officer and the Chair, Human Research Ethics Committee, has allowed the site to return to a quieter version of its former self for the time being.

What this case study makes clear is that communities are brought into existence in new media contexts and they behave in both good and bad ways, like human communities in other settings. There has been a lot of discussion (including a number of publications from the HeartNet project) about the positive benefits and round-the-clock accessibility of online communities. These perspectives are valid. Less publicised are the consequences of major discord among community members. Researchers in the field intending to find ethical ways to investigate these issues would be wise to consider worst-case scenarios.

Reflection: the role of moderators

Do you think that online communities need moderators?
Which people or organisations operate as 'moderators' in F2F community?

Summary

- This chapter examined the notion of online community and placed it in the context of being a collaborative space where people offer each other support and emotional engagement.
- The first two case studies typically involve gendered groups of teenagers and young adults. LAN FPS online game-play culture is traditionally male, whereas fan fiction writing and reading is more likely to attract young women. Both involve the development of expertise and skills in collaboration.
- The final case study investigated a crisis in a research community set up to support recovering heart patients. The crisis was unable to be resolved satisfactorily and the community fractured. It is suggested that this parallels processes that also happen in F2F community.

Chapter 9 moves the book forward from considering community to a consideration of family contexts for internet use.

9 INTERNET IN FAMILY LIFE

INTRODUCTION

This chapter is concerned with the internet in everyday life. It is in the home that internet use is most likely to express the choices, pleasures and preferences of the user; rather than the requirements of their employment. Even so, the home is a site of work for some members of the family; especially the mother, but also including children at school who have 'homework'. For these domestically bound workers, the internet can be a 'home away from home' – a place of relaxation within the world of domestic labour. According to Morley, 'For many men, the home is principally a site of leisure and rest (in contrast to their work obligations in the public sphere); for many women (if not most) the home is a site of labour (both physical and emotional) and responsibility' (Morley 1995: 316).

An examination of ICT use in families with children provides a wealth of information about power and priorities across axes of age/generation and gender. A generation ago, Livingstone argued (1992: 113) that:

> The accounting practices through which people understand and explain the role of domestic technologies in their lives reflect their gender relations and family dynamics. Talk about television or the telephone, for example, is imbued with notions of who lets who use what, of moral judgements of the other's activities, of the expression of needs and desires, of justifications and conflict, of separateness and mutuality.

The same dynamics are equally true of the internet as they were of television and the telephone, particularly in homes where there is only one computer online.

Researchers addressing technology flows into and out of the domestic sphere often refer to the Domestication model offered by Silverstone et al. (1992: 19), discussed in Chapter 1, involving appropriation, conversion, objectification and incorporation. Whereas appropriation examines the processes through which a technology enters the home, conversion marks the exporting of the benefits of the technology from inside the household to the wider public sphere. It demonstrates that ICTs offer significant social benefits, as well as educational and entertainment opportunities.

While better grades in school may be one way of benefiting from the conversion of domestic ICT access, ICT use is also harnessed to build social status and networks of interactions, sometimes through such activities as opinion leadership (see below). This dynamic is evident in the discussion of LANing circles in Chapter 8. According to Silverstone (1994: 130), conversion 'defines the relationship between the household and the outside world – the boundary across which artefacts and meanings, texts and technologies pass as the household defines and claims for itself and its members a status in neighbourhood, work and peer groups in the "wider society"'. Silverstone's discussion of texts and meanings underlines the fact that the different frameworks used in this book can interrelate with each other.

A technology is integrated within the home – sitting on a table, connected to a specific power socket – spatially located through the process of objectification. In a complementary manner, incorporation describes the way in which use of the technology is integrated within the temporal rhythms of the household's daily life. It also marks the way in which the household, or its members, incorporate themselves into audiences and communities that produce and consume the chosen media and technologies. In this way, the members of the household can be related to various online communities such as those discussed in Chapter 8. For example, using a computer to access 24-hour coverage of a Big Brother household, and contributing to chat, converts online access into an audience membership as part of an imagined community of viewers and participants (Anderson 1991). Audience participation provides access to information and opinions that, through conversion, can be traded in F2F discussions and social exchanges in the days to come (Hill 2002).

Reflection: Applying the domestication model

Thinking of your most recent ICT acquisition, can you identify the processes and decisions through which it was appropriated, incorporated, objectified and converted?

Many commentators have investigated the gendered dimension of domestication processes, and one particularly useful contribution to this debate is that of Ann Moyal. In researching people's uses of communication technologies, Moyal (1995) draws a useful distinction between 'instrumental' and 'intrinsic' uses of technology. An instrumental use occurs when the technology's role is to achieve a particular outcome such as 'making appointments, shopping, seeking information, timetables, entertainments, making business arrangements, dealing with emergencies, accidents

[and] household crises' (Moyal 1995: 285). ICTs and digital media permit further value-adding over and above other instrumental communication channels. One example of this might be the utilisation of web-based business directories that allow potential clients to browse catalogues and order online. E-tailer Amazon, through its use of cross-selling to market book B to purchasers who have already bought book A, is one example of an online service that has product advantages for many consumers. Online shopping services such as Amazon can simplify complex instrumental activities such as researching, 'wish-listing' and ultimately acquiring goods.

In contrast, Moyal's intrinsic uses included 'personal communication with relatives, friends, volunteer work, counselling, and intimate discussion and exchange' (Moyal 1995: 285). The fact that instrumental and intrinsic uses are very different was indicated by Ann Moyal's in-depth interviews plus diaries of phone use. Two hundred Australian women aged from 15 to over 75 were involved in the research. Except for those who worked from home, who made 10–12 instrumental calls per week, women averaged 2–6 instrumental calls over a seven day period (ibid.: 287). This instrumental activity contrasted with 20–28 intrinsic calls per week averaging about 15–20 minutes, but which could last up to an hour (ibid.: 288). There is likely to be regional and generational variation here, especially since Moyal's work was carried out before the domestication of internet access, but the grounds for distinction between instrumental and intrinsic are likely to apply across ICTs.

The major purpose served by Moyal's respondents' intrinsic calls was 'kinkeeping' (Moyal 1995: 289). This was the term she used for the process by which callers used prolonged and frequent communication to maintain and strengthen their links with family and friends ('kith and kin'). Kinkeeping means that people who are emotionally connected with one another are also closely aware of what is going on in each other's lives. Friendship and affection are strengthened and deepened as a result of extended contact. Moyal identified a major gender aspect to this emotional work, whereby kinkeeping was particularly recognised as 'women's business'. She cites Lana Rakow's (1988) US studies to comment that intrinsic phone calls are 'both "gendered work" and "gender work", in that it is work that women do to hold together the fabric of the community, build and maintain relationships, and accomplish both care-giving and receiving functions' (Moyal 1995: 304).

This pattern of kinkeeping usage continues into internet activities, where women are far more likely than men to be found using email, chat and Skype in intrinsic ways (see, for example, Dare 2006). This kinkeeping communication, carried out between women to strengthen and nurture them in their emotional and relational labour of supporting friends, families and each other, extends the domestic sphere beyond the confines of the home and constructs a virtual domestic environment in which the private and personal of the everyday flows freely and easily.

In addition to including case studies that address the internet in domestic family life, debates around internet 'addiction' and the importance of innovation in family uses of ICTs, this final section of the book highlights how much the majority world's experience of technology differs from that of the West's. In particular, this chapter considers ways in which families, separated by nations and sometimes continents, use ICTs to sustain dependencies and supportive relationships. For example, remittances sent from family members in richer countries to their relatives in poorer ones span transnational distances and link migrants in new countries and their partly dependent relatives left behind. First, however, we return to the consideration of online risk, first encountered in Chapter 6, to investigate further the 'who lets who use what' dynamics of children's use of the internet in domestic spaces. The focus now moves to the parent–child relationship in terms of the regulation of risk.

FAMILY REGULATION OF THE INTERNET

Does someone you know worry about the time you spend online? Are they concerned that your digital life is impacting badly upon your everyday life? Maybe time seems to disappear when you're on a social network site, or in a game, or blogging, and other priorities are left untouched? These are displacement issues. The fear in displacement is that time spent online may take the place of more valuable activities, and such concern is grounded in a notion of an appropriate balance between the time spent online and the time offline. Once issues of values and appropriateness are raised in a discussion, it becomes clear that we are talking about subjective judgements. Judgements indicate a struggle over possible choices and they replay old arguments that have also been applied to other media – such as the time spent watching television, or playing music, or reading books. You, or the people making the judgements, are constructing an image of what life might be like if you used the internet less, or differently. Such judgements are one way to communicate people's priorities.

Maybe you see the idea of a distinction between online and offline as an old-fashioned throwback to the 1990s: after all, internet use is real life, and the two aspects blur. It can be the same with perceptions of positives and negatives. What one family perceives to be the development of technical skills and media literacy, another may judge to be 'internet addiction'. As we saw with the discussion of press coverage in Chapter 6, and the classification of content, contact and conduct risks, people are more likely to worry about negative consequences of the internet while taking positive benefits as a given. Hasebrink et al. (2009: 8–9) identify the positives and negatives of children's online activities as indicated in Table 9.1

Table 9.1: Opportunities and risks of children's online activities

Opportunities		Risks	
Motivations	*Consequences*	*Motivations*	*Consequences*
General usage	Technical skills, media literacy	General usage	Time addiction, dependency
Education and learning	Knowledge, skills, career advancement	Commercial interests	Financial consequences, exploitation of personal data
Participation and civic engagement	Civic engagement	Aggression	Harm, anxiety, aggressiveness
Creativity	Creative skills	Sexuality	Personal contact with strangers, harm, sexual concerns
Identity and social connection	Identity and social connection	Values, ideology	Distorted understandings (of health, politics etc)

Source: Based on Hasebrink et al. (2009: 8–9).
Note: Figure 9.1 adapts two Hasebrink tables that also integrate the perspectives of: Content, 'child as recipient;' Contact, 'child as participant;' and Conduct, 'child as actor,' roles.

Many issues of greatest concern to parents and policy makers, although they may occur infrequently, involve a range of risks. For example, a child might access inappropriate content, and then go on to use chat and messaging services to talk about what they have seen. As a result, they might come into contact with strangers and conduct themselves inappropriately, possibly revealing personal information, publishing personal photos or agreeing to meeting offline. The fact that some of these risks are experienced within the child's home might make the activities seem less real or less dangerous. Further, Lobe et al. (2007: 17) argue that 'children's lives are often lived in the interstices of adult spaces and timetables, and ... children may be expected to circumvent, evade or subvert adult expectations or norms for their behaviour'. It can be suggested that risk-taking is a normal part of child development.

Discussions of these kinds of online 'stranger danger' risks rarely emphasise how infrequently they occur, that their incidence – in the US, at least – is heavily in decline. Schrock and boyd (2008: 10) cite Finkelhor (2008) when they say 'the [minus] −53 per cent change in reports of sexual offences against children from 1992 to 2006 ... is both significant and real'. The final report of the Internet Safety Technical Task Force, commissioned by the State Attorneys General of the United States in response to a perceived increase in risky behaviour as a result of children's participation in social networking sites notes that children at risk online are also more likely to be at risk in other situations: 'Depression, abuse and substances are all strongly correlated with various risky behaviors that lead to poor choices with respect to online activities. A poor home environment that includes conflict and poor parent–child relationships is correlated with a host of online risks' (Wolak et al. 2003; Ybarra and Mitchell 2004; SNS Safety 2008: 20).

There is also concern that young people growing into adulthood risk being judged by future employers and others on the basis of their teenage postings, photographic and otherwise, on public or password-protected websites. This happened to 22-year old Ray Lam, a New Democratic Party candidate for an elected role in Canada, whose Facebook party photos were the centre of a media storm and provoked his resignation from the provincial election (CBC News 2009). Consequently, risks of online activity can be projected into the future as well as being located in the present. Such risks have led to work from, for example, Ann Cavoukian (2009), the Information Privacy Commissioner for Ontario, to educate younger users about their privacy, including the creation of an interactive website MyPrivacy, MyChoice, Mylife (Youthprivacy.ca).

It is unsurprising that in a context of the internet being a risky place, most parents attempt to regulate the ways in which their children go online. This is often done in terms of the placement of the internet-connected computer – for example, by putting it in a public area, and by restricting when it can be used and what it can be used for. The final report of the EU Kids Online project cautions, however, that 'Rules and restrictions do not fit well with the ethos of modern parenting, especially in some countries, and it is unclear that parental strategies are effective in reducing children's exposure to risk or increasing their resilience to cope' (Livingstone and Haddon 2009: 4). Later, the report goes on to say that parents adopt a range of strategies for mediating online activity: 'First, imposing rules and restrictions; second, social approaches – watching, sharing, talking about the internet with their children; and third, using technical tools such as filtering, monitoring' (Livingstone and Haddon, 2009: 27).

Often, family rules centre on the use of the internet for specific activities. The use of social media such as internet messaging, chat, social networking, email and blogging (SNS Safety 2008: 21) tend to be the 'top online activities [... of] youth who are solicited and harassed,' according to Ybarra and Mitchell (2008), and these activities are often regulated within the family. It should be noted that the majority of cases of sexual solicitation and harassment are thought by the victims to be people of their own age (minors) or of unknown age, and some of these could be construed as 'flirting' (SNS Safety 2008, pp. 15–16). Harassment is not straight-forwardly related to the amount of time online, however, since 'youth who are not solicited are much more likely to indicate that gaming is one of their top Internet uses as compared to those who are solicited (Ybarra and Mitchell 2008)' (SNS Safety 2008: 44–5). This is an interesting inversion of many media-sponsored 'moral panics' (Cohen 1980) about games taking over the lives of adolescents. Such stories are often circulated by the 'old media', in newspaper articles and on television, even though there is growing evidence that online game play may offer benefits.

Although we looked at gamer communities in Chapter 8, we have not addressed the pervasive media commentary about problems associated with online game-play. Such reports stretch back to at least 1993 (Kelly and Rheingold 1993) and can be readily uncovered with an internet search (e.g. Freeman 2008), although there are alternative perspectives that counter this dominant trend (Johnson 2005) arguing that many adolescents gain considerable social and educational benefits from game-playing. As well as links into their peer group community, gamers are more likely to be sociable teenagers with positive family relationships (Durkin and Barber 2002). Telephone research conducted by the Pew Internet and American Life project with 1,102 children aged 12–17, and their parents, suggests that 'Fully 97 per cent of teens age[d] 12–17 play computer, web, portable or console games … for most teens, gaming is a social activity and a major component of their overall social experience' (Pew 2008: i, iii). In making positive statements about the social aspects of gaming, researchers do not always have a high opinion about the actual narrative subtlety of such games as Grand Theft Auto: 'the actual content of the game is often childish or gratuitously menacing … much of the role play inside the gaming world alternates between drive-by shooting and princess rescuing' (Johnson 2005: 39–40).

All these issues are brought to bear in the family context because of contests over power and autonomy; the intentions and responsibilities of parents to supervise and regulate online activity, and the fun and freedoms of maturing adolescents, chafing against family restrictions. Parents and children negotiate these parameters, which change over time as children get older (ACMA 2007: 14). Interestingly, many parents say they trust their children to choose appropriate internet activities most of the time. In a 2007 Australian study of 751 households, involving telephone interviews with parents and 1,003 children of the households aged between 8–17 completing diaries, researchers found that 'Most parents trust their child's judgement about the internet and, at least some of the time, leave it up to him/her to choose what is done on the internet (83 per cent). This includes two-thirds who trust their child's judgement all/most of the time (66 per cent)' (ACMA 2007: 21).

This does not mean that there are no rules around internet use in the home. Many families include some or all of the following rules and restrictions: '[not allowed to] talk to people they don't know online, use email, instant messaging, chat rooms, create profile, access certain websites, download music, films, games, buy online, give out personal information' (Livingstone and Haddon 2009: 28 n.26). Such strategies may become less viable as more houses adopt wireless connectivity and as more teenagers get mobile access to the internet. Further, no domestic regime can guarantee to prevent children's access to undesirable material, since restricted children will often access the internet in other locations, such as the homes of their relatively less-supervised friends. Indeed, there is often disagreement between parents and children about the very kinds of rules that are in place. Livingstone and Bober (2005) found that: 'children and parents gave different answers to questions of the incidence of risk (children report more online risk than parents) and to questions of domestic rules (parents report more rules about internet use than children)' (summarised in Lobe et al. 2007: 24).

Parents accept that children change as they mature, and parental rules and behaviour reflects this. For example, in a qualitative Australian research study involving in depth interviews with parents and children, separately, one parent commented that 'He used to let me see the [onscreen] conversations but he won't let me see them now. But that's fine. If I come up and talk to him, he clicks the button and takes the screen off' (Green et al. 2004: 90). Domestic rules about internet use reveal the ways in which the family unit prioritises and models particular behaviours and attitudes. They are a locale through which family relations are tried, tested, negotiated and changed; particularly around axes of gender (ACMA 2007: 7), age (ACMA 2007: 10), and generation in terms of an ongoing discussion between children and their mothers and fathers; together and separately.

Parents' attitudes to online activity can usually be placed on a continuum from seeing their children as autonomous individuals who are able to make appropriate choices, through to more authoritarian approaches where 'parents know best'. As supervisors, parents negotiate their children's access to the internet and work to develop agreement around a hierarchy of uses. This hierarchy includes parents' preferred and promoted uses of the internet for work and study purposes, acceptable leisure activities, and forbidden or illegitimate usage of the internet. In the qualitative study mentioned above, given that parents are generally trusting of children's activities, the most common concern they express is that children spend too much time online. Interviewing parent and child separately reveals the differing perceptions at work (Holloway et al. 2004):

> Father of two, Xavier, expressed his concern about (what he perceived as) his
> teenage son's excessive use of the internet: 'Well I think there's far too much

time ... Gavin'll spend a whole day on it. I try to get him to come to the footy on Sunday. No. He's available for friends [for online gaming and chat on the internet]. He'll spend all day on the computer' (Xavier).

Son Gavin (16), in a separate interview, anticipated that this criticism had been made and felt compelled to counter it: 'Well he [dad] makes comments like saying I'm not fit enough 'cause I spent too much time on the computer but I play soccer a lot. Like, I do sport perhaps everyday at school ... I mean, I think, such a piece of crap (Gavin).

Father and son here are in an age-old contest about who wants whom to do what when. The internet is just one location in which these family-life dynamics are explored, and the son, Gavin, is clearly aware of the explicit accusation that he spends 'too much time on the computer'. For some parents, and their children, the accusation is that the child is actually addicted to game-playing.

'INTERNET ADDICTION'

Lobe et al. argue that, in addition to various forms of specific content, contact and conduct risks, a perceived risk of internet use is the possible development of 'time addiction, dependency' (Lobe et al. 2007: 9). There has been considerable discussion over the past decade as to whether the internet in general, and online gaming in particular, is addictive (e.g. Widyanto and Griffiths 2007). A part-UNESCO-funded report which looks at the effects of game-playing on gamers comments that 'addiction in a non-medical sense is an extremely controversial concept ... for example, the concept is almost exclusively used by people who perceive the activity in question as a deviation from the norm and a deviation from the desirable' (Nordicom 2004: 34). While such statements leave open the possibility that people can become 'addicted' to the internet, they highlight the fact that people make judgements about others' internet activity. Such judgements can lead to complicated interpersonal power struggles, especially between older children and their parents, and result in conflict and concern.

Allison et al. (2006) discuss at length the clinical case of an 18-year-old North American student from the Pacific Northwest. 'Mr A's' parents referred him for psychiatric assessment concerning his online game playing; initially in Diablo II and subsequently World of Warcraft. He had been playing games for several years at the point where his parents and he had sought psychiatric assessment:

Mr A's parents were particularly hoping that the evaluation team would view his game playing as a manifestation of treatable obsessive-compulsive disorder (OCD), but they worried that it might be a form of addiction. Mr A reported that his life had been taken over by the game-playing: 'I play 12–16 hours a day, I do not sleep and I've never had a girlfriend'. (Allison et al. 2006: 381)

While Mr A's internet activities were certainly associated with a range of behaviours that impacted upon his family relationships and his everyday life, the issue of cause and effect was left unresolved in the analysis. The case study stops short of arguing in favour of the existence or otherwise of a clinical condition of 'internet addiction' and instead leaves open the possibility that Mr A's extensive engagement with online games might be a coping strategy which allowed him to avoid a range of psychological challenges identified by the clinical team, none of which could clearly be established as an effect of his game-playing. Instead, there was some suggestion that Mr A's early experience of gaming was as a retreat from the pressures of his parents' continuous house moves (14 times in 18 years) and a refuge from problems at school.

In the early days of public take-up of the internet, Storm King, a US online theorist, asked a key question: 'Is the internet addictive, or are addicts using the internet?' (King 1996). Case studies of internet 'addiction' tend not to deal with this salient perspective. In particular, they discount the pleasurable effect for some internet users of identifying an activity in which they are recognised for their skill and competency. This sense of enjoyment is likely to be heightened where other aspects of an internet user's life make them feel powerless or marginalised.

Reflection: Internet addiction

Do you know anyone who you would say is 'addicted' to the internet?
Does their online life offer them an opportunity for recognition and respect?

INNOVATIVE FAMILIES

Families with school-aged children are a site for a huge amount of innovation and creativity. Two reasons help account for this. First, parents try to equip dependent children with access to the technologies and experiences that they feel are important for their children's future. Second, as children grow older and develop their own income streams, they often use that money to buy goods and technologies that enhance their lives, add value to the equipment provided in their parents' household(s) and establish their status as people with independent spending capacity. These dynamics prompt the acquisition of new and upgraded technologies and the family dynamics supporting technological innovation are considered here.

We have already noted the power contests between parents and children as children mature and claim autonomy and independence. We have also noted, in

Chapter 8, the importance of peer groups in the lives of young people. Essentially, in forming the tight-knit communities (Jin and Chee 2008: 39) characteristic of much teenager society, young adults are negotiating a 'family' of peers able to offer support as they move into the next stage of life and prepare to leave home. The success with which older children negotiate this 'leaving home' phase is important to their parents' sense of self-esteem as well as their own. Research carried out among parents indicates that 'self evaluations in the middle years of adulthood are strongly linked to perceptions of adult children, particularly children's personal and social adjustment' (Ryff et al. 1996: 417). It is relevant here that parents value their children's perceived happiness, rather than narrower measures concerning their financial success.

Teenagers and young adults are often in paid employment, part-time or full-time, while still resident in their parents' family home. In these circumstances young adults in affluent families may enjoy disposable resources that will not be matched for some decades in terms of discretionary spending power. With the infrastructure expenses of daily life – accommodation, food and services – mainly funded by their parents, most of what they earn can be spent as they choose. Many young people are consequently in a key position to be innovators and early adopters of new technologies. The characteristics of such technology users include:

> being risk-takers (they are less likely to perceive risk, and are more able to cope with loss) opinion leaders, younger, educated, with a higher disposable income, socially mobile ('upscale') and socially involved (in formal and informal groups). They are active information seekers in their area of interest and likely to be less dogmatic than non-innovators, more open-minded and 'inner-directed' (follow their own judgement). They may seek variety and stimulation. They may need to feel (or self-identify as) 'unique'. (Green 2002: 31, citing Schiffman et al. 1997)

They are also most likely to be male (Wajcman 1991). The fortuitous economic circumstances of some older children still living in the family home coincide with strong pressures to 'keep up' with other members of their social circle, as well as to make a specific contribution to collective activities, such as improved technology for one person that can then be accessed by the group.

Internationally, in western countries, the demographic most likely to have internet access are couple-families with school-aged children (Kennedy et al. 2008). The relevance of the couple, rather than the single parent household is one of resources: couples usually have more money. In a recent study, being a couple with children at home was an equivalent indicator of internet access as having high education qualifications (88 per cent) and being in the highest income bands (89 per cent) (ABS 2008). Maria Bakardjieva (2005) cites one of her Canadian interviewees as saying 'When we got the computer first, it was basically for the kids' (ibid.: 93).

Although there are likely to be more financial resources available to couples of the same age who do not have children, couples with children are more likely to have internet access. It's the presence of children that increases internet access rates.

This perception is underlined by the fact that although internet access is high in these couple-with-children households, it is not necessarily driven by the parents' usage: 'The high access and lower usage rates for people aged 35–54 years may be related to the presence of children in the household. Parents may acquire internet access for educational and entertainment purposes for their children, but may not use it themselves' (ABS 2008). Parents feel a sense of obligation to provide the best possible start for their children. It is comparatively easy for both parents and children to tap into this desire to be 'future-proof' through proficiency with new and emerging technology (Kennedy et al. 2008).

Children and their parents are involved in social and work-based circles that introduce them to the benefits of technological advances. For example, many schools and workplaces introduced broadband technologies in advance of most homes, introducing workers and students to the benefits of speedy access to online materials. Such exposure outside the home has domestic implications. As 16-year-old Evana, an interviewee in a qualitative study of Australian families' internet use, commented, regarding her father's thoughts about upgrading to broadband, 'We might be getting broadband 'cause he's in real estate so he needs it for his work to catch up with other companies' sales and everything' (Green and Holloway 2004: 180).

A mother, whose children lived during the week with her ex-husband told researchers that she 'was the only parent with access to the internet: "a lot of times, the kids will ring us during the week and say 'I've got an assignment to do. I've got to use the internet', so I go, pick them up and they do their assignments here" (Jasmine)' (Green and Holloway 2004: 180). This study indicated that the usual priorities in the home for access to the internet were: paid work, followed by study needs, followed by entertainment, chat and games. In practice, there was some stratification in time bands since children could often get unfettered access to the internet after school, before parents got in from work, and they tended to use the computer for fun activities at that time, especially if they had friends over.

A desire to regain the family phone line proved a significant driver for families to transfer from dial-up to broadband. Once broadband is connected in affluent households, the irritations of slow internet speeds and competing requirements for the domestic phone connection soon give way to frustrations with having to share a single computer connected to the internet. Whereas during the 1990s most families had only one computer in the home, this changed in the 2000s according to the age of family members and the occupations of parents. Given increased laptop reliability, and with students and some employees taking portable computers between home and work, many households soon had more than one computer, and some had one computer per person. In these circumstances, where there was only one broadband connection point it became increasingly frustrating for family members to wait their turn to go online.

This set the scene for replicating the dynamic of the 1970s TV access. Moving from black and white reception in the 1960s, to colour in the 1970s, middle-class families also began to buy more television sets to help settle arguments about who was going to watch what when programme choices clashed. The profusion of different sets in different rooms helped solve this problem in the days before the widespread take-up of videotape technology allowed time-shifting. Although the access point has recently narrowed again with the adoption of cable TV services (Holloway and Green 2008), there is a pressure within families to avoid situations in which people have to queue for limited access to a service if there are alternative options available. For a family home serviced by a broadband connection, that alternative solution was either to install a local area network or a wireless modem. The advantage of wireless was that family members with laptops could work anywhere in the house they chose, within signal range.

This 'always on for everyone' wireless capability does not let children escape from their parents' priorities and regulation, however. One tech-savvy family, where the children and parents each had their own laptops, still felt the need to restrict internet access for the oldest son, Theo,

> who is in his final year at high school, [and] consistently challenges the implicit work/study/entertainment hierarchy within the home by participating in long gaming sessions with online friends. His mother Jenny, who oversees her children's educational activities, spends time tutoring Theo in his weakest subjects in preparation for his final school examinations. She considers his computer use (gaming and 3D modelling) excessive in that it interferes with the time Theo needs to study and get adequate sleep for the next day's schooling. (Green et al. 2004: 98)

In an interview setting, Theo was philosophical about the restrictions. 'I understand it. I don't like it. I know it's [the right thing], I'd be happy just playing games' (Green et al. 2004: 98). Naturally, such parental control does not go unchallenged. Leslie Haddon discusses how research has demonstrated children's creativity in overcoming parental controls (2005: 62) using some examples from mobile use. Unwilling to be contacted by their parents, children claimed that 'the mobile signal was lost, the mobile battery was dead, or else they sent parents' calls directly to voice mail'. In internet usage, children soon learn to: minimise questionable screens; argue that multiple screens are required for active research; that they are using

Internet Messenger to get tips for homework; and to delete search histories from their web browsers. Citing Nicola Green's work (Green 2001), Haddon comments that approaches such as these are 'all part of "parent management strategies" to avoid surveillance and gain some privacy' (Haddon 2005ibid.: 62–3).

Within this culture of technology adoption and innovatory use, people can be identified as 'lead users' (Haddon 2005: 56); those who lead others by modelling new and emerging uses. This term would equate to Rogers' (2003, [1962]) terms of innovators and early adopters from his Diffusions of Innovations theory, discussed in Chapter 4. According to this model, the diffusion of an innovation occurs over a period of time whereby the (approximately) 16 per cent of innovators and early adopters influence the 84 per cent of early majority, late majority and laggards/contents. Within the moment, this influence occurs between co-present parties involved in networks of communication. In these networks people learn from each other, and particularly from key informants and enthusiasts, what the new technologies are and how they offer benefits.

Opinion leadership and the fostering of technology aspirations is an activity that happens in the present, in terms of prompting awareness, raising interest, developing desire and resulting in action. Long before the majority move to broadband or investigate wireless connections, they have been influenced by someone whose views and experience they respect. Key influences upon the household can occur at the level of either a parent or a child, but within the family home the person influenced has to argue the case for the adoption of the new technology or the new way of organising something. Networks of influence influence both the appropriation and the conversion phases of domestic technology acquisition.

Reflection: opinion leaders

Are you an opinion leader in any field? Why do people seek out your opinions in that area?
Are you an opinion seeker for some activities or purchases? What makes you choose one person to approach for advice, rather than another?

Let's consider this material in terms of our domestication model of appropriation, in-corporation, objectification and conversion (Silverstone et al. 1992: 19). The western household is well integrated within local and national information and technology flows, and a decision to appropriate technology involves seeking and evaluating information from others and from a range of sources such as the internet and consumer stores. Decision-makers become more involved in researching a decision depending upon how expensive it is to carry through, and the perceived risks. 'High-involvement' decisions require a significant investment of time and energy as well as money. Incorporation relates to the way the innovation is taken up in terms of the temporal patterns of the home. Moving from a single internet access point to allowing multiple computers to go online simultaneously, via a broadband router for example combined with a cabled LAN network, means that family members no longer have to negotiate who has access to the internet, when and for what purpose.

Objectification sees the physical environment of the home altered to accept the new technology. For example, cables may be taken up and discarded as a family moves from a cable LAN access pattern to a wireless one. Finally, conversion sees the benefits of the new innovation translated into other forms: enhanced ICT access might result in better school results, or more flexible work hours with some telecommuting from the home, or the chance to send and receive family videos and speak online to family members far away, as well as a greater capacity to offer opinions, advice and support to others leading to increased social standing. It may also constitute an important element of the socialisation of the next generation of online users, communicating the message that innovation is to be welcomed and that change is excitingly dynamic. Families, both within the same household and extended in geographical space, are consequently central to much innovation and technology adoption.

REMITTANCES AND THE INTERNET

We have examined the role of the internet as a catalyst for helping to reveal the priorities and dynamics of people living in a shared space in family relationships. We have concentrated upon the wealthy West although we have also considered how the internet is used by the homeless; people who are essentially excluded from family life (Chapter 4). Here we attend to the different issue of generally poorer, majority-world people who have left their families behind in order to work overseas so that they can generate an income stream to support those they care for at a distance. The payments sent home from one country to another by a family member working in a richer economy to support their loved ones in a poorer country are called 'remittances'. It is estimated that ten per cent of the world's population is subsidised in these ways, by absent family workers who live abroad (IFAD 2009a). Remittance flows have been called 'the human face of globalization' (IFAD 2009b).

Even though these migrant workers are generally among the poorest communities in the countries in which they work, their contribution to some of the economies of majority nations is astonishing. Although most migrant workers would have mobile-phone communications, rather than internet-based contact, with the families they have left behind, the remittances traffic by which they send money home has an internet dimension and may start its journey as an online transfer in the worker's host country. It is to a discussion of these issues of informal but critical distance communication between dispersed family members that we now turn.

According to World Bank data, the poorest nations in the world rely disproportionately on remittance income. As a percentage of national Gross Domestic Product (GDP), Tajikistan received an estimated 45 per cent of their total GDP in remittances during 2008, Moldova 38 per cent and Tonga 35 per cent. In this ranking of dependence, it is not until the tenth country is reached, Jamaica at 19.8 per cent, that the proportion of estimated GDP falls below 20 per cent. On average, over a quarter of the national productivity of the top ten recipient countries was voluntarily supplied by citizens living and working abroad. The total amount of money estimated to have been transferred in remittances sent through formal channels in 2008 was US$283 billion according to the World Bank, which notes that 'These flows do not include informal channels, which would significantly enlarge the volume of remittances if they were recorded' (WB Press Release 2008; Kumar 2008). Remittances are among the most resilient forms of income for recipient countries: 'While capital flows tend to rise during favourable economic cycles and decline in bad times, remittances tend to be counter-cyclical' (World Bank 2008: 12). Which is to say that, as the world goes into a recession, migrant workers send more money home since they know their families are among the most adversely affected people globally.

The costs of remitting money to the developing world can be very high (AusAID 2007: ix), and new delivery mechanisms are constantly being investigated by both the senders and receivers of micro-finance remittances. In many cases the options are limited by poor technological infrastructure and security issues in terms of accessing money from ATMs in urban locations. The key features in desirable services are cost, security, convenience and speed, as these impact upon both senders and receivers (AusAID 2007: 24). Researchers note, however, that 'high rates of mobile phone ownership in [...poorer] countries offer the potential for improving access and reducing transfer costs through SMS-based transfer technologies' (AusAID 2007: 21).

Although it will be some time before remittances can be sent internationally by phone (ABC BB 2008), since all phone traffic of this kind has to happen within national borders, the combination of e-banking transfers plus mobile phone access offers the potential to improve the lives and the incomes of the one-in-ten people involved in the global remittances economy. International Food and Development researcher Dilip Ratha enthused about seeing a prototype system in operation in Africa:

I have seen it operating in Kenya and I was so impressed. I saw people, including the taxi drivers and the hotel people who worked there, and men on the street and women on the street, actually use the cell phone transfers, and it's very convenient and it is almost instantaneous, and they were using this at a fee of about 50-cents per transaction. (ABC BB 2008)

These possible uses of mobile phones constitute an innovation 'unanticipated' (Haddon 2005: 55) by those industry players who first designed and developed the mobile phone. At the same time, it makes the mobile phone even more likely to be the pervasive inclusion-building technology in terms of its use among the world's poor (Parreñas 2005). The internet may be the powerful connector of the world's wealthy nations, but it may also be integral in supporting other technologies in delivering benefits to the world's poor. In many ways, and increasingly, it is a tool for integrating and connecting individuals within the family, the family within the community, and the family within its global networks.

Summary

- This chapter examined the role of the internet in everyday family life since it is through the examination of the domestic that we discover people's individual priorities and values. By looking at the internet in family life we learn about families, as well as about the internet.

- Discussions about the domestication of the internet within the family home led to consideration of parents' strategies for regulating internet use and the question of internet addiction. People continually upgrade their internet equipment and services, and the processes through which this takes place were examined.

- Although the internet has predominantly been constructed in terms of the lives of the world's richer citizens, in that it is available to a minority of the globe's population, it plays an important role in the lives of the poorest by facilitating the operation of the remittances economy.

- It is worth remembering that we are only at the end of the beginning when it comes to understanding what the internet means to human society, and what it may yet mean. Even in the most technologically advanced nations on earth, general access to the internet is less than a generation old: and what is accessed keeps developing and changing. This is an exciting time to be using, and studying, new media.

The final chapter of the book sums up the issues we have explored, and brings the various threads together as we cement our understanding of the internet as an introduction to new media.

10 CONCLUSION

INTRODUCTION

Only recently established as an academic discipline, the study of new media is an exciting area of research. The term 'new media' is applied to digitally based information and communication technologies, which are increasingly mobile. It is constantly changing and evolving, has many facets, and applies to many technologies and practices. Within the total range of new media, the internet and online communication are a particular focus of investigation. Some people are paid to be experts in one aspect of new media or other, but many of the most passionate users of new media consume it and develop their skills in their spare time – or at times when they should be engaged in other activities (like homework). Such people have been referred to in this book as prosumers (e.g. Hartley 2006), but they may also be referred to as prod-users (producer-users, Bruns 2003) or pro-ams (professional-amateurs; people who are amateurs, but who work to professional standards). As is clear, internet-user enthusiasts have stimulated the coining of new words to describe key user groups. New media prowess is also associated with being future-savvy: while we may not know what the future will look like we can be confident it is digital.

Researchers in this field use approaches and research methodologies from a variety of disciplinary fields, often informed by the aspect of internet use they wish to study. Psychologists, marketers, sociologists, designers, anthropologists, educators, managers, information scientists, technologists, linguists, and practitioners from every other discipline have a legitimate interest in internet research and a valid toehold and contribution to make to new media studies. This diversity is demonstrated in the case studies included in this volume. In this concluding chapter we draw together the different strands of the book by examining issues from across a range of chapters and ask what we have learned about new media, and ourselves, as a result of studying the internet. At the same time, we will review the tools of the trade for critically examining our own new media use, seeing ourselves as the subjects of an immersive, longitudinal engagement with new media.

The internet is a medium that is constantly being reinvented as social and economic space, with its roots in computer networks, defence strategies, freedom of information and frontier mythologies. Unsurprisingly, it also raises fundamental questions around gender, family, community, and old media in relation to the new.

From a theoretical and conceptual perspective, this book has adopted a Social Constructionism framework which argues that our understandings of the world and the ways in which we relate to it are constructed through social and cultural forces. Such an approach positions the socio-cultural as the predominant determiner of meaning. Within the Social Constructionism framework, the social shaping of technology perspective acknowledges the power of user agency in fashioning technology, alongside those political and economic elites located in the armed services, bureaucracies and the corporate world, who finance and hothouse many developments later taken up by innovative publics. Software and technology developments provide examples of distributed collaboration, while everyday innovations include the creativity inherent in social media practices (see mnemonic in Chapter 1). Technological advance is consequently positioned as an outcome of social dynamics and, at least theoretically, susceptible to scrutiny, regulation, accountability and democratic change. Ultimately, a Social Constructionism framework complements a user-driven development agenda and offers an optimistic approach to technological change.

Within the over-arching approach of the social shaping of technology perspective, a range of specific micros-theories inform the methodological frameworks evident in the case studies that are the backbone of this book. The micro-theories of greatest relevance are the Theory of Consumption, the Domestication framework, the Social Construction of Technology (SCOT) perspective and Actor-Network Theory (ANT).

This theoretical canon presupposes an inclusive definition for the notion of 'technology'. That definition includes not only the physical object of the technology but also the uses for which it is designed and to which it is put, and the knowledge, skills and practices through which it is used. Once we talk about the ways in which people learn to use something and are given access to a limited resource, such as technology, we are talking about the social and the political, and implicating the process within broader issues of education, economics, power and gender (Wajcman 1994: 6). This is another reason for using case studies to examine the internet.

In tying together some themes raised in the book, and introducing a new one on the brain, which provides a specific prompt for consideration and reflection, this chapter suggests ways in which to create a series of integrated research-based expectations concerning new media use. The examples to be considered below are articulated around aspects of gender, family and community, and some psychological implications of internet use. Such research-driven overviews might serve as a touch-stone for readers' investigations, and promote further research and study including examination of individual practices using new media. The book and the chapter conclude with an over-arching consideration of the internet.

GENDER

This book does not address gender and new media as a stand-alone topic, but it is difficult to discuss new media, and especially access to and uses of the newest media, without recognising that gender constitutes a specifically social dimension of new media use. It is beyond the scope of this book to engage in debates about how much gender is constructed in social interactions compared with the extent to which it is biologically determined. Even so, it is clear that boys and girls, men and women, use the internet differently when they have the opportunity to choose their online activities. Hasebrink et al. (2009: 51), discussing children's internet use in research projects reported from across Europe, note that 'while both boys and girls enjoy a range of online opportunities, there is clear evidence of gender differences in online activities and preferences. Girls prefer activities that involve communication, content creation and collaboration. Boys prefer competition, consumption and action'.

Comments about gender differences will vary with the age of the people con-cerned and their cultural context, while in many instances such differences may be smaller than indicated above. Even so, the differences noted for children have their equivalents in older age groups with women, for example, having the major responsibility for 'kinkeeping', using both old and new media to maintain links with friends and family (Chapter 9). Noting gendered activities for groups of teenage boys (game-players) and groups of teenage girls (fan-fiction writers and readers), as discussed in Chapter 8, does not preclude men from active careers as successful fan-fiction authors, or prevent women from being exceptionally skilled in first-person shooter games. Such against-the-grain activities are well outside the norm, however.

The case studies addressed in the book have often recognised a gendered dimen-sion in technology use, including an acknowledgement of the preponderance of men in accounts of the development of the internet (Chapter 2). In cultures around the world, prowess with high-technology is generally associated with young, wealthy, well-educated males (Kidder 1982), who are also seen as proactively preparing for and guiding the emergence of the future (Wajcman 1991: 144). In the early days of new media adoption within a national context (Chapter 4), this masculine privilege is expressed in differential rates of take-up between males and females, with men having far greater access to technology and greater confidence in its use.

In countries where pornography is legal it has been shown to be a major driver of internet service investment and uptake, particularly among young male consumers, as well as prompting the development of innovative business models and internet pricing strategies (Chapter 6). In some other countries, pornography is entirely prohibited and heavily prosecuted, constituting a serious content risk. Given multiple jurisdictions and a range of different legal frameworks, what is illegal and prosecutable in one country might be legal and acceptable in another. Most liberal, free-market economies permit adults to access pornography while restricting its use by children and young people and strictly forbidding its creation except between freely consenting adults.

Men's opportunities to use new media in early-adopter societies are associated with the fact that men are more likely to have higher education and gain employment in environments where internet use is expected and supported, and where they are appropriately trained as part of their work role. This removes many of the barriers to gaining skills and competence. In contrast, people outside the digital workforce, including many women, have to overcome barriers of access, training and support, as well as looking for opportunities to practice and develop their skills over time as new programs and technologies come online. Once internet use is more pervasive and found in most home, school and work environments, as is currently the case with the majority of western nations, the difference between the proportions of males and females accessing the internet tends to disappear (Hasebrink 2009: 20) and gender is instead expressed through the purposes for which individuals use the internet.

Partly because of differences in gendered use, the content, contact and conduct risk profiles of boys and girls usually differ and change over time. One example of this is that girls are more likely to be harassed through solicitation, for example, and boys more likely to be the harassers, with the figures from one study indicating that 75 per cent of victims were girls and 99 per cent of perpetrators were boys (Wolak et al. 2004, cited in SNS Safety 2008: 20). It is possible to find online activities where the gender balance is comparatively equal and some MMORPGs (massively multiplayer online role-playing games) would provide examples of this, but again there are gendered dimensions to the preferred virtual game world: fantasy as opposed to sci-fi, for example.

Within gendered environments online, MMORPG players often gender swap their game character, but give different reasons for doing so. In a recent online survey involving 119 participants (83 males, 32 females, 4 undeclared), over half the male respondents (54 per cent) had swapped gender in-world, while two-thirds of females had done so (68 per cent). A male respondent reported that 'playing a female character meant that male gamers treated him far better' (Hussain and

Griffiths 2008: 52), while a female commented that she played as a man 'to prevent unsolicited male approaches on her female characters' (ibid.: 52).

Hasebrink et al. (2009: 20) comment, regarding the multi-country EU Kids Online research network findings, that 'in almost every country, boys are more likely than girls to spend greater amounts of time online, have more places to access the internet from, have their own computer and internet access and have access to a PC and internet in their bedrooms'. This material also reinforces other research which demonstrates some (slight) differences in family regulations about internet use affecting boys and girls, which changes with the age of the child and with cultural factors. Even where families agree that there are rules in place, however, research has repeatedly indicated that children and their parents disagree on what the rules are (Chapter 9). The consideration of regulation moves the focus from one of gender to one of the family, and it is to a consideration of family to which we now turn.

FAMILY

Even with internet-connected computers available in schools and community-based resources such as libraries, or affordably accessible in cyber cafés, families remain a key influence in terms of younger members developing computer skills and using their internet competencies. This may be clear for families with school-aged children living at home, but is also the case in other contexts where the family influence may be more tenuous. Within the lives of the Scottish homeless, for example (Chapter 4), some younger homeless people used their irregular access to the internet as a fixed place for family contact. Similarly, the internet is one means of communicating with distant family members, keeping in touch with each others' lives and performing kinkeeping at a distance (Chapter 9), exchanging photos, videos, chat and email. Maintaining a deep sense of commitment and connectivity means that family members are more likely to make themselves available in times of crises, including travelling to be of physical help to distant family members (Baldassar 2007).

The Scottish homeless was one case study supporting our consideration of the digital divide, and highlighted the particular circumstances of a loss of internet access due to a change in circumstances such as retirement, redundancy, separation and divorce, or even in terms of young adult children moving away from home (Green 2002: 106–7). Another family-related case study centred on the experiences of people who were (in the main) registered carers of seriously ill or disabled family members (Chapter 4). Younger carers, and male carers, were more likely to have had access to the internet, as were the adult care-givers of younger people, whose charges were more likely to be involved in education, leaving their carers with greater opportunities to develop new skills themselves. In this context, however, the household as a whole was generally poorer and more stretched financially, and significant poverty is a serious inhibitor of much new media access and use.

Family was also implicated in discussion of the customisation of the internet to support languages other than English (Chapter 5). For example, according to Fleming and Debski's study (2007), much of the motivation for using Irish in internet-based communication is centred on maintaining contact with other family members, and using the same language online as would be used in face-to-face discussion. Elsewhere, as discussed in Chapter 6, the internet was constructed as a place to which people retreat as 'an escape' from the 'drudgery of maintaining self and family,' even an 'aphrodisiac for everyday life' (Rival et al. 1998: 304).

The family home and the internet café are the primary sites of volunteer online activity, and since the home is generally where people do what they choose with their leisure, rather than what they are required to do, it becomes a locale within which preferred internet activity takes place. The activities of LAN clans and fan-fiction communities are unlikely to be carried out at work or school. Indeed, many schools and employers ban game-play and other 'entertainment' uses of the internet. A study of internet use in domestic spaces thus becomes, particularly, a study of how people negotiate the internet when they have a choice. It also becomes a study of the family since the internet is one of the catalysts which reveal the dynamics of family life in terms of Livingstone's (1992: 113) 'who lets who use what' (Chapter 9).

The family is connected into the wider society through social, emotional, econ-omic and political processes and is directly impacted by the moral panics that circulate in the mass media about such fears as internet addiction, and rising rates of obesity. For these and other reasons, parents feel obliged to regulate their children's use of the internet, particularly emphasising ways that maximise the educational and skills-based opportunities provided by online interaction while minimising perceived content, contact and conduct risks. For younger children especially, these dynamics result in a series of family rules and regulations around internet use, although such rules become less enforceable once children get wireless or networked access in private domestic spaces, and with the growing accessibility of the internet via use of mobile media. Chapter 9 includes discussion of a case study where regulation failed and a young adult within the family circle was investigated for 'internet addiction'.

Where internet activity is seen as a positive within family life, and where families or individuals within them have sufficient financial resources, the purchase and upgrading of online equipment can become a major priority. With older children within their parents' home, but especially young men who are not themselves responsible for the household's daily expenses, the family becomes a site for sign-ificant innovation and creativity. In turn, as new technologies and practices are adopted in one family so they are modelled to others within a community, spurring demand for similar innovations in other households and establishing an opinion leader dynamic.

The capacity to innovate depends upon family wealth, education and cultural contexts. Some of the dynamics through which decisions are made about investments in new media were addressed in the 'domestication' framework of appropriation, objectification, incorporation and conversion (Chapter 9). It is through the domestication of a technology that a family integrates their new media usage within the temporal and spatial configuration of their home, and harnesses the benefits of consumption for activities within the wider social realm. Although the domestication framework operates at the level of the household, and is thus broader than applying solely to families, many households are built around family groups.

The internet is also critical to families at the other end of the global wealth scale, where ICTs including the internet are critically implicated in the international remittance flows that are sent by family members working in distant, richer countries to relatives in their home communities. Although comparatively under-discussed, these remittance flows affect about 10 per cent of the world's population, some 700 million people. The recipients are generally among the three in four people globally who remain cut off from the internet due to a combination of poverty, and lack of education, opportunity and infrastructure.

COMMUNITY

Community is important to internet activity in a number of ways, two of which are considered here, the first of which also involves the family, the second of which focuses on shared interests. Family is implicated within notions of the wider physical community, partly as a conduit through which individual members relate to community, and also in terms of the conversion phase of technology domestication. Community-based narratives may reveal specific aspects of internet use and sometimes these are at odds with, or disruptive of, the generally accepted stories of how the internet works or why it has developed in the ways it has. A personal history of a new media technology can demonstrate a richness of engagement specific to the individual and their community. Such a history may involve the social minutiae of the wider community of opinion leaders and supporters who influenced the technology's purchase and helped set it up and get it working. It would include details of who was first communicated with and why, integrating the technology and its use within the family, community and society.

An example from the early days of consumption studies may indicate this. Igor Kopytoff is an American academic who has carried out anthropological research in Africa. He suggested that 'things' have a 'social biography' relating to the ways in which they are integrated and consumed in people's lives and gave this example to illustrate his argument:

> The biography of a car in Africa would reveal a wealth of cultural data: the way it was acquired, how and from whom the money was assembled to pay for it, the relationship of the seller to the buyer, the uses to which the car is regularly put, the identity of its most frequent passengers and of those who borrow it, the frequency of borrowing, the garages to which it is taken and the owner's relation to the mechanics, the movement of the car from hand to hand over the years, and in the end, when the car collapses, the final disposition of its remains. All of these details would reveal an entirely different biography from that of a middle-class American, or Navajo, or French peasant car. (Kopytoff 1986: 67)

In this vignette, Kopytoff has taken the social history of a specific car as a 'text' that can be used to illustrate ways in which some people in Africa might live their lives differently from people in other contexts, and in other parts of the world. Internet use and the acquisition of new media skills can similarly construct a relevant text for comparison with others and for analysis. Such a text would include the reasons given for the acquisition of the ICT concerned, the people consulted, the shops and sites through which the purchase was researched, the insurance taken out, the set up and installation arrangements, the funding sources, the first people communicated with and how, the uses to which it is actually put rather than those anticipated. In all these ways the community contributes to the individual construction of a particular technology.

Physical community is therefore an important part of the domestication and consumption of ICTs. Online community can also be critically important to these processes in terms of providing a context within which technology is acquired. It may be that the technology has been purchased in order to keep in touch with a distant other, such as when middle-aged children buy their elderly parents a computer. As well as helping elderly people keep in touch by using new media, such a purchase might be a strategy to fill empty hours created by family moving away or by other significant life events. Online communities can offer a range of supports in diverse circumstances to supplement, replace and compensate for interaction, or lack of interaction, with people living locally. This may be particularly relevant at times when people nearby may be at work or asleep, or otherwise inaccessible, since an online community may have a round-the-clock availability.

Communities can take shape offline and then become active online, or can form online around shared passions and practices. As a consequence, the range of possible communities that can be considered as having an internet dimension is innumerable. The communities considered in Chapter 8 were primarily articulated with gender and youth, and particularly harnessed online practices. LANing culture implicates teenage and young adult males, such as those who responded to the viral video memes of 'All your chocolate rain are belong to us' (discussed in Chapter 7). In contrast to the LANers, and underlining the gendered nature of some online interaction, fan-fiction communities generally involve teenage and young adult women who create and share stories within a particular fan realm, such as *Harry Potter* or *Twilight*. Some commentators, such as Tosenberger (2008), see the erotic aspects of many of these stories as expressing a gendered counterpoint to the visual pornography consumed by many young males (Chapter 6).

Reciprocal commitment to community members is developed when 'enough people carry on those public discussions long enough, with sufficient human feeling, to form webs of personal relationships in cyberspace' (Rheingold 2000: xx). Such comments can be taken as a reference to the development of social capital, which is central to the uses of social media as well as to the development of specific online communities. A discussion of social capital (Chapter 5) helps explain the dynamics through which people construct the internet as a supportive environment, building linkages of mutual obligation using social structures beyond the family.

BRAIN-CHANGING

There have been some suggestions, for example in research studies cited by Steven Jones (2005), that new media is making us more intelligent. It is, in effect, good for the brain, and that might be sufficient reason for a middle-aged child to buy their elderly parent a computer. Neurologists believe they have demonstrated that even adult brains grow according to how they are used. The brains of London taxi drivers, for example, change in response to the experience of navigating the inner city (Maguire et al. 2006). It now seems probable that everything we do, including using the internet, has subtle effects upon our brain. The more we do something, the greater the impact it will have on our brain's physiology. At the same time we rewrite our neuronal wiring, we help rewrite our consumer culture. The choices we make online mean that some consumer products are developed in certain ways, practices evolve to suit our priorities, and companies providing services come into existence and thrive, or decline and are closed. As our usage patterns drive changes in the information and experiences available on the internet, so the activities of engaging with the internet and its various aspects are changing us.

Well over a decade ago, when the internet was still a minority experience even in the wealthy West, David Porush, an MIT-trained cyber-theorist, suggested that cyberspace is 'brain changing'. Writing in the late 1990s, Porush suggested that society was embarking upon a momentous journey. He sought 'an analogous moment in history when culture found itself in possession of an equally new and revolutionary cybernetic technology ... for getting thoughts from one mind to another' (1998: 46) and argued that the invention of the internet is of equivalent importance to the invention of language and writing. Given the impact upon human culture of these communications tools, it is unsurprising that there is a perception that we have fallen behind in our capacity to understand the impact of ICTs on society.

Such a perspective, of the internet having an incredible social impact, gives credence to the attempts by minority language speakers and members of numerically smaller cultures to use online resources to support cultural maintenance. This might be done by creating culturally specific web-based content (Chapter 5) to strengthen a culture that feels under threat from social and linguistic communities that have particular traction on the internet (Chapter 2). Some policy makers are concerned that the power of the cultures dominating the internet may distort minority cultural influences, particularly through the impact of the English language. Also implicated are the large transnational corporate cultures, some of which are themselves ICT companies (Bryan 1994: 146), such as IBM, Microsoft and Google (Chapter 2). Indeed, commentators have suggested that technology operates a little like a genetic code, transferring the DNA of the originator community into the cultural heritage of the societies that adopt the technology (Bissio 1990, in Chapter 4).

By following certain choices and web-pathways that reflect their perceptions of the internet, users create patterns of access and consumption that effectively construct their online experience as a model of their own preferences and priorities, rather like synaptic pathways are laid down in the brain (Maguire et al. 2006). Internet access and use is a choice that both expresses and moulds individual and community identity and this prompts a critical examination of what an individual's internet usage says about them as social and cultural actors; and what would constitute the major highways, routes and byways of each person's internet use.

Alongside these varied analogies, the model of the brain has another relevance to the development of the internet. It was not self-evident that a computer network would be developed along the lines of a distributed grid (Chapter 2). On the contrary, both the telephone and the earlier telegraph system had used hubs, nodes and spokes (or trunks, branches and twigs) as their organising principles. The hub, as with the centre of a wheel, provided services, support and control for all the spokes radiating from it. Some of those spokes ended in mini-hubs, or nodes, allowing a number of additional spokes to radiate from that point. However, given the importance of keeping communications open after a critical incident, such as an attack on a national communications system, engineers were looking for ways to develop self-mending frameworks.

The structure of the brain was offered as a possible model for the internet, partly because it is remarkably resilient in accommodating and compensating for partial damage. The networks through which neurones are connected became the pattern for proposed computer inter-connectivity. If one link between computers was down, or congested, other links offered a way forward. Such a model included built-in redundancy, the term used for when there is more capacity than can be reasonably needed. This model also meant that cheaper, less robust connections could be utilised since the chance of all of these being broken at the same time was reduced with the large number of possible connections available. The use of the brain metaphor as a way of envisaging the internet, and the indication that the internet is itself brain changing, ties into Rheingold's statement (Chapter 6) about online community allowing a member to tap 'into this multibrained organism of collective expertise' (Rheingold 2000: 109).

OLD MEDIA AND NEW MEDIA

Whereas the public sphere (Chapter 7) of old media, such as broadcasting and newspapers, was characterised by professional access and rigorous 'gatekeeping' that restricted the kinds and numbers of voices heard, the internet allows a space for multiple voices of varied credibility. In particular, blogging has been identified as a collaborative activity which is particularly related to Web 2.0 (Bruns 2008a), examined here through the case study of the Iraqi citizen-journalist Salam Pax (Chapter 7). One perceived strength of new media as opposed to old media is that there are no space constraints, and generally no cost implications, in reading and writing multiple blogger-stories. With a limited resource such as newsprint, access to good information is ensured when everything accepted for printing is of a specific quality. With an effectively unlimited resource such as the online environment, a single form of quality control is replaced by access to large amounts of information and the exercise of careful judgement on the part of the reader.

The example of cyber-stalking addressed in Chapter 6 focuses upon the deliberate use of the public sphere to harm a person's reputation and employment prospects. Whereas most print and broadcast media are published and consumed in specific jurisdictions, and court action is comparatively straightforward, new media engages readers, writers and recipients across national and jurisdictional boundaries. This leads to potential clashes of national information cultures and illustrates the difficulty of developing relevant regulations (Chapter 6). Even given a court order in one country which declared a range of statements to be defamatory lies, the victim in the study was unable to prevent continued cyber-harassment emanating from another country. Instead, his attempt to stop someone from saying something on the internet could be seen as an attempt to 'chill' debate and thus constructed as a restriction upon free speech. The difficult balancing act relating to the celebration of free speech, while allowing for the legitimate protection of people's reputations, is a long way from being resolved.

In the context of the expanded public sphere, Wikipedia is an example of a quality-controlled collaborative project that aims to establish self-correcting processes to support a continuously-updatable resource which functions as a flawed repository of human knowledge (Chapter 7). The acknowledgement of flaws recognises that the project cannot afford to aim for perfection. Peer-reviewed perfection was established to be problematic in the pre-wiki days and now Wikipedia aims to get better with each iteration, rather than achieving perfection. This approach differs from the vision which inspired YouTube, which was to create a showcase for short digital videos which attracted audiences on the basis of viewers' quality recommendations and the numbers of times a video has been viewed.

National policy makers (Chapter 3), influential opinion leaders (Chapter 8) and individuals within their domestic contexts (Chapter 9) all have differing constructions of the internet, and different ways of relating to and using it. There is no single, stand-alone, agreed way of understanding new media. Instead, the internet can generally be constructed as the result of a series of choices, and a dialogue, between the user, the regulator, the technology manufacturer and supplier, the access portal, the search engine and the website designers – often with a host of advertisers, as well. This is very different from the situation with the press and broadcasting where the readership or audience has limited capacity to engage with the medium itself and has little opportunity to use the media to share ideas except through newspapers' letters pages and radio talk-back.

It is notable that many of the moral panics about the internet (Cohen 1980) are circulated by the old media. Panics can start using a range of emotive triggers, such as paedophiles preying on young girls they befriend on social networking sites. Old media would almost never undermine a good panic-promoting story by citing Finkelhor's (2008) work (Chapter 9) to the effect that there has been a 53 per cent reduction in sexual offences against children between 1992 and 2006 (Schrock and boyd 2008: 10). Old media are far more likely to talk about the risks of internet use than they are about its opportunities and benefits (Chapter 6). Some people might argue that it is old media that is panicking at present since they have yet to find an economic model that makes newspaper publishing viable in the post-internet world, and advertising revenues are increasingly used to support internet sites, rather than newspapers.

LOOKING FORWARD

It is impossible to confidently predict the future development of the internet. Whilst it is clear that, in internet terms, the first decade of the twenty-first millennium marked the conjunction of Web 2.0 and social media, this would not have been predictable in the late 1990s. It will only be clear in retrospect what elements of the internet will spawn the defining path for new media in the coming decade (Chapter 3). Even so, some predictions centre around the development of a 'Semantic Web', and this has been discussed as one possibility among many others (Chapter 5).

Constructed as an immensely versatile technological system, the internet has energised creativity, collaboration and commercialisation on a global scale in unexpected and unpredictable ways and impacted all areas of human life. Over the course of the previous chapters, as well as this one, *The Internet: An Introduction to New Media* has analysed and explained research into people's uses of 'the network of networks' at the global, national, community, family and individual levels. In taking this big-picture perspective, the volume has raised and addressed issues of policy, regulation and legislation, and also considered the digital divide and the internet's contribution to the public sphere. Through these considerations we have developed a complex understanding of the internet, its development, and possible trajectories.

There is intense social interest and concern focused upon the internet, as was also true of other information and communication technologies in the critical stages of early adoption and take-up. Such concern implicates politicians, lawyers, corporations, opinion leaders, educators, parents and consumers in a debate about issues of control, access, regulation, (dis)advantage, cultural imperialism and the economic implications of internet use. Whilst it is evident that the internet supports new ways of seeking information and relating to others socially, there is little evidence that this technology rewrites human society and sociability any more than did television, radio or the invention of printing. Instead, the internet offers new ways through which different social entities (both nation-based and interest-based) can connect and express themselves.

Building upon major and current research, such as that in the US and the EU examining the opportunities and risks presented by the internet to children and young people (SNS Safety 2008; Livingstone and Haddon 2009), this book has offered an account of the internet as it currently stands whilst acknowledging that it represents the epitome of a fast-developing medium. In developing an awareness of the complex content, contact and conduct risks which characterise this technology, the volume has also sought to showcase the immense benefits offered by a medium which engages its users' creativity and allows access to communities untrammelled by issues of time and space, even though users in individual communities may be limited by access. During the time that this book was being written, however, global take-up of the internet rose from one in five to one in four people (*Internet World Statistics* 2009), and this statistic demonstrates that while many people are still unable to access the internet, it has a growing relevance around the world.

Researchers and students should feel confident and conversant with the use of key technical and policy terms germane to debates about the internet as it was, as it is, and as it will be (Chapter 3). Such an ambition requires a more explicit engagement with technological policy than is usually addressed in social and cultural explorations of the internet. A glossary is supplied as an aid to help the reader understand both the physical and the policy infrastructures of the internet, better to engage with public debates about further ICT policy in local, regional and national contexts. Demystifying this language allows students and researchers to make informed choices as to the debates they engage with, and the terminologies they use.

Citizens are an early focus of Chapter 4, which starts by considering the situation of some sections of the population that are not sufficiently settled and prosperous to make good consumers. Citizens have rights, while consumers access products and services according to their capacity to pay. As the internet continues to develop in its scope and relevance, the right to access and use information has never been more important. This book has positioned the internet in relation to readers' daily lives, so that researchers and students who use this volume will be better able to analyse the implications of new media for themselves, for their societies, and for the future.

ANNOTATED GUIDE TO FURTHER READING

Readers are encouraged to use the web to investigate these issues further. Although most recommendations are for old media – printed books and journals – many of these are available through the web and often link through to further resources.

Chapter 1: Introduction

A general introduction to the social shaping of technology is provided by MacKenzie and Wajcman (1999), which is foundational in this field. The domestication framework, which looks at ways in which technologies become integrated within people's homes and lives, has been linked to the social-shaping approach in Silverstone and Haddon (1996). Haddon (2004) offers a range of studies of ICT use in daily life.

Wajman's books (1991, 2004) are a good starting point for discussions about technology as a masculine culture, while Gray (1992) provides a classic account of the gendering of the video recorder.

The nature and characteristics of the information society have been theorised over the past thirty years with Bell's (1973) *The Coming of the Post-Industrial Society*, a foundational text. Masuda (1981) offers a futurist view of the information society, while Jones (1995) examines some implications for the future of work – as seen in the early years of the WWW.

Chapter 2: History

The book and the film *October Sky* (Johnston 1999), based on a true story, give some indication of the Sputnik launch in the US from the perspective of a teenage boy, Homer Hickham Jnr, who was inspired to become an American rocket scientist as a result of seeing Sputnik 1 in orbit. Similarly, *Thirteen Days* (Donaldson 2000), recreates the drama of the Cuban Missile Crisis.

Maney (2003) and Gerstner (2002) between them cover much of the history of IBM, while Whol (2006) provides a brief and accessible overview of the implications in computer and software development for those who used the technology. Paul Ceruzzi's *A History of Modern Computing* (2003, 2nd edn) is an engaging chronological narrative dealing with critical events from WWII to the dot.com crash.

Some of the excitement of 'directing the future' through involvement with the development of computers and the internet is communicated in the work of Hafner and Lyon (2003), who interviewed many of the key inventors and pioneers and also engaged in extensive archival research. Their work contributes significantly to the chapter. Berners-Lee with Fiscetti (1999) and Battelle (2006) carry this exciting history forward.

Raymond (2001) outlines the differences between the processes of open-source software production and the large proprietary software houses, while Bruns (2008a) examines the implications of participatory culture for everyday internet practices such as blogging and wikis.

Chapter 3: Policy

There is a growing literature on innovation and creativity including Florida (2002), Kuhn (1996) and Howkins (2001). In terms of national responses to the challenge of fostering creativity throughout the innovation system, the UK's National Endowment for Science Technology and the Arts (NESTA n.d.) probably sets the agenda.

Although this chapter relies upon a range of sources to compare and contrast the working of regulatory regimes in China and Australia, the purpose of this discussion is to indicate the value in being aware of equivalent debates in the context of these and other countries. It may be useful to choose a country other than China or Australia and use the internet to research the major agencies and regulatory bodies charged with overseeing the operation of regulation in the fields of broadcasting, telecommunications and the internet. This strategy will result in a range of relevant reports and recommendations. Some regions also have over-arching bodies, such as the EU's COST 298 action: *Participation in the Broadband Society* (COST 298 n.d.), and the part-UN funded *Digital Review of Asia-Pacific* (DirAP n.d.). Such sources can provide useful starting points to individual country's regimes and to the issues affecting a region.

Green (2002) contains a detailed discussion on the active process of regulating, building on Palmer (1994).

Chapter 4: The Digital Divide

Bell (1973) is often considered as the first person to systematically demonstrate that the economies of western countries had shifted inexorably from an agricultural and manufacturing base to the development and delivery of information goods and services. Beniger (1986) added value to this concept by tracing a detailed history of the shift. Van Dijk (2005) offers a conceptual framework and policies to address the digital divide, while Rooksby and Weckert (2007) are editors of a volume that examines the implications of the digital divide for social justice issues.

The Pew Internet and American Life project has been documenting the impact of the internet upon segments of the US population, and upon aspects of American life since 2000 (Pew 2009). The range of reports, from online dating to teleworking, is fascinating. Rogers' (2003) *Diffusion of Innovations Theory* is one way to explain the take-up of internet goods and services charted by the Pew Internet and American Life project.

Chapter 5: Customising the Internet

Herb Schiller's seminal theory of cultural imperialism (1991) makes a useful starting point for discussions of the potential of new media for the strengthening of Irish Gaelic (Fleming and Debski 2007), and *La Francophonie* (Jeanneney 2006).

Tapscott and Williams's (2006) popular volume on *Wikinomics* is a useful introduction to the implications of Web 2.0 collaborative engagement, while Hendler and Golbeck (2006) and Berners-Lee et al. (2001) offer an accessible and brief introduction to visions of Web 3.0 and the workings of the Semantic Web. Crawford's (2009) account of the emerging practice of Twitter is a fun and readable study of the incorporation of a new digital application into everyday domestic life.

Chapter 6: Regulation and Legislation: Pornography and Cyber Stalking

Culler's (2001) introduction to discourse analysis is a classic of the field, while Morgan's *Images of Organization* (2006) demonstrate the additional power and versatility of metaphor.

Some risks faced by children and teenagers in their internet activities have prompted much government research and many landmark reports including the EU Kids Online outputs (EU Kids Online n.d.); the US report *Enhancing Child Safety and Online Technologies* (SNS Safety 2008) and *Media and Communications in Australian Families* (ACMA 2007). As part of the EU Kids Online project, Staksrud et al. (2009: 18–19) summarise perceived risks in their report on available data about children's activities online. Specialist centres such as the US National Center for Missing and Exploited Children (e.g. Finkelhor et al. 2000; Wolak et al. 2006) and the Pew Internet and American Life project also publish reports that address risk (e.g. Lenhart 2005; Lenhart et al. 2007). Perceived risk is often raised and handled in family contexts, thus Chapter 9 also comments on this theme.

Chapter 7: The Public Sphere

The radical differences in conceptions of the public sphere put forward by Habermas (1989b) and McKee (2004) repay detailed consideration, especially when considered in the context of changes in ICTs and social organisation over the past few decades. The Electronic Frontier Foundation (EFF 2009) has branches in many countries and campaigns actively for internet freedoms (but see Chapter 6). While caution is in order when using information found on the internet, Clegg (2006) offers a how-to guide to using the web for study purposes.

Bruns (2008a) addresses citizen-journalism, blogging and wikis in his wide-ranging book on prod-usage, while Tapscott and Williams (2006) examine the implications of voluntary collaborative organisation for business practices. Burgess and Green's (2009) analysis of YouTube is usefully positioned in the context of participatory culture.

Chapter 8: Community

Rheingold's *Virtual Community* (2000) remains one of the key discussions of online social connection, while Anderson's *Imagined Community* (1991) examines the impact of mediated connections in building a sense of belonging to a community.

Nichols et al. (2006) consider the potential value of gaming communities to brands and to business, while Jenkins's book *Convergence Culture* (2006) examines a range of case studies indicating the growing influence of digital media upon individuals, society and politics. Hills's *Fan Culture* (2002) offers an in-depth look at the working of fandom. Like Jenkins, Johnson (2005) sees significant value in many aspects of digital culture that are minimised or decried by the formal education establishment.

In terms of participant-based research and writing, Green and Guinery (2004) address fan fiction while Green and Guinery (2006) investigate a FPS LAN clan. A range of complex issues is raised when we think about the ethics and practicalities of online research. Hine (2005) provides an invaluable guide to this minefield.

Chapter 9: Internet in Family Life

Morley's *Family Television* (1986) is a landmark study in accounts of the domestication of technology, even though it precedes the development of the classic domestication framework (Silverstone et al. 1992, Silverstone and Haddon 1996). Bakardjieva's (2005) examination of the internet in everyday life adds to these accounts. ACMA (2007) offers a detailed, recent account of family-based uses of ICTs, including the internet, while the Pew Internet and American Life (Pew 2009) Project provides a wealth of specific research findings across gender and generational axes.

Although some parents have strong fears that the internet is addictive, discussions still continue. Allison et al. (2006) indicate that the subject of their case study, Mr A, had a range of problems underlying his condition. Bocij (2006) includes a section on addiction; Johnson (2005) offers an alternative viewpoint.

The International Fund for Agricultural Development (IFAD 2009a) and the World Bank (2008) provide information on families and remittances and this is often backed up by country-specific reports, such as AusAID (2007).

Chapter 10: Conclusion

EU Kids Online (n.d.) reports investigate gender and family influences upon children's internet usage. Moyal's (1995) work on the gendered use of the telephone is relevant for older age groups when considering the ways in which women's uses of ICTs typically differ from those of men.

Porush's (1998) article about the brain-changing nature of internet activity is an intriguing one, especially alongside the recent findings of neurobiology (Maguire et al. 2006).

McKee (2004) and Bruns (2008a) offer detail that helps identify a range of differences between old and new media, while Castells' book on *The Rise of the Network Society* (2009), a revised and updated edition and the first volume of the Information Age series, provides a philosophical perspective on the social, cultural and economical implications of these changes.

Between them, the thirty-one chapters in *The Handbook of New Media*, edited by Leah Lievrouw and Sonia Livingstone (2002), engage with many of the issues raised here and can offer supplementary and contrasting perspectives.

EXERCISES AND QUESTIONS

Chapter 1: Introduction

Exercises

1. Is it possible to develop a truly inclusive digital technology, accessible to people all over the world? What issues and problems would need to be addressed? What would the benefits and costs of such a project be?
2. Using a global perspective, give examples of social, political and cultural factors that influence whether any particular individual is more or less likely to have the opportunity to use the internet.
3. List some of the ways in which new media differ from old media. Is the internet an archetypal new medium? Why?

Questions

1. In 1994, Theodore Roszak suggested that the information age involves a range of unacceptable risks:

   > the price we pay for its benefits will never outweigh the costs. The violation of privacy is the loss of freedom. The degradation of electoral politics is the loss of democracy. The creation of the computerized war machine is a direct threat to the survival of our species. (Roszak 1994: 233)

   Would you agree with Roszak? Please give your reasons.
2. Why has the digitisation of information triggered a huge explosion of goods, services and convergent technologies? What issues are raised by the speed with which technology changes?

Chapter 2: History

Exercises

1. What do you see as the key components of the technological system that we call the internet? How would the components of that technological system change if

we took time lines of 1975, 1995 and 2010? What are the implications of adding human inputs in terms of the roles played by key influencers?

2. Do you think of the internet as being a US-controlled entity? What evidence would you offer in favour or against such a proposition? What would be the implications of a 'split' internet that was fractured along nationalistic or political lines? (Might the internet reflect an economic divide?)

3. What factors build the wealth and the influence of successful 'internet start-up entrepreneurs'? What aspects of the digital economy mean that their labour is rewarded so extravagantly?

Questions

1. Compare the development process of a proprietary brand of software with that of an open source application. What are the implications for producers and for users?

2. 'Thousands of computer scientists had been staring for two decades at the same two things – hypertext and computer networks. But only Tim conceived of how to put those two elements together' (Dertouzos 1999: x). How would you explain the implications for the internet of the development of the World Wide Web? What else might explain the exponential growth in popular internet use since the mid-1990s?

3. In 2004 Judy Wajcman argued that women who wish to participate in fields that are traditionally masculine preserves, such as computer science and electronic engineering, are asked 'to exchange major aspects of their gender identity for a masculine version without prescribing a similar "degendering" process for men'. Do you agree? Why do you think that women are under-represented in the history of the development of computing and the internet?

Chapter 3: Policy

Exercises

1. Do you believe we can identify features that lead to a society being especially creative? What social influences would you see as helping to build innovation?

2. What kinds of debates about the internet are currently circulating in your society? How are they likely to affect policy development and your government's approach to regulating the internet? How might a person in your position, individually or as part of a group, make a contribution to a policy debate?

3. Is it possible to censor the internet? What would be the positives and the negatives of trying to do so? What kind of social, economic, political and personal price would be paid by those trying to enforce such censorship and those trying to resist it?

Questions

1. Think about Thomas Kuhn's (1996 [1962]) notion of the paradigm shift. Do you consider that the notion of the internet as we understand it today has 'shifted' significantly from that of its first developers? If so, where do you think that paradigm shifts can be identified? If not, explain how the internet today is implied in the internet as it took shape in the late 1960s and early 1970s.
2. What kinds of policy approaches characteristic of western democracies have fostered the rapid take-up and fast adoption of the internet? How did the policy environment drive consumer response?

Chapter 4: The Digital Divide

Exercises

1. What are the implications of being in the 25 per cent of people without internet access in a rich, western-style country? What are the implications of being in a poor country, where few people have internet access, and being part of the 75 per cent of the world's population without internet access? How do these two circumstances differ from the point of view of an individual unconnected citizen?
2. Statistics can go out of date very quickly. (Indeed, most are already out of date at the time that they are first published.) Taking your country as your case study, research the statistics for broadband use, dial-up use, and for the proportion of people who have no internet connection at all. What factors explain relative advantage? How quickly is the situation changing?
3. This chapter uses a number of technical terms which might be seen by some people as 'jargon'. Make a list of the terms that are unfamiliar to you and construct your own glossary of definitions. (This is often done best with a group of people sharing the tasks, and comparing their results.)

Questions

1. If you were a legislator responsible for communications policy and infrastructure, what factors would you take into account when determining which groups of people most need your help to connect to the internet? Why?
2. 'There are more computers around, but the digital divide is getting wider because of broadband'. Discuss the implications of this statement in terms of (i) those with no access to a computer, and (ii) those with access to a computer and a dial-up service.

Chapter 5: Customising the Internet

Exercises

1. How important is it that minority languages are supported in their home territories? In what ways are new media a help in preserving minority languages? In what ways a hindrance?
2. Do you agree that Google has a 'perceived Anglo-centric bias'? Is this a problem? Why? What might be done to reassure someone who thinks it is a problem? Can you recommend steps that would address their concerns?
3. Compare the workings of a heterarchical folksonomy with those of a hierarchical taxonomy. Why is it so difficult to think in terms of a taxonomy of internet information?

Questions

1. 'If the web is a library, why do we need a building full of books? Why do we need librarians?' What would you say in response to this post from 'Blake', a blogger librarian?
2. Discuss the characteristics of 'social media'. What is it about the way that some people use certain technologies that makes some media social?

Chapter 6: Regulation and Legislation: Pornography and Cyber Stalking

Exercises

1. Where do you see the intersections and cross-overs between your online and offline life? Do other people make judgements about your online activities? What impacts do such judgements have on you?
2. The decision to change an ISP contract, or to buy a new piece of software or technology, often centres around the need for more or better or faster service. In your experience, what kinds of reasons and rationales have been given for domestic technology upgrades? Did these upgrades deliver as expected?
3. Drawing upon your own experience, or using the Cullen case study, what advice would you give to someone who was being bullied online? Do you think that Cullen could or should have responded differently?

Questions

1. '[T]here can be no single theory or metaphor that gives an all-purpose point of view. There can be no "correct theory" for structuring everything we do' (Morgan 2006: 338). Relate this quotation to your experience of using the internet. What metaphor(s) do you find helpful, and why?

2. Do you see a difference between 'real life' and 'life online'? Give reasons for your answer. How do you see the relationship between your online and your offline life?

Chapter 7: The Public Sphere

Exercises

1. McKee paints a chaotic image of the contemporary public sphere but seems to suggest that there is greater strength in its inclusivity and diversity than is the case with the unitary public sphere championed by Habermas. What are the advantages and disadvantages of these competing visions?
2. What are the key differences between a professionally produced encyclopedia and Wikipedia? When would those differences be advantageous, and when would they be drawbacks?
3. After buying YouTube, Google has become increasingly likely to offer video segments in response to a search enquiry. What strategies would you use to integrate a database of images with a database of words?

Questions

1. Reflecting upon the statement that 'authenticity has since been validated by an American newsperson' (Hamilton and Jenner 2003: 131), discuss the differences that characterise professional journalists and citizen-journalists. How would you justify the contribution of citizen-journalists?
2. Is all information equal? What aspects of information need to be considered when judging its value?

Chapter 8: Community

Exercises

1. Ideologically based internet communities are a new force in politics, alongside big business and employers, and workers and trades unions. How might these online organisations impact upon the political system?
2. What rules would you put in place so that members of an online community would be accountable and take appropriate responsibility for their actions?
3. Is it acceptable to join an online community for the purpose of researching and writing about it? What ethical issues are raised?
4. How difficult would it be to hide your identity online over a protracted period, like 'Julie' did? What would make it easy? What would make it hard?

Questions

1. Do you agree with Jenkins's proposition that some people learn more from their voluntary internet activities than they do from school-based classwork? What might the implications be for the organisation of education?
2. In richer countries, internet participation is no longer gendered, both sexes participate equally. It seems, however, that certain activities are gendered: fan fiction writing and FPS gaming are two such activities. What issues are raised by the identification of gender as an important aspect of some internet activity?

Chapter 9: Internet in Family Life

Exercises

1. Why might some children see their family as being without internet rules, while the parents in that family see themselves as having internet rules? Is it surprising that most parents seem to 'trust' their children in terms of their internet use?
2. One consistent piece of advice for parents is to have the internet-accessible computer in a public space so that usage can be monitored. What are the implications of the growing prevalence of mobile phone-based internet access for this strategy? How can children be protected from risk if they have 'anytime, anywhere' connectivity?
3. How would you see a family's media use, and its conversion into social currency, influencing 'the relationship between the household and the outside world – the boundary across which artefacts and meanings, texts and technologies pass as the household defines and claims for itself and its members a status in neighbourhood, work and peer groups in the "wider society"'? Give examples from one or more of the case studies in this book.

Questions

1. Accepting that internet use follows phone use, comment on Moyal's claim that intrinsic communication is 'both "gendered work" and "gender work", in that it is work that women do to hold together the fabric of the community, build and maintain relationships, and accomplish both care-giving and receiving functions'. What do these kinds of communication look like in an internet context? Is it gendered work?
2. Do you believe that people can get addicted to the internet? How would that be recognised? What treatment would you see as useful?

Chapter 10: Conclusion

Exercises

1. A generation ago, parents and care-givers might have worried that children spent too much time 'in front of the television'. Now the concern is that they spend too much time 'on the computer'. Is this essentially the same kind of concern or are there important differences?
2. Some commentators have used the idea of the brain to explain the workings of the internet. What other ways can you think of to explain how the internet works?
3. There's a popular saying attributed to the open source movement to the effect that 'Information just wants to be free'. Do you agree with this sentiment? What are the implications of such freedom for old media? Are the implications for new media different?

Questions

1. 'Our technology – computerized weapons systems, medical scanners, the Internet – sets the standard to which developing countries aspire' (Schiller 2000: 149). Critique Schiller's argument that we have moved into an era of 'soft' colonialism where poorer countries are unnecessarily driven by the desire to adopt elements of richer culture, including the internet.
2. Is the internet particularly 'brain changing'? Justify your answer.
3. 'Your legal concepts of property, expression, identity, movement, and context do not apply to us [in cyberspace]. They are all based on matter, and there is no matter here' (Barlow 1996). Do you agree?

ABBREVIATIONS AND GLOSSARY

This glossary should be read in conjunction with the index, where readers are pointed to uses of critical terms in the text. Further understanding will be gained from the web and by following concepts of interest through the indexes of other books, cross-referencing different authors' usages. High profile brand name products such as Google, Facebook and Twitter are not included here, but are indexed. I have written two previous Abbreviations and Glossaries (Green and Guinery 1994, Green 2002), and this work draws on those earlier versions.

1G/2G/3G ... XG – used to refer to first, second, third, etc., generation technology, often used as a way of referring to mobile phone advances

24/7 – around the clock; twenty-four hours a day, seven days a week; all the time

3D – 3-dimension

a/synchronous – synchronous activity (a phone call) occurs with two or more people interacting at the same time while asynchronous activity is interaction separated by lapsed time (for example, leaving a message and waiting for a reply)

ACE – Automatic Computing Engine (early UK computer)

ACMA – Australian Communications and Media Authority

ADS – asymmetrical digital subscriber line

algorithm – step-by-step logical sequence which embodies the rules for interpreting the information it contains. Different algorithms serve different purposes. When a communication is digitised, it is encoded algorithmically. Digital data travels in algorithmic form, and algorithmic rules dictate decoding back to the original form at the destination, for example, to computer data, sound waves, etc.

analogue – something analogous to, or representative of, the original; continuously changing, like hands on a watch face, or a sound wave. Digital representation is on/off (or high/low), i.e. two states only

ANT – Actor-Network Theory; a theoretical approach to understanding how people interact with each other and with networks

AOL – America Online

ARPANET/DARPANET – the computer network created by ARPA, the Advanced Research Projects Agency of the US Department of Defense, renamed DARPANET (Defense ARPA Network) in 1972. Designed to overcome the lack of interactivity between different types, kinds, and models of early computers

ATM – automatic teller machine

Avatar – a digital persona that can take a 3D form, as in a computer game; a 2D form, as an icon; or a 1D form as a nickname or pseudonym

AVS – adult verification system, identifies the age of an internet user for access to restricted websites, typically 'adults only'

BBC – British Broadcasting Corporation

BBN – Bolt Beranek and Newman Inc.; consultancy which helped develop ARPANET

BDP – Big Dikk Pimpz, a LAN clan

BitTorrent – P2P file-sharing network that makes it possible to source large multimedia files by using a protocol to near-equalise the time taken by traffic in both directions, uploading and downloading, and also makes it increasingly necessary with use that the hard drive collections of members that are downloading content be accessible to other community members for uploading

Broadband ISDN – an example of an intelligent communications system. The 'broadband' prefix indicates that the system is designed to include many channels (bands). See ISDN

BT – British Telecom

CASS – Chinese Academy of Social Sciences

CD – compact disk; compact storage of digital information on a disk

CDA – Communications Decency Act (US)

CEO – chief executive officer

CERN – European particle physics research centre, near Geneva, Switzerland

communications system/intelligent communications system – an intelligent communications system has artificial intelligence built in, monitoring the flow and quality of the information communicated and making sure that it reaches the destination in the correct form. Broadband ISDN is an example of such a system. See ISDN

communications technology – technology used for communicating – but also storing, retrieving and packaging (manipulating) – information. The communications revolution, the progressive separation of communication from transport is an integral part of the information revolution

construction of meaning – a perspective which argues that meaning is a construct or product of social processes shared by individuals and groups. Thus the meaning of 'computer' includes elements of 'the technological', unlike the meaning of 'pen' (even though, during the decline of the quill, the pen would have been seen as technological)

CPU – central processor unit, the 'guts' of a computer

cross-subsidy – the use of profits from one sector to subsidise an unprofitable sector, usually to permit the possibility of universal service at an affordable price

CSO – community service obligation

CTSS – compatible time-sharing system

customer service – presumes that the consumer is rich enough to be a customer. Citizenship is not sufficient, and wealth is also required. See **public interest** for more

cyber- (for example, **cyberspace**) – something constructed from digital components thus cyberspace, a digital construction of space

cyberspace – term coined by William Gibson to refer to the cyberworld created by the convergence of IT/computers, digital media and telecommunications

Cyclades – early French computer network

DDD – direct distance dialling (US)

determinism – the notion that something is so powerful that it is beyond human control, for example, in technological determinism

digital divide – the gap between the haves and have-nots of the information society following the advent of ICTs and digitisation

digitisation – the rendering of information in digital form. For example, in analogue phone services the sound is modulated at the mouthpiece, retaining the pattern of sound waves as digital information until it is converted back into waves at the earpiece of the listener. Digital sound is encoded algorithmically, using on/off states, which compacts the signal and means that more data can travel at the same time, with consequent benefits in terms of carriage capacity and cost

discourse – given that understanding depends upon the construction of meaning, a discourse frames the parameters within which meaning is shared with other/s – it involves the concept of communication. Feminism, for example, assumes that gender is a political as well as social construction and that to be feminine is to struggle with dominant masculine and patriarchal discourses

DNA – dioxyribonucleic acid (a nucleic acid) plus protein molecules make up chromosomes

DoCoMo – 'DO COmmunications over the MObile Network' (Japan)

DSL – digital subscriber line

DVD – digital video disk

EFF – Electronic Frontier Foundation

effects research – a branch of audience/readership research which attempts to describe and quantify media effects, such as the effect of violent television images upon children, or of pornography upon sex-offenders. There is a tendency to assume that there is an effect (see **construction of meaning**), although most effects described are subtle and highly conditional

electronic and microelectronic – applied to microchip technologies where the electrical circuits have been progressively miniaturised to allow quantum leaps in available processing capacity while minimising physical size; often used to indicate some element of in-built computer control as in robotics

ENIAC – the Electrical Numerical Integrator and Calculator (an early computer) (US)

ethnography – the study of patterns of living of a series of individuals, or of a group of people. Tends to provide large amounts of data, which are affected by the presence of the observer/researcher, and which reflect their priorities. Often associated with postmodern discourses, and also the foundation for early structuralist analysis

EU – European Union

EU Kids Online – a multi-country EU research network led by Professor Sonia Livingstone and Dr Leslie Haddon at the LSE and co-sponsored by the LSE and the European Community Safer Internet Plus Programme

F2F – face to face

F2S – face to screen

fan fiction – fiction produced by fans for fans as a voluntary response to their immersion in a specific fictional world. It commonly adds unexpected and potentially subversive themes to established story lines

fanzine – fan-produced magazine for consumption by other fans

FF – See **fan fiction**

fibre optic/optical fibre – pulses of laser light travel along superfine glass strands to communicate information. Laser energy travels at the speed of light and its power is concentrated as a result of the photons all having the same wavelength. Digitisation allows optic fibres to carry immense amounts of information

FPS – first person shooter, a digital game in which the gamer's main aim is to shoot opponent avatars. See RTS

frequency – the frequency of, for example, a radio signal is related to its wavelength; the point on the broadcasting spectrum at which that signal is transmitted and can be received. Longer wavelengths travel at lower frequencies. The frequency (the number of waves per second) is measured in hertz (Hz). A range of neighbouring frequencies make a spectrum, such as that of visible light (each colour has its own frequency)

FTP – file transfer protocol

FTTH/FTTP/FTTN – fibre to the home, fibre to the premises, fibre to the node

gatekeeping – the process through which experts, such as news editors, restrict access to the mass media – newspapers, radio, television, etc. – usually on grounds of ensuring professionalism, quality and relevance

GDP – gross domestic product, a measure of a country's productivity

gender – a social construction with political implications, justified by biological difference. Conceptualisations of biological difference are also social constructions (see **discourse**)

global/isation – the notion that a networked world is interconnected rather than divided – by satellites, by fibre optics, by digital information – and that the whole is greater than the sum of the parts. Usually associated with such terms as information flows and information power within the global context

GNU – free software platform with the acronym meaning Gnu's Not Unix

gTLD – generic top-level domain

heterarchy – a flat organisational structure in which position does not determine relative status

hierarchy – a trunk, branch, twig, type of classification system with different levels of power

HIV/AIDS – human immunodeficiency virus/auto-immune deficiency syndrome

host, network host – a computer connected into the network as a network node (or internet node). Each host has a unique IP address while data is sent and received according to TCP parameters

HP – Harry Potter, J.K. Rowling's schoolboy wizard character

HTML – hypertext mark-up language

http:// – hypertext transfer protocol – protocol that allows pages of text held on servers accessible via the WWW to be accessed by remote computers

IBM – International Business Machines

ICANN – Internet Corporation for Assigned Names and Numbers

ICTs – information and communication technologies, digital by nature, including computers and mobile phones

IGF – Internet Governance Forum

IM – internet messaging, such as MSN messenger

IMP – interface message processor (see Diagram 2.3). IMPs connected hosts into the early ARPANET network

imperialism – associated with the domination by one culture or country – the colonial power – of other countries or cultures, the colonies. Involves the enrichment of the imperial power by the impoverishment of the oppressed

information – a surprisingly ambiguous term in that, according to the semantic definition, information is organised data with the capacity to inform people. Classic information theory sees information as data; it needs to be measurable, but doesn't need to be understood to be processed, for example, by machines

information revolution – the process by which the material base of industrialised nations became based upon an information economy. Conceived broadly this can include libraries, education, law, administration, media. etc. Information societies were originally defined as over 50 per cent dependent upon information, and were sometimes referred to as post-industrial societies, because the industrial base was no longer judged to be the prime constituent

information rich/poor – as the knowledge explosion accelerates, those with access to the information produced – the information rich – become richer. At the same time the information gap widens between the information rich and poor (see **global/isation, digital divide**)

information technologies – especially computers, databases and telecommunications (see **communications technologies**) means that information societies are characterised by a knowledge explosion, with the amount of information in the (developed) world estimated to be doubling every five years

intelligent communications system – See **broadband ISDN**

interactive – the capacity of a communication medium to be altered by, or to have its products altered by, a user or audience

interface – the coupling of hardware and software which is negotiated by network/ computer users before they use the technology to communicate, store, retrieve or manipulate information

internet – an interconnecting, global-wide series of inter/national networks – based on the first ARPANET – into which all computers can be connected at a cost. Stand-alone PCs can access the internet via modems (modulator-demodulators) or routers, and an appropriate software gateway/interface, to get information onto and off from the telecommunications channels. IMPs and TIPs used to serve the purposes now served by routers (see Diagram 2.3)

IP – internet protocol, the protocol that manages the transfer of information from one network to another via a gateway (see Diagram 2.4)

IP – intellectual property

IPO – Initial Public (stock) Offering, a process and a document required to transform, or 'float', a privately owned company into one that is listed on the stock exchange

IRC – internet relay chat. Synchronous (= same time) chat over the internet using text and/or images and sound. Sometimes called simply 'chat'

IRI – internationalised resource identifiers, unique identifiers for information which will help to structure the (anticipated) semantic web

ISDN – integrated switched digital network (an intelligent system). ISDN pathways utilise a variety of communications media – for example, satellite and/or fibre optics

ISP – internet service provider – an organisation that sells access to the internet

ISTTF – Internet Safety Technical Task Force (US)

IT – information technology

Kbps – kilobits per second

kinkeeping – the process by which regular calls concerning everyday domestic activities and subjects bind together people who are distant from each other within reciprocal ties of caring and involvement

LAN – local area network (see **network**), but more usually applied to a 'clan' of game-players who regularly get together and set up a LAN to play games and exchange files

LANfest – a gathering of LAN clans for immersive engagement in a gaming tournament, typically over a weekend. Similarly, LAN party

LANing – engaged in the process of LAN playing

liberalisation – used to indicate the commercial marketplace will play a bigger part in regulating goods and services – for example, in telecommunications

Linux – currently the leading open-source software platform

MAD – mutually assured destruction, a strategy promoted as a means for avoiding nuclear war

MAKO – movement against kindred offenders, Australian organisation publicising the crimes and whereabouts of sex offenders

Mbps – megabits per second

meaning – meanings formed by an individual or group are often revealed through analysing the myths and narratives which that group shares

media diversity – used both to mean a diversity of media, for example, internet, print, television, radio – and diversity within a given medium, for example, a variety of different newspapers, and viewpoints, including minority opinions and ideas. The internet showcases greater diversity of opinion than any other medium in history

meme – the smallest possible element of culture, analogous to the gene in biology

microchip – See **electronic and microelectronic**

MIT – Massachusetts Institute of Technology (US)

MMORPGs – massively multiplayer online role-playing games

modem – *mo*dulator-*dem*odulators, used to transfer digital data between computers using analogue phone lines. See **internet**

moral panic – when a society or mainstream group reacts to a change in the environment, as of it 'threatens life as we know it'

MS-DOS – Microsoft disk operating system

MSN – Microsoft network

MSP – minimum service provision; a service so central to society that regulators work to make it universally available (sometimes USP, universal service provision), for example, telephone, television, mail

multimedia – the use of interactive multiple media components which respond to inputs, for example, a computer program through which a user can trigger text, graphics, pictures and sound

multiplexing – interweaving of different digital elements during data transfer to achieve efficiencies of communication

mythology – myths involve shared social understandings which help inform members of a cultural group as to the nature of that group, and to unite the group, for example, in the creation of a national identity. Sometimes associated with the suspension of disbelief of something which would usefully be true, for example, equality between the sexes might be seen as mythic. Myths often work below the level of consciousness. Stories, fictions, narratives and legends frequently serve mythic ends

narrative theory – readers bring to an event or experience a sense of before and after required to understand the story. If an event is un-narratable. it is beyond the context of the rules and understandings which society uses to construct meaning

NASA – National Aeronautics and Space Administration agency (US)

NASDAQ – US (mainly) technology-based stock exchange

NCP – network control protocol, precursor of TCP/IP

NES – Nintendo Entertainment System (Japan)

net – the totality of networks, email, proprietary (for example, AOL), WWW. etc., a contraction of 'internet'

network – networks come in a range of typologies and specifications and the passage of data through different networks is controlled by the internet protocol (IP)

newbie – newcomer to the net, or to a chat room, or to a discussion area

nouveau information poor – people who lose access to ICTs as a result of sudden poverty or change in life circumstances; for example, unemployment, divorce

NPL – National Physical Laboratory (UK)

NSFNET – The National Science Foundation Network (US)

NTT – Nippon Telegraph and Telephone (Japan)

OECD – Organisation for Economic Co-operation and Development

ONI – Open Net Initiative, an international index of freedom on the internet sponsored by Harvard, Toronto, Cambridge and Oxford Universities

open source – where the source code is available for any skilled person to work with a program to improve or adapt it

P2P – peer-to-peer

paradigm – a framework of understandings within which discourses are constructed and communicated. Analysing a paradigm can be the first step to resisting or subverting the power of the elite whose interests that paradigm serves. A paradigm is analysable through its discourses

PC – IBM-compatible 'personal computer'

PC bangs – Korean internet café

post-industrial – See **information revolution**

POTS – plain old telephone system (paired copper wires)

privatisation – the passing into private ownership, usually by share float, of publicly (government) owned industries

protocol – a series of program commands by which sender and recipient hosts communicate regarding the status and destination of a specific data set to be transferred between the two machines

PTT – postal, telegraph and telephone service

public interest – when an aspect of a debate requires consideration of wider social costs and benefits than company profitability or government efficiency. 'Citizen' implies that people have certain civic rights regardless of their financial status and these are often honoured through public services. 'Customer service' considers the needs of people rich enough to be customers. The introduction of user-pays changes a public service into customer service

RAND Corporation – Research ANd Development Corporation, based in Santa Monica, California (US)

reader – one who reads, but also a term making visible the active power of the person constructing meaning and interpreting a text

RFC – Request for Comments, started in the development phase of ARPANET

RFLAN – Red Flag LAN, a specific LANfest (Australia)

RIM – Research in Motion (Blackberry software, Canada)

RL – 'real life'

RTS – Real Time Strategy, a more strategic game genre than some online gaming; for example, FPS tests fast reflexes as much as strategy

sci-fi – science fiction: often used to explore social and moral issues related to technology

SCOT – Social Construction of Technology: a theoretical approach to the understanding of technology and society

semantic – this refers to the communication of meaning. The semantic web implies a belief that machine-understandable meaning can be built into the web and its components, such as web pages. See **Web 3.0**

slash – erotic fan fiction usually with homosexual themes

SMS – short message service

SNS – social networking sites, such as Facebook, MySpace and Bebo

social determinism – sees technology as expressing the priorities of the social elites which create or utilise the technology. See **determinism**

SRI – Stanford Research Institute (US)

STD – subscriber trunk dialling system (UK)

switched-packet system – each message is broken into smaller packets of data with a standardised 'header' containing information about destination and sequence for reassembly. The header switches the packet along lines in a network which allocates bandwidth on the connecting communications cables according to the requirements of the message/data to be sent (known as 'dynamic allocation')

TCP – transmission control protocol, the protocol that manages the communication of data at the sending host and the receiving host, standardising packet size, sequencing, and confirmation

technological determinism – constructs technology as outside social control, determining future social development and direction. Media determinism is a specialist application of technological determinism to communication media

telecommunications – communications at a distance, usually implying cable, satellite, broadcasting spectrum, fibre optics, etc.

text – this need not be written, or be a media product; it can be any human/social construct, Alan Turing's life say, or a car. To view such entities as texts, a reader would normally subscribe to a constructionist approach and use appropriate discursive practices to analyse meaning

TIP – terminal interface message processor. TIPs allowed 'dumb' terminals to access a host built into the TIP and allowed multiple access to the ARPANET network (see Diagram 2.3)

TV – Television

UCLA – University of California, Los Angeles (US)

UK – United Kingdom

UNESCO – United Nations Educational, Scientific and Cultural Organisation

UNIVAC – early, room-sized computer made by Remington Rand (US)

UNIX – multi-user, multi-tasking operating system used by many powerful computers and the basis for much open-source programming. Unix contains many subprograms that perform network operations transparently between several machines

URL – uniform resource locator

US – United States

USO – universal service obligation

USSR – Union of Socialist Soviet Republics

viral (video) – viral communication is when groups of internet users are 'infected' with an enthusiasm for some digital product to the extent that they cannot help but pass that infection on

VL – 'virtual life'

WAN – wide area network. See **network** and **LAN**

wavelength – electromagnetic waves travel out in every direction from the point where they are generated. The distance between the peaks of the waves (where the electrical energy is strongest) determines the wavelength. Wavelength is related to frequency: the longer the wavelength the lower the frequency; the higher the frequency the shorter the wavelength

Web 1.0 – the name which has been retrospectively given to the early versions of 'the web'

Web 2.0 – the development of the internet beyond the straightforward accessing of websites and files to fostering interactivity through the use of collaborative and social media including wikis and blogs

Web 3.0 – more speculated than delivered, but seen as a combination of the sociality of Web 2.0 plus a layer of coded information carried in each element of the web which makes it 'meaningful' to computers and other ICTs. A web which has 'embedding meaning' accessible to computers is termed the 'semantic web'

WELL – early online community: Whole Earth 'Lectronic Link

WSIS – World Summit on the Information Society

WWII – Second World War

WWW – World Wide Web; an accessible, connected, searchable, updatable web of information with elements of the whole widely dispersed among the networked computers

XXX – triple X-rated: Adults only

REFERENCES

Aaronovitch, D. (2003), 'Why We Love Wife Swap', *The Observer*, 5 October, p. 23.

ABC BB (2008), 'Remittances – Flying Money', *Background Briefing*, ABC Radio National, 5 October, http://www.abc.net.au/rn/backgroundbriefing/stories/2008/2375175.htm (accessed 3 October 2009).

Abraham, R. (2008), 'Mobile Phones and Economic Development: Evidence From the Fishing Industry in India', *Information Technologies and International Development*, 4(1): 5–17.

ABS (2001), *Use of the Internet by Householders, Australia.* 8147.0 http://www8.abs.gov.au/ausstats/abs@.nsf/PrimaryMainFeatures/8147.0?OpenDocument (accessed 3 October 2009).

ABS (2008), 'Internet Access at Home', *4102.0 Australian Social Trends*, Australian Bureau of Statistics, July, http://www.abs.gov.au/AUSSTATS/abs@.nsf/Lookup/4102.0Chapter10002008 (accessed 3 October 2009).

ACMA (2007), *Media and Communications in Australian Families: Report of the Media and Society Research Project*, Australian Communications and Media Authority, Canberra: ACMA. http://www.acma.gov.au/webwr/_assets/main/lib101058/media_and_society_report_2007.pdf (accessed 3 October 2009).

ACMA (2008), 'Internet Codes Index', Australian Communications and Media Authority website, http://www.acma.gov.au/WEB/STANDARD/pc=IND_REG_CODES_INT (accessed 3 October 2009).

Adler, P. S. and Kwon, S. W. (2002), 'Social Capital: Prospects for a New Concept', *Academy of Management Review*, 27(1): 17–40.

Aizu, I. (2003), '.jp Japan', in Chin Saik Yoon (ed), *Digital Review of Asia Pacific 2003/2004*, Penang: Southbound; Kuala Lumpur: Asia-Pacific Development Information Programme, UN Development Programme; Ottawa: Pan Asia Networking Programme, International Development Research Centre; Montreal: Orbicom Network of UNESCO Chairs in Communications, pp. 120–9.

Albanese, A. (2009), 'Authors Guild Slams Amazon Over Its Google Settlement Stance: Other Groups Opt Out of Settlement', *Publishers Weekly*, 3 September, http://www.publishersweekly.com/article/CA6687448.html (accessed 3 October 2009).

Albury, K. (2003), 'The Ethics of Porn on the Net', in C. Lumby and E. Probyn (eds), *Remote Control: New Media, New Ethics*, Melbourne: Cambridge University Press, pp. 196–211.

All your … (n.d.) All Your Chocolate Rain Are Belong To Us [music video], *YouTube*, http://www.youtube.com/watch?v=dUyxurUWtSQ (accessed 3 October 2009).

Allison, S., Wahlde, L. von, Shockly, T. and Gabbard, G. (2006), 'The Development of the Self in the Era of the Internet and Role-Playing Fantasy Games, Clinical Case Conference', *American Journal of Psychiatry*, March, 163 (3): 381–5.

ALP (2007), 'A Computer for Every Student, Federal 07 Campaign', *Australian Labor Party*, http://www.alpvictoria.com.au/News-and-Media/Federal-07-Campaign/Archived-News/ A-Computer-For-Every-Student-.html (accessed 3 October 2009).

Amnesty International (n.d.), 'Shi Tao Background', *Amnesty International: Action for Human Rights. Hope for Humanity* [website], http://www.amnestyusa.org/business-and-human-rights/internet-censorship/yahoo-action-background/page.do?id=1011510 (accessed 3 October 2009).

Anderson, B. (1991 [1983]), *Imagined Communities*, 2nd edn, London: Verso.

Anderson, D. (2007), 'Max Newman: Topologist, Codebreaker and Pioneer of computing', *IEEE History of the Annals of Computing*, July–Sept, 29 (3): 76–81.

Anderson, M. (1971) *Sociology of the Family*, Harmondsworth: Penguin.

Ang, P. H. and Yeo, T. M. (1998), *Mass Media Laws and Regulations in Singapore*, Singapore: Asian Media Information and Communication Centre [AMICC].

Apted, M. (dir.) (2001), *Enigma* [Film], Miramax.

Arensberg, C. M. and Kimball, S. T. (2001 [1940]), *Family and Community in Ireland*, 3rd edn, Clare: CLASP Press.

AusAID (2007), *Leveraging Remittances with Microfinance: Synthesis Report*, Monash Asia Institute; Institute for regional development and University of Tasmania; Foundation for development cooperation, December, http://www.ausaid.gov.au/publications/pdf/ remittances.pdf (accessed 3 October 2009).

Avaaz (2009), *Avaaz: The World in Action* [website], http://www.avaaz.org/ (accessed 3 October 2009).

Bakardjieva, M. (2005), *Internet Society: The Internet in Everyday Life*, London: Sage.

Baldassar, L. (2007), 'Transnational Families and the Provision of Moral and Social Support: The Relationship Between Truth and Distance', *Identities: Global Studies in Culture and Power*, 14: 385–409.

Barcan, Ruth (2002), 'In the Raw: "Home-Made" Porn and Reality Genres', *Journal of Mundane Behavior*, 3(1) February http://www.mundanebehavior.org/issues/v3n1/barcan. htm (accessed 3 October 2009).

Barlow, J. P. (1996), 'A Declaration of the Independence of Cyberspace', *Electronic Frontier Foundation*, 8 February, http://homes.eff.org/~barlow/Declaration-Final.html (accessed 3 October 2009).

Barter, Peter (2002), Peter Barter's open letter regarding Bill White's Anti-Divine Word Uni campaign, *VoyForums: Clown* [website], http://www.asiapac.org.fj/cafepacific/resources/ aspac/clownindex2.html (accessed 3 October 2009).

Battelle, J. (2006 [2005]), *The Search: How Google and its Rivals Rewrote the Rules of Business and Transformed our Culture*, UK revised edn), London: Nicholas Brealey Publishing.

Baym, N. (1995), 'The Emergence of Community in Computer-Mediated Communication', in S. Jones (ed.), *CyberSociety: Computer-Mediated Communication and Community*, Thousand Oaks: Sage, pp. 138–63.

BBC News (2000), 'Tech Stock Meltdown', *Business Stories of the Year*, 15 December, http://news.bbc.co.uk/1/hi/in_depth/business/2000/review/1058175.stm (accessed 3 October 2009).

BBC *Newsnight* (2008), 'Talk About Newsnight: Return of the Baghdad Blogger', *Newsnight*, 17 June, http://www.bbc.co.uk/blogs/newsnight/2008/06/return_of_the_baghdad_blogger.html (accessed 3 October 2009).

BBC Press Office (2008), 'Next Generation BBC iPlayer Launches', *BBC Press Releases: New Media*, 25 June, http://www.bbc.co.uk/pressoffice/pressreleases/stories/2008/06_june/25/iplayer.shtml (accessed 3 October 2009).

BBN (2008), 'About BBN, BBN Technologies', *Bolt Beranek and Newman Inc.*, [website] http://www.bbn.com/about/timeline/ (accessed 3 October 2009).

Bearman, D. (2006), 'Jean-Nöel Jeanneney's Critique of Google: Private Sector Book Digitization and Digital Library Policy (Opinion)', *D-Lib Magazine*, 12 December (12), http://www.dlib.org/dlib/december06/bearman/12bearman.html (accessed 3 October 2009).

Beavis, C. (2007), 'New Textual Worlds: Young People and Computer Games', in N. Dolby and F. Rizvi (eds), *Youth moves, Identities and Education in Global Perspective*, London: Routledge, pp. 53–66.

Bell, D. (1973), *The Coming of Post-Industrial Society: A Venture in Social Forecasting*, New York, NY: Basic Books.

Beniger, J. R. (1986), *The Control Revolution: Technological and Economic Origins of the Information Society*, Cambridge, Mass: Harvard University Press.

Berners-Lee, T. (with Fiscetti, M.) (1999), *Weaving the Web: The Original Design and Ultimate Destiny of the World Wide Web by its Inventor*, San Francisco: Harper San Francisco.

Berners-Lee, T; Hendler, J., and Lassila, O. (2001), 'The Semantic Web: A New Form of Web Content that is Meaningful to Computers Will Unleash a Revolution of New Possibilities', *Scientific American*, 5 (1): 28–37.

Bijker, W., Hughes, T. and Pinch, T. (eds) (1987), *The Social Construction of Technological Systems: New Directions in the Sociology and History of Technology*. Cambridge, MA: MIT Press.

Bill White exposed (n.d.), *Bill White Info* [website], http://bill_white1.tripod.com/ (accessed 3 October 2009).

Bissio, R.R. (1990), Third World Guide 1991/92: The World as seen by the Third World. Facts, Figures, Opinions, Montevideo, Uruguay: Institut del Tercer Mundo.

Blackburn, C., Read, J. and Hughes, N. (2005), 'Carers and the Digital Divide. Factors Affecting Internet Use Among Carers in the UK', *Health and Social Care in the Community*, 13 (3): 201–10.

Blake (2004), 'Our Battle for Hearts and Minds, LISNews Blog/Blake's Blog', *Librarian and Information Science News*, 5 November, http://www.lisnews.org/node/24580 (accessed 3 October 2009).

Bocij, P. (2006), *The Dark Side of the Internet: Protecting You and Your Family From Online Criminals*, Santa Barbara, CA: Praeger Publishers.

Bonniface, L., Green, L. and Swanson, M. (2006a), 'Communication on a Health-Related Website Offering Therapeutic Support: Phase 1 of the HeartNET Intervention', *Australian Journal of Communication*, 33 (2,3), pp. 89–108.

Bonniface L., Omari A. and Swanson M. (2006b), 'Shuffling Buddies – How an Online Community Supports Healthier Lifestyle Choices: An Early Indication of Physical Activity and Exercise Outcomes from the HeartNET Intervention', in F. Sudweeks, F. H. Hrachovec and C. Ess (eds), *Proceedings of the Fifth International Conference on Cultural Attitudes Towards Technology and Communication*; Estonia, Tartu: School of Information Technology/ Murdoch University; pp. 90–101.

Bonniface, L., Green, L. and Swanson, M. (2005), 'Affect and an Effective Online Therapeutic Community', *M/C: A journal of Media and Culture*, 'Affect', 8 (6), http://journal. media-culture.org.au/0512/05-bonnifacegreenswanson.php (accessed 3 October 2009).

boyd, d. (2006), 'Friends, Friendsters, and Top 8: Writing Community into Being on Social Network Sites', *First Monday*, 11 (12), http://131.193.153.231/www/issues/issue11_12/ boyd/index.html (accessed 3 October 2009).

Brain, M. (n.d.) 'How Analog and Digital Recording Works', *How Stuff Works*, http:// communication.howstuffworks.com/analog-digital.htm/printable (accessed 3 October 2009).

Branwyn, G. (1999), 'How the Porn Sites Do It', *The Industry Standard*, 22 March, pp. 36– 8, http://www.danni.com/press/industrystan_032299.html (accessed 3 October 2009).

Brin, S. and Page, L. (n.d.), *The Anatomy of a Large-Scale Hypertextual Web Search Engine*, Stanford: Stanford University, http://infolab.stanford.edu/~backrub/google.html (accessed 3 October 2009).

Bringers (n.d.), 'The Potter War Campaign', *The Bringers: Fighting For the Rights of Fans Online* [website], http://web.ukonline.co.uk/bringers/temp/c-potter.html (accessed 3 October 2009).

Bruns, A. (2003), 'Gatewatching, Not Gatekeeping: Collaborative Online News', *Media International Australia Incorporating Culture and Policy*, May, 107: 31–44.

Bruns, Axel (2008a), *Blogs, Wikipedia, Second Life and Beyond: From Production to Produsage*, New York: Peter Lang.

Bruns, Axel (2008b), 'News Blogs and Citizen Journalism: New Directions for e-Journalism', in K. Prasad (ed.), *e-Journalism: New Directions in Electronic News Media.*, New Delhi: BR Publishing, http://snurb.info/files/News%20Blogs%20and%20Citizen%20Journalism. pdf (accessed 3 October 2009).

Bryan, D. (1994), 'The Multilocals, Transnationals and Communications Technology', in L. Green and R. Guinery (eds), *Framing Technology: Society, Choice and Change*, Sydney: Allen and Unwin pp. 145–60.

BuddeComm (2009), *Global - Key Telecoms Mobile and Broadband Statistics* (6th ed), Paul Budde Communication Pty Ltd, http://www.budde.com.au/Research/Global-Key-Telecoms-Mobile-and-Broadband-Statistics.html (accessed 3 October 2009).

Bure, C. (2005), 'Digital Inclusion Without Social Inclusion: The Consumption of Information and Communication Technologies (ICTs) within Homeless Subculture in Scotland', *The Journal of Community Informatics*, 1 (2): 116–33.

Burgess, J. (2008), '"All Your Chocolate Rain Are Belong to Us"? Viral Video, YouTube and the Dynamics of Participatory Culture', in G. Lovink and S. Niederer (eds), *The VideoVortex Reader: Responses to YouTube*, Amsterdam: Institute of Network Cultures, pp. 101–10 http://networkcultures.org/wpmu/portal/files/2008/10/vv_reader_small.pdf (accessed 3 October 2009).

Burgess, J. and Green, J. (2009) YouTube: Online Video and Participatory Culture, Cambridge: Polity Press.

Burkeman, O. (2004), Plug Pulled on Live Website Seen by Millions, *The Guardian*, 3 January, http://www.guardian.co.uk/technology/2004/jan/03/usnews.internationalnews (accessed 3 October 2009).

Burman, E. (2003), *Shift! The Unfolding Internet – Hype, Hope and History*. Chichester, UK: John Wiley and Sons.

Buzan, T. and Buzan, B. (1996) *The Mind Map Book: How to Use Radiant Thinking to Maximise Your Brain's Untapped Potential* New York: Plume.

Carey, J. (1988), 'Technology and Ideology: The Case of the Telegraph'. In *Communication as culture, essays on media and society*. London and Boston: Unwin Hyman, pp. 201–30.

Carr, D., Buckingham, D., Burn, A. and Schott, G. (2006), *Computer Games: Text, Narrative and Play*, Cambridge: Polity Press.

Castells, M. (2010), *The Rise of the Network Society* (rev. ed, new preface) Oxford: Wiley-Blackwell.

Castells, M., Fernández-Ardèvol, M., Qui, J. L. and Sey, A. (2007), *Mobile Communication and Society: A Global Perspective*, Cambridge, MA: MIT Press.

Cavoukian, A. (2009), *Online Privacy: Make Youth Awareness and Education a Priority*. Toronto: Information and Privacy Commissioner of Ontario. http://www.ipc.on.ca/images/resources/youthonline.pdf (accessed 3 October 2009).

CBC News (2009) 'NPD Candidate in BC Election Quits Over Racy Photos in Facebook', *CBC News*, 20 April, http://www.cbc.ca/canada/bcvotes2009/story/2009/04/20/bc-election-lam-facebook.html (accessed 3 October 2009).

Center for Internet Addiction Recovery (2006), 'Cybersex/Cyberporn Addiction', *Center for Internet Addiction Recovery* [website], http://www.netaddiction.com/cybersexual_addiction.htm (accessed 3 October 2009).

Cerf, V. and Kahn, R. (1974), 'A Protocol for Packet Network Intercommunication', *IEEE Transactions on Communications*, May, Com–22 (5): 637–48.

CERN (2008) 'How the Web Began', *CERN: European Organization for Nuclear Research* [website], http://public.web.cern.ch/public/en/About/WebStory-en.html (accessed 3 October 2009).

Ceruzzi, P. (2003), *A History of Modern Computing*, Cambridge MA: MIT Press.

CFR (2009) About, *Council on Foreign Relations* [website], http://www.cfr.org/about/ (accessed 3 October 2009).

Cheal, D. J. (1988), *The Gift Economy*. New York: Routledge.

Chmielewski, D. (2007), 'Search Site Moves at the Speed of China', *LA Times Business*, 10 December, http://articles.latimes.com/2007/dec/10/business/fi-baidu10 (accessed 3 October 2009).

Clegg, B. (2006), *Studying Using the Web: The Student's Guide to Using the Ultimate Information Resource*, Oxford: Routledge, Routledge Study Guides.

Cohen, S. (1980 [1972]), *Folk Devils and Moral Panics: The Creation of the Mods and Rockers*, 2nd edn, Oxford: Martin Robertson.

Computer Economics (2007), 'Internet and Broadband Growth Accelerates Worldwide', *Computer Economics: Metrics for Management*, March, http://www.computereconomics.com/article.cfm?id=1206 (accessed 3 October 2009).

Conroy, T. and Hanson, J. (2007), *Constructing America's War Culture: Iraq, Media and Images at Home*, Lanham, Maryland: Lexington Books.

Coopersmith, J. (2006), 'Does Your Mother Know What You Really Do? The Changing Nature and Image of Computer Based Pornography', *History and Technology*, 22 (1): 1–25.

COST 298 (n.d.), *Participation in the Broadband Society* [website], http://www.cost298.org/ (accessed 3 October 2009).

Crawford, K. (2009), 'These Foolish Things: on Intimacy and Insignificance' in G. Goggin and L, Hjorth, Mobile Media, *Mobile Technologies: From Telecommunications to Media*, Oxford: Routledge, pp. 250–63.

Culler, J. (2001 [1981]), 'Story and Discourse in the Analysis of Narrative', *The Pursuit of Signs: Semiotics, Literature, Deconstruction*, London: Routledge, Routledge, Classics edn, pp. 188–208.

CyberAngels (2009), 'Homepage', *CyberAngels: A Program of Guardian Angels, Keeping It Safe* [website], http://www.cyberangels.org/ (accessed 4 October 2009).

Dare, J. (2004), 'Online Defamation: A Case Study in Competing Rights', *Cultural Studies Association of Australasia Annual Conference*, Murdoch University, Murdoch, W.A. http://wwwmcc.murdoch.edu.au/cfel/docs/Julie_Dare_FV.pdf (accessed 4 October 2009).

Dare, J. (2005), 'Cyberharassment and Online Defamation: A Default Form of Regulation?' *Transformations*, 11 (Nov), http://www.transformationsjournal.org/journal/issue_11/article_04.shtml (accessed 4 October 2009).

Dare, J. (2006), 'Connections in the Private Sphere: Women's Use of ICTs in Sustaining and Enriching Connections and Communion', *Making and Keeping Connections: Life, Learning and Information Networks*, Proceedings of the Transforming Information and Learning Conference, 30 September, Perth, Australia, pp. 61–72, http://conferences.scis.ecu.edu.au/TILC2007/documents/2006/tilc2006_dare.pdf (accessed 4 October 2009).

Dertouzos, M. (1999), Foreward, in T. Berners-Lee, *Weaving the Web: the Original Design and Ultimate Destiny of the World Wide Web by its Inventor*, New York: Harper SanFrancisco, pp. ix–xi.

DiMaggio, P. and Hargittai, E. (2001), 'From the "Digital Divide" to "Digital Inequality": Studying Internet Use as Penetration Increases', *Working Paper Series, 15*, Princeton University: Center for Arts and Cultural Policy Studies, Princeton University, http://www.

princeton.edu/~artspol/workpap/WP15%20-%20DiMaggio%2BHargittai.pdf (accessed 4 October 2009).

DirAP (n.d.), *Digital Review of Asia-Pacific* [website], http://www.digital-review.org/ (accessed 4 October 2009).

Donaldson, R. (dir.) (2000), *Thirteen Days* [Film], New Line Cinema.

Durkin, K. and Barber, B. (2002), 'Not So Doomed: Computer Game Play and Positive Adolescent Development', *Applied Developmental Psychology*, 23: 373–92.

EDL Project (n.d.) 'About EDL project', *European Digital Library Project*, http://www.edlproject.eu/about.php (accessed 4 October 2009).

EFF (2009), *Electronic Frontier Foundation* [website], http://www.eff.org/ (accessed 4 October 2009).

Endeshaw, A. (2004), 'Internet Regulation in China: The Never-Ending Cat and Mouse Game', *Information and Communication Technology Law*, 13 (1) March: 41–57.

Enough Rope (2004), 'Salam Pax', *Enough Rope with Andrew Denton*, 42, ABC, 17 May http://www.abc.net.au/tv/enoughrope/transcripts/s1110359.htm (accessed 4 October 2009).

Ephron, N. (dir.) (1998), *You've Got Mail* [Film], Warner Bros.

Ernkvist, M. and Ström, P. (2008), 'Enmeshed in Games with the Government: Governmental Policies and the Development of the Chinese Online Games Industry', *Games and Culture*, 3 (1): 98–126.

Estabrooks, M. (1995), *Electronic Technology, Corporate Strategy and World Transformation*, Westport, CT: Greenwood Publishing Group.

EU Kids Online (n. d.), *EU Kids Online* [website], London: London School of Economics/ EC Safer Internet Plus Programme, http://www.eukidsonline.net/ (accessed 4 October 2009).

Evangelista, B. (2003), 'The Other Shared Files: Pornography. Adult Film Industry Profits from Services', *SFGate/San Francisco Chronicle*, 19 May http://www.sfgate.com/cgi-bin/ article.cgi?file=/chronicle/archive/2003/05/19/BU248597.DTLandtype=business (accessed 4 October 2009).

Finkelhor, D. (2008), *Childhood Victimization: Violence, Crime and Abuse in the Lives of Young People*, New York, NY: Oxford University Press.

Finkelhor, D., Mitchell, K.J., and Wolak, J. (2000), *Online Victimization: A Report on the Nation's Youth*. Alexandria, VA: National Center for Missing and Exploited Children, http://www.unh.edu/ccrc/pdf/jvq/CV38.pdf (accessed 4 October 2009).

Fisher, W. A. and Barak, A. (2001), 'Pornography, Erotica and Behaviour: More Questions than Answers', *International Journal of Law and Psychiatry*, 14: 65–83.

Fishkin, J., He, B., Luskin, R. and Siu, A. (2006), *Deliberative Democracy in an Unlikely place: Deliberative Polling in China*, Stanford University: Center for Deliberative Democracy http://cdd.stanford.edu/research/papers/2006/china-unlikely.pdf (accessed 4 October 2009).

Fleming, A. and Debski, R. (2007), 'The Use of Irish in Networked Communications, A Study of School Children in Different Language Settings', *Journal of Multilingual and Multicultural Development*, 28 (2): 85–101.

Flickr (2009), 'Flickr tour', *Flickr* [website], http://www.flickr.com (accessed 4 October 2009).

Florida, R. (2002), *The Rise of the Creative Class: And How It's Transforming Work, Leisure, Community and Everyday Life*, New York: Basic Books.

Fraunholz, B; Unnithan, C; and Jung, J. (2005), 'Tracking and Tracing Applications of 3G for SMEs', in M. Pagani (ed.), *Mobile and Wireless Systems Beyond 3G*, Hershey, PA: IRM Press, pp. 130–54.

Freeman, C. B. (2008), 'Internet Gaming Addiction', *The Journal for Nurse-Practitioners*, 4 (1), January: 42–47.

Gerstner, L. (2002), *Who Says Elephants Can't Dance? Inside IBM's Historic Turnaround*, NY: HarperCollins.

Get Up (2009), *Get up! Action for Australia* [website], http://www.getup.org.au/ (accessed 4 October 2009).

Gettys, J. (1999) *Re: GNU/Linux* [Blog], http://www.ussg.iu.edu/hypermail/linux/kernel/9904.0/0497.html (accessed 4 October 2009).

GNU (n.d.) *The GNU Manifesto* [website], http://www.gnu.org/gnu/manifesto.html (accessed 4 October 2009).

Goggin, G. (2006), *Cell Phone Culture: Mobile Technology in Everyday Life*, Oxford: Routledge.

Google (2006), 'Google To Acquire YouTube for $1.65 Billion in Stock: Combination Will Create New Opportunities for Users and Content Owners Everywhere', *Google Press Center*, Google, 6 October, http://www.google.com/press/pressrel/google_youtube.html (accessed 4 October 2009).

Google Books (n.d.) 'About Google Book Search', *Google*, http://books.google.com.au/intl/en/googlebooks/about.html (accessed 4 October 2009).

Gorman, M. (2004), 'Google and God's Mind, Opinion', *Los Angeles Times*, B–15, 17 December, http://articles.latimes.com/2004/dec/17/opinion/oe-nugorman17 (accessed 4 October 2009).

Gray, A. (1992), *Video Playtime: The Gendering of a Leisure Technology*, London: Routledge.

Green, L. (1999), 'The End of the Virtual Community', *M/C Journal: A Journal of Media and Culture*, 'End', 2 (8), http://journal.media-culture.org.au/9912/virtual.php (accessed 4 October 2009).

Green, L. (2001), 'The Work of Consumption: Why Aren't We Paid?', *M/C: A Journal of Media and Culture*, 'Work', 4 (5), http://journal.media-culture.org.au/0111/Green.php (accessed 4 October 2009).

Green, L. (2002), *Technoculture: From Alphabet to Cybersex*, Sydney:Allen and Unwin (published concurrently as *Communication, Technology and Society*, London: Sage).

Green, L. (2003), 'Attempting To Ground Ethnographic Theory and Practice', *Australian Journal of Communication*, 30 (2): 133–45.

Green, L. and Costello, L. (2009), 'Fractures Between an Online and Offline Community (and the Ethical Responses)', *International Journal of Web-based Communities*, 5 (3): 462–75.

Green, L. and Guinery, B. (2006), 'Play Up! Play Up! and Play the Game!' *Cultural Studies Association of Australasia,* Canberra, 6–8 December, http://www.unaustralia.com/electronicpdf/Ungreenandguinery.pdf (accessed 4 October 2009).

Green, L. and Guinery, C. (2004), 'Harry Potter and the Fan Fiction Phenomenon', *M/C: A Journal of Media and Culture,* 'Fame', 7 (5), http://journal.media-culture.org.au/0411/14-green.php (accessed 4 October 2009).

Green, L. and Holloway, D. (2004), 'The Role of Everyday Life in Confounding Expectations in Communication Research', *Australian Journal of Communication,* 31 (2): 167–84.

Green, L. Holloway, D. and Quin, R. (2004), '@ Home: Australian Family Life and the Internet', in G. Goggin (ed.), *Virtual Nation: the Internet in Australia,* Sydney: UNSW Press, pp. 88–101.

Green, N. (2001), 'Information Ownership and Control in Mobile Technologie', *'e-Usages' Conference,* June 12–14, Paris.

Green, N. (2009), 'Mobility, Memory and Identity', in G. Goggin and L.Hjorth (eds), *Mobile Technologies: From Telecommunications to Media,* Oxford: Routledge, Oxon, pp. 266–81.

Guardian (2008), 'China and the Internet: The Great Firewall', *The Guardian,* Monday 22 December, http://www.guardian.co.uk/commentisfree/2008/dec/22/china-internet-comment (accessed 4 October 2009).

Gunther, M. (2006), 'Tech Execs Get Grilled Over China Business', *Fortune,* 16 February http://money.cnn.com/2006/02/15/news/international/pluggedin_fortune/index.htm?cnn=yes (accessed 6 October).

Haas, T. (2005), 'From "Public Journalism" to the "Public's Journalism"? Rhetoric and Reality in the Discourse on Weblogs', *Journalism Studies,* 6 (3): 387–96.

Habermas, J. (1989a), 'The Public Sphere: An Encyclopedia Article', in S. Bronner and D. Kellner (eds), *Critical Theory and Society: A Reader,* trans. S. Lennox and F. Lennox, New York: Routledge, pp. 136–42, in M. G. Durham and D. Kellner (eds) (2005), *Media and Cultural Studies: Keyworks,* 2nd edn), Oxford: Wiley-Blackwell, pp. 73–9.

Habermas, J. (1989b), *The Structural Transformation of the Public Sphere: An Inquiry into a Category of Bourgeois Society,* trans. T. Burger, Cambridge, MA: MIT Press.

Haddon, L. (1988), 'The Home Computer: The Making of a Consumer Electronic', *Science as Culture,* 2: 7–51, http://www.lse.ac.uk/collections/media@lse/whosWho/LeslieHaddon/HomeComputer.pdf (accessed 6 October 2009).

Haddon, L. (2000), Social Exclusion and Information and Communication Technologies: Lessons from Studies of Single Parents and the Young Elderly, *New Media and Society,* 2 (4): 387–406.

Haddon, L. (2004), *Information and Communication Technologies in Everyday Life: A Concise Introduction and Research Guide,* Oxford: Berg.

Haddon, L. (2005), 'The Innovatory Use of ICTs', in L. Haddon, E. Mante, B. Sapio, K-H Kommonen and L. Fortunati (eds), *Everyday Innovators: Researching the Role of Users in Shaping ICTs,* Netherlands: Springer, pp. 54–66.

Haddon, L. and Stald, G. (2008), 'A Comparative Analysis of European Media Coverage of Children and the Internet', *Association of Internet Researchers (AoIR) Annual Conference*, Denmark: IT University, Copenhagen, 16–19 October, http://www.lse.ac.uk/collections/EUKidsOnline/EU%20Kids%20I/Presentations/EUKidsPressAnalysisAoIR.pdf (accessed 6 October 2009).

Hafner, K. and Matthew L. (2003 [1998]), *Where Wizards Stay Up Late: The Origins of the Internet*, London: Simon and Schuster.

Hamilton, J. M. and Jenner, E. (2003), 'The New Foreign Correspondence', *Foreign Affairs*, 8 (5): 131.

Hartley, J. (2006), 'Journalism as a Human Right: The Cultural Approach to Journalism', in M. Loffelholz and D. Weaver (Eds), *Journalism Research in an Era of Globalization*, London: Routledge, pp. 40–50.

Hasebrink, U., Livingstone, S., Haddon, L. and Ólafsson, K. (2009), *Comparing Children's Online Opportunities and Risks Across Europe: Cross-National Comparisons for EU Kids Online*, Deliverable D3.2., 2nd edn, LSE, London: EU Kids Online, http://eprints.lse.ac.uk/24368/ (accessed 6 October 2009).

Hearn, G., Mandeville, T., and Anthony, D. (1997), *The Communication Superhighway: Social and Economic Change in the Digital Age*. Sydney: Allen and Unwin.

Hellard, P. (2003), 'Cyber Victim Seeks Payout', *Sunday Times*, 27 July.

Hendler, J. and Golbeck, J. (2008), 'Metcalfe's Law, Web 2.0, and the Semantic Web', *Web Semantics: Science, Services and Agents on the World Wide Web*, 6 (1): 14–20.

Herz, J. C. (2002), 'Harnessing the Hive: How Online Games Drive Networked Innovation', *Release 1.0*, 18 October, 20 (9): 1–22.

Hill, A. (2002), '*Big Brother*, The Real Audience', *Television and New Media*, August, 3 (3): 323–340.

Hills, M. (2002), *Fan Cultures*, Oxford, UK: Routledge.

Hindley, R. (1990), *The Death of the Irish Language: A Qualified Obituary*, Oxford, UK: Routledge.

Hine, C. (ed.) (2005) *Virtual Methods: Issues in Social Research on the Internet*, Oxford: Berg.

Hodges, A. (1992 [1982]), *Alan Turing: The Enigma*, rev. edn, London: Vintage.

Holloway, D. and Green, L. (2008), 'Room to View: Family Television Use in the Australian Context', *Television and New Media*, 9 (1): 47–61.

Holloway, D. Green, L. and Quin, R. (2004), 'What Porn? Children and the Family Internet', *M/C: A Journal of Media and Culture*, 'Porn', 7(4), http://journal.media-culture.org.au/0410/02_children.php (accessed 6 October 2009).

Holt, J. (2006), 'Code-Breaker: The Life and Death of Alan Turing', *The New Yorker*, 6 February, http://www.newyorker.com/archive/2006/02/06/060206crbo_books (accessed 3 October 2009).

Horrigan, J. (2008a), 'Home Broadband 2008. Adoption Stalls for Low Income Americans Even as Many Broadband Users Opt for Premium Services That Give Them More Speed', *Pew Internet and American Life Project*, July, http://www.pewinternet.org/Reports/2008/Home-Broadband-2008.aspx (accessed 6 October 2009).

Horrigan, J. (2008b), 'Obama's Online Opportunities: What Our Research Suggests About Where President-Elect Obama's Technology Policy May Lead', *Pew Internet and American Life Project*, 4 December, http://www.pewinternet.org/Reports/2008/Obamas-Online-Opportunities.aspx (accessed 6 October).

Howkins, J. (2001), *The Creative Economy: How People Make Money From Ideas*. London: Penguin.

Hussain, Z. and Griffiths, M. (2008), 'Gender Swapping and Socialising in Cyberspace: An Exploratory Study', *CyberPsychology and Behavior*, February, 11 (1): 47–53. doi:10.1089/cpb.2007.0020.

Hutchins, B. (2008), 'Signs of Meta-Change in Second Modernity, The Growth of e-Sport and the World Cyber Games', *New Media and Society*, 10 (6): 851–69.

Hwang, J. S. and Park, S.-H. (2009), '.kr Korea, Republic of', *Digital Review of Asia-Pacific 2009/2010*, Shahid Akhtar (ed.), India: Sage; Ottawa: Pan Asia Networking Programme, International Development Research Centre; Montreal: Orbicom Network of UNESCO Chairs in Communications, pp. 234–40.

Hyman, S. (2003), 'Cyberspace. Last Frontier for Settling Scores?' *Los Angeles Times*, 27 July.

IFAD (2009a), 'Sending Money Home: Worldwide Remittance Flows to Developing Countries', *International Fund for Agricultural Development*, http://www.ifad.org/remittances/maps/index.htm (accessed 6 October 2009).

IFAD (2009b), 'Global Forum on Remittances 2009', *International Fund for Agricultural Development*, http://www.ifad.org/remittances/events/forum09.htm (accessed 6 October 2009).

Indymedia (n.d.), *The Independent Media Center* [website], http://www.indymedia.org/en/index.shtml (accessed 6 October 2009).

Internet World Statistics (2009), *Internet World Stats* [website], http://www.internetworldstats.com (accessed 3 October 2009).

Ishii, K. (2004), 'Internet Use Via Mobile Phone in Japan', *Telecommunications Policy*, 28 (1): 43–58.

Jeanneney, J.-N. (2006), *Google and the Myth of Universal Knowledge: A View From Europe*, trans. T. L Fagan, Chicago: University of Chicago Press.

Jenkins, H. (2004), 'Why Heather Can Write', *Technology Review*, 6 February http://www.technologyreview.com/business/13473/?a=f (accessed 3 October 2009).

Jenkins, H. (2006), *Convergence Culture: Where Old and New Media Collide*, New York: New York University Press.

Jennings, T. (2009), 'Global outlook for video games', [video] *Insights and Analysis: Global Entertainment and Media Outlook 2009-2013*, PriceWaterhouseCoopers, http://www.pwc.com/gx/en/global-entertainment-media-outlook/insights-and-analysis.jhtml (accessed 3 October 2009).

Jin, D. Y. and Chee, F. (2008), 'Age of New Media Empires: A Critical Interpretation of the Korean Online Game Industry', *Games and Culture*, January, 3 (1): 38–58.

Johnson, S. (2005), *Everything Bad is Good For You*, London: Penguin, Allen Lane.

Johnston, J. (dir.) (1999), *October Sky* [Film], Universal Pictures.

Jones, B. (1995 [1981]), *Sleepers, Wake! Technology and the Future of Work*, 4th edn, Melbourne: Oxford University Press.

Jordan, L. (2007), 'The Google Book Search Project Litigation: "Massive Copyright Infringement" or "Fair Use"?', Arts, Communications, Entertainment and Sports Law, *Michigan Bar Journal*, September: 32–4 http://www.michbar.org/journal/pdf/pdf4article1210.pdf (accessed 3 October 2009).

Justia.com (n.d.), 'Featured Cases: The Author's Guild et al. v Google, Inc', *Justia.com News and Commentary*, http://news.justia.com/cases/featured/new-york/nysdce/1:2005 cv08136/273913/#20081002 (accessed 3 October 2009).

Kalathil, S. and Boas, T. (2003), *Open Networks Closed Regimes, The Impact of the Internet on Authoritarian Rule*, Washington, DC: Carnegie Endowment for International Peace.

Kasesniemi, E.-L. and Rautiainen, P. (2002), 'Mobile Culture of Children and Teenagers in Finland', in J. E Katz and M. A. Aakhus (eds), *Perpetual Contact: Mobile Communication, Private Talk, Public Performance*, New York: Cambridge University Press, pp. 170–92.

Kelly, K. and Rheingold, H. (1993), 'The Dragon Ate My Homework', *Wired*, 1.03, July/August, http://www.wired.com/wired/archive/1.03/muds.html (accessed 3 October 2009).

Kennedy, T., Smith, A., Wells, A. and Wellman, B. (2008), *Networked Families*, October, Washington, DC: Pew Internet and American Life, http://www.pewinternet.org/Reports/2008/Networked-Families.aspx (accessed 3 October 2009).

Kenny, C. (2005) 'Sùil Eile: Another Way of Seeing Minority Language Broadcasting', *Language and Intercultural Communication*, 5 (3/4): 264–73.

Kidder, T. (1982), *The Soul of a New Machine*, London: Penguin, Harmondsworth.

King, S. A. (1996), 'Is the Internet Addictive, or Are Addicts Using the Internet?' *Storm King* [website], http://webpages.charter.net/stormking/iad.html (accessed 3 October 2009).

Kopytoff, I. (1986), 'The Cultural Biography of Things: Commoditization as a Process', in A. Appadurai (ed.), *The Social Life of Things: Commodities in a Cultural Perspective*, Cambridge: Cambridge University Press, pp. 64–91.

Kuhn, T. (1996 [1962]), *The Structure of Scientific Revolutions*, 3rd Edn, Chicago: University of Chicago Press.

Kumar, A. (2008), Indians Abroad Send $27 bn Home to Make India Top Receiver, *Thaindian News*, 20 March, http://www.thaindian.com/newsportal/uncategorized/indians-abroad-send-27-bn-home-to-make-india-top-receiver_10029300.html# (accessed 3 October 2009).

Kump, P. (1999), *Breakthrough Rapid Reading*, revised edn, New Jersey: Prentice Hall.

Lampe, C., Ellison, N. and Steinfield, C. (2006), 'A Face(book) in the Crowd: Social Searching vs. Social Browsing', *Computer Supported Cooperative Work*, Proceedings of the 2006 20th anniversary conference on Computer Supported Cooperative Work, Canada: Banff, pp. 167–70.

Latour, B. (1987), *Science in Action: How to Follow Scientists and Engineers Through Society*, Milton Keynes: Open University Press.

Layden, J. (2003), 'Content is King for 3G. But What Content?' *The Register*, 1 April, http://www.theregister.co.uk/2003/04/01/content_is_king_for_3g/ (accessed 3 October 2009).

Lenhart, A. (2005), *Protecting Teens Online*, Pew Internet and American Life Project, 17 March, http://www.pewinternet.org/Reports/2005/Protecting-Teens-Online.aspx (accessed 3 October 2009).

Lenhart, A., Madden, M., Macgill, A. R. and Smith, A. (2007), *Teens and Social Media*, Pew Internet and American Life Project, 19 December, http://www.pewinternet.org/Reports/2007/Teens-and-Social-Media.aspx (accessed 3 October 2009).

Leonard, M. (2008a), 'Inside China's New Intelligentsia', *Prospect Magazine*, 144 (28 March), http://www.prospect-magazine.co.uk/article_details.php?id=10078 (accessed 3 October 2009).

Leonard, M. (2008b), *What Does China Think?* London: Fourth Estate.

Lievrouw, L. and Livingstone, S. (eds) (2002), *The Handbook of New Media*, London: Sage.

Litwark, E. and Szelenyi, I. (1969), 'Primary Group Structures and Their Functions: Kin, Neighbours and Friends', *American Sociological Review*, 34 (August): 465–81.

Livingstone, S. (1992), 'The Meaning of Domestic Technologies: A Personal Construct Analysis of Familial Gender Relations', in R. Silverstone and E. Hirsh (eds), *Consuming Technologies: Media and Information in Domestic Spaces*, London: Routledge, pp. 113–30.

Livingstone, S. and Bober, M. (2005), *UK Children Go Online*, Economic and Social Research Council, April, http://www.citizensonline.org.uk/site/media/documents/1521_UKCGO-final-report.pdf (accessed 3 October 2009).

Livingstone, S. and Haddon, L. (2009), *EU Kids Online: Final Report*, LSE London: EU Kids Online (EC Safer Internet Plus Program Deliverable D6.5) http://eprints.lse.ac.uk/24372/ (accessed 3 October 2009.

Lobe, B., Livingstone, S. and Haddon, L. (2007), *Researching Children's Experiences Online Across Countries. Issues and Problems in Methodology*, LSE London: EU Kids Online (EC Safer Internet Plus Program Deliverable D4.1) http://eprints.lse.ac.uk/2856/ (accessed 3 October 2009).

MacKenzie, D. and Wajcman, J. (eds) (1999 [1985]), *The Social Shaping of Technology: How the Refrigerator Got Its Hum*, 2nd edn, Milton Keynes: Open University Press.

Madden, M. and Fox, S. (2006), 'Finding Answers Online in Sickness and in Health', *Pew Internet and American Life Project Report*, 2 May, http://www.pewinternet.org/Reports/2006/Finding-Answers-Online-in-Sickness-and-in-Health.aspx (accessed 3 October 2006).

Maguire, E. A., Woollet, K. and Spiers, H. J. (2006), 'London Taxi Drivers and Bus Drivers: A Structural MRI and Neuropsychological Analysis, *Hippocampus*, 16: 1091–1101 http://193.62.66.20/Maguire/Maguire2006.pdf (accessed 3 October).

Maney, K. (2003), *The Maverick and His Machine: Thomas Watson Sr. and the Making of IBM*, New Jersey: John Wiley and Sons.

Marcus, A. and Perez, A. (2007), 'M-YouTube Mobile UI: Video Selection Based on Social Influence', in J. Jacko (ed.), *Human Computer Interaction, HCI Intelligent Multimodal Interaction Environments*, Berlin/Heidelberg: Springer, pp. 926–32.

Marshall, P. D. (1997), 'Technophobia: Video Games, Computer Hacks and Cybernetics', *Media International Australia*, 85 (November): 70–8.

Marvin, C. (1990), *When Old Technologies Were New: Thinking About Electric Communication in the Late Nineteenth Century*, New York: Oxford University Press.

Masuda, Y. (1981), *The Information Society as Post-Industrial Society*, (English Ed.), Bethesda, US: World Future Society.

McCarthy, R. (2003), 'Salam's Story', *The Guardian*, Friday 30 May, http://www.guardian.co.uk/world/2003/may/30/iraq.digitalmedia (accessed 3 October 2009).

McKee, A. (2004), *The Public Sphere: An Introduction*, Melbourne: Cambridge University Press.

McKee, A., Albury, K. and Lumby, C. (2008), *The Porn Report*, Melbourne: Melbourne University Press.

MCT (2004), *The Rise of Korean Games: Guide to Korean Game Industry and Culture*, Ministry of Culture and Tourism, Seoul: Korea Game Development and Promotion Institute.

Mercury (1992), *Fibre Optic Technologies*, Mercury Communications Ltd, August, accessed at *Technology Watch* http://www.gare.co.uk/technology_watch/fibre.htm (accessed 3 October 2009).

MIC (2007), *Subscribers of High Speed Internet by Region*, Seoul, Korea: Ministry of Information and Communication.

Milian, M. (2008), '"Numa Numa" Kid and Rihanna and T.I.'s Hyper-Viral New Song', *Los Angeles Times: Entertainment*, 9 September, http://latimesblogs.latimes.com/webscout/2008/09/numa-numa-song.html (accessed 3 October 2009).

Miller, C. C. (2008), 'How Obama's Internet Campaign Changed Politics', Technology BITS, *New York Times*, 7 November, http://bits.blogs.nytimes.com/2008/11/07/how-obamas-internet-campaign-changed-politics/ (accessed 3 October 2009).

Miller, D. (1987), 'Towards a Theory of Consumption (chapter 10)', *Material Culture and Mass Consumption*, Oxford: Basil Blackwell pp. 178–217.

Miller, D. (1994), *Modernity, an Ethnographic Approach: Dualism and Mass Consumption in Trinidad*, Oxford, UK: Berg.

Miller, D. and Slater, D (2000), *The Internet: An Ethnographic Approach*, Oxford, UK: Berg.

Molyneux, G. J., McCarthy, G. M., McEniff, S., Cryan, M. and Conroy, R. M. (2008), 'Prevalence and Predictors of Carer Burden and Depression in Carers of Patients Referred to an Old Age Psychiatric Service', *International Psychogeriatrics*, 20: 1193–1202 doi:10.1017/S1041610208007515.

Morgan, G. (2006 [1986]), *Images of Organization* (Rev. ed), Thousand Oaks, CA: Sage.

Morley, D. (1986), *Family Television: Cultural Power and Domestic Leisure*, London: Routledge.

Morley, D. (1995), 'Theories of Consumption in Media Studies', in D. Miller (ed.), *Acknowledging Consumption: A Review of New Studies*, London: Routledge, pp. 293–324.

Morris, S. (2004), 'Shoot First, Ask Questions Later: Ethnographic Research in an Online Computer Gaming Community', *Media International Australia*, 110 (February): 31–41.

Moses, A. (2008), 'Don't Be Evil or Don't Loose Value?' *Sydney Morning Herald*, 15 April, http://www.smh.com.au/news/biztech/dont-be-evil/2008/04/15/1208025168177.html?page=fullpage#contentSwap1 (accessed 3 October 2009).

Move On (2008), 'Celebrating 10 Years of People Power', *MoveOn.org Political Action* [Slideshow], http://pol.moveon.org/10years/ (accessed 3 October 2009).

Moyal, A. (1989), 'The Feminine Culture of the Telephone: People, Patterns and Policy', *Prometheus*, 7 (1): 5–31.

Moyal, A. (1995), 'The Feminine Culture of the Telephone: People Patterns and Policy', in N. Heap, R. Thomas, G. Einon, R. Mason and H. Mackay, (eds), *Information Technology and Society*, London, UK: Sage Publications, in association with The Open University, pp. 284–310.

Mullins, J. (2007), 'iMode: A Case Study', *The New Business Road Test: What Entrepreneurs and Executives Should Do Before Writing a Business Plan*, 2nd edn, Harlow, UK: Pearson Education, pp. 29–33.

Murdock, G., Hartmann, P. and Gray, P. (1992), 'Contextualising Home Computing: Resources and Practices', in R. Silverstone and E. Hirsch (eds), *Consuming Technologies: Media and Information in Domestic Spaces*, London: Routledge, pp. 146–60.

NESTA (n.d.), *National Endowment for Science, Technology and the Arts: Making Innovation Flourish* [website], http://www.nesta.org.uk/about-us/ (accessed 3 October 2009).

Nichols, D., Farrand, T., Rowley, T. and Avery, M. (2006), *Brands and Gaming – The Computer Gaming Phenomenon and its Impact on Brands and Businesses*, Basingstoke, UK: Palgrave Mcmillan.

Nohe, R. (1995), 'A Different Time, a Different Place: Breaking up Telephone Companies in the United States and Japan', *Federal Communications Law Journal*, 48: 307–37.

Nordicom (2004), *Playing with Fire: How Do Computer Games Influence the Player?*, Gothenburg University, Sweden: Nordicom, The International Clearinghouse on Children, Youth and Media.

November, A. (2008), *Web Literacy for Educators*, Thousand Oaks, CA: Corwin Press.

O'Donnell, M. (2003), 'Perth Academic Takes "Cyberstalker" to Court', *7.30 Report*, ABC Television, 12 August, http://www.abc.net.au/7.30/content/2003/s922886.htm (accessed 3 October 2009).

O'Leary, C. (2003), 'Cyber-Stalker Traps Perth Lecturer in Web of Deceit', *The West Australian*, (11 October): 13.

O'Rourke, B. (2005), 'Expressing Identity Through Lesser Used Languages, Examples from the Irish and Galician Contexts', *Language and Intercultural Communication*, 5 (3and4): 274–83.

OECD (2008), *OECD Broadband Subscribers per 100 Inhabitants, by Technology, June 2008*, Organisation for Economic Co-operation and Development, http://www.oecd.org/dataoecd/21/35/39574709.xls (accessed 3 October 2009).

Ohmori, S., Yamao, Y. and Nobuo N. (2000), 'The Future Generations of Mobile Communications Based on Broadband Access Technologies', *IEEE Communications Magazine*, (December): 134–42, http://www.comsoc.org/ci/public/preview/ohmori.html (accessed 3 October 2009).

ONI Australia (n.d.), 'Australia and New Zealand', *Open Net Initiative* [website], http://opennet.net/research/regions/au-nz (accessed 3 October 2009).

ONI China (n.d.), 'China (including Hong Kong)', *Open Net Initiative* [website], http://opennet.net/research/profiles/china (accessed 3 October 2009).

Palmer, L. (1994), 'Regulating Technology', in L. Green and R. Guinery (eds), *Framing Technology: Society, Choice and Change*, Sydney: Allen and Unwin, pp. 77–90.

Parreñas, R. (2005), 'Long Distance Intimacy: Class, Gender and Intergenerational Relations Between Mothers and Children in Filipino Transnational Families', *Global Networks*, 5 (4): 317–36.

Parsons, T. (1943), 'The Kinship System of the Contemporary United States', *American Anthropologist* (New Series), 45 (1) Jan–March: 22–38.

Passerini, K., Patten, K., Bartolacci, M. and Fjermestad, J. (2007), 'Reflections and Trends in the Expansion of Cellular Wireless Services in the US and China: Charting the Evolution of Business Capabilities and Communication Technology and Standards', *Communications of the ACM*, 50 (10): 25–8.

Pesce, M. (2006), 'The Tags Within', *The Human Network: What Happens After We're All Connected?* 7 Oct, http://blog.futurestreetconsulting.com/?p=18 (accessed 3 October 2009).

Pew (2008), 'Teens, Video Games and Civics: Teens' Gaming Experiences are Diverse and Include Significant Social Interaction and Civic Engagement', *Pew Internet and American Life Project with the MacArthur Foundation*, 16 September, http://www.pewinternet.org/Reports/2008/Teens-Video-Games-and-Civics.aspx (accessed 3 October 2009).

Pew (2009), *Pew Internet and American Life Project* [website], http://www.pewinternet.org (accessed 3 October 2009).

Pinch, T. and Bijker, W. (1984), 'The Social Construction of Facts and Artefacts: Or How the Sociology of Science and the Sociology of Technology Might Benefit Each Other', *Social Studies of Science*, (14) August: 399–441.

Pink, D. (2005), 'The Book Stops Here', *Wired*, 13.03 (March), http://www.wired.com/wired/archive/13.03/wiki.html?pg=1andtopic=wikiandtopic_set= (accessed 3 October 2009).

Porush, D. (1998), 'Telepathy: Alphabetic Consciousness and the Age of Cyborg Illiteracy', in J. Dixon and E. Cassidy (eds), *Virtual Futures: Cyberotics, Technology and Post-Human Pragmatism*, London: Routledge, pp. 45–64.

Pouzin, L. (1973), 'Presentation and Major Design Aspects of the Cyclades Computer Network', *Proceedings of the NATO Advanced Study Institute on Computer Communication Networks*, Sussex, United Kingdom: Noordhoff International Publishing, pp. 415–34.

Rakow, L. (1988), 'Women and the Telephone: The Gendering of a Communications Technology', in C. Kramarae (ed), *Technology and Women's Voices*, New York: Routledge and Kegan Paul, pp. 207–28.

Rakow, L. (1992), *Gender On The Line: Women, the Telephone and Community Life*, Illinois: University of Illinois Press.

Raymond, E. S. (2001), *The Cathedral and the Bazaar: Musings on Linux and Open Source by an Accidental Revolutionary*, revised edn, Sebastopol, CA: O'Reilly and Associates, also at http://www.catb.org/~esr/writings/cathedral-bazaar/cathedral-bazaar/index.html#catbmain (accessed 3 October 2009).

Reimer, J. (2005), 'Total Share: 30 Years of Personal Computer Market Share Figures', *Ars Technica*, December 14, http://arstechnica.com/articles/culture/total-share.ars/10 (accessed 3 October 2009).

RFLAN (2006), 'WA Red Flag LAN 16', *Red Flag LAN* [Unauthorised Documentary], YouTube, http://www.youtube.com/watch?v=qUMLsjGP5yY (accessed 3 October 2009).

Rheingold, H. (2000 [1993]), *The Virtual Community: Homesteading on the Electronic Frontier*, Cambridge, MA: MIT Press, also at http://www.rheingold.com/vc/.

Rival, L., Slater, D. and Miller, D. (1998), 'Sex and Sociality: Comparative Ethnographies of Sexual Objectification', *Theory, Culture and Society*, 15 (3–4): 295–321.

Roberts, L. (1967), *Multiple Computer Networks and Intercomputer Communication*, http://www.packet.cc/files/multi-net-inter-comm.html (accessed 3 October 2009).

Roberts, L. (1978), *The Evolution of Packet Switching*, http://www.packet.cc/files/ev-packet-sw.html (accessed 3 October 2009).

Rogers, E. (2003 [1962]), *Diffusion of Innovations*, 5th edn, New York: Simon Schuster.

Rogers, E. and Larsen, J. (1984), *Silicon Valley Fever: Growth of High-Technology Culture*, New York: Basic Books.

Rooksby, E., and Weckert, J. (Eds.), (2007), *Information Technology and Social Justice*. Hershey, PA.: Information Science Publishing.

Rosenberg, M. (2009), 'The Number of Countries in the World', *About.com: Geography*, http://geography.about.com/cs/countries/a/numbercountries.htm.

Roszak, T. (1994), *The Cult of Information: A Neo-Luddite Treatise on High Tech, Artificial Intelligence and the True Art of Thinking*, California: University of California Press.

Rotunda, R. (n.d.), 'Legal Analysis: On the Facts', *Google Perspectives* [website], http://www.google.com/googlebooks/legal.html (accessed 3 October 2009).

Ryff, C. Schmutte, P. and Lee, Y (1996), 'How Children Turn Out: Implications for Parental Self-Evaluation', in C. Ryff and M. Saltzer (eds), *The Parental Experience in Midlife*, Chicago: University of Chicago Press, pp. 383–422.

Schiffman, L. Bednall, D. Watson, J. and Kanuk, L. (1997), *Consumer Behaviour*, Sydney: Prentice Hall.

Schiller, H. (1991), 'Not Yet the Post-Imperialist Era', *Critical Studies in Mass Communication*, 8 (1) March: 13–28.

Schiller, H. (2000), *Living in the Number One Country: Reflections from a Critic of American Empire*, New York, NY: Seven Stories Press.

Schonfeld, E. (2009), 'Watch Out Google, Obama's Antitrust Chief is Looking to Make an Example out of You', *TechCrunch*, 11 May, http://www.techcrunch.com/2009/05/11/watch-out-google-obamas-antitrust-chief-is-looking-to-make-a-big-case/ (accessed 3 October 2009).

Schrock, A. and boyd, d. (2008), 'Online Threats to Youth: Solicitation, Harassment and Problematic Content, Appendix C: Research Advisory Board Literature Review', *Enhancing Child Safety and Online Technologies*, http://www.danah.org/papers/ISTTF-RABLitReview.pdf (accessed 3 October 2009).

Silverstone, R. (1994), *Television and Everyday Life*, London: Routledge.

Silverstone, R. and Haddon, L. (1996), 'Design and the Domestication of Information and Communication Technologies: Technical Change and Everyday Life', in R. Silverstone and R. Mansell (eds), *Communication by Design. The Politics of Information and Communication Technologies*, Oxford: Oxford University Press, pp. 44–74.

Silverstone, R., Hirsch, E. and Morley, D. (1992), 'Information and Communication Technologies in the Moral Economy of the Household', in R. Silverstone and E. Hirsch (eds), *Consuming Technologies: Media and Information in Domestic Spaces*, London: Routledge, pp. 15–31.

Singel, R. (2009), 'The Fight Over the Google of All Libraries: A Wired.com FAQ', *Wired: Epicenter*, 30 April, http://www.wired.com/epicenter/2009/04/the-fight-over-the-worlds-greatest-library-the-wiredcom-faq/ (accessed 3 October 2009).

Skeldon, P. (2002), '"Sex and the City": It Is the US Adult Services Industry Currently Making the Most Money from Broadband', UK: *Communications International*, 1 October: 18–25.

SNS Safety (2008), *Enhancing Child Safety and Online Technologies*, Final Report of the Internet Safety Technical Task Force to the Multi-State Working Group on Social Networking of the State Attorneys General of the United States, Harvard: Internet Safety Technical Task Force, 14 January, http://cyber.law.harvard.edu/pubrelease/isttf/ (accessed 3 October 2009).

Somerville, P. (1998), 'Explanations of Social Exclusion: Where Does Housing Fit In?', *Housing Studies*, 13 (6): 761–780.

Staksrud, E., Livingstone, S., Haddon, L. and Ólafsson, K. (2009), *What Do We Know About Children's Use of Online Technologies?* 2nd edn, A Report on Data Availability for the EC Safer Internet Plus programme, EU Kids Online, London, UK. http://eprints.lse.ac.uk/24367/ (accessed 3 October 2009).

Stone, A. R. (1991), 'Will the Real Body Please Stand Up?' in M. Benedikt (ed.), *Cyberspace: First Steps*, Cambridge: MIT Press, pp. 81–118, http://molodiez.org/net/real_body2.html (accessed 3 October 2009).

Streeter, T. (2003), 'The Romantic Self and the Politics of Internet Commercialization', *Cultural Studies*, 17(5): 648–68.

Stvilia, B., Twidale, M., Smith, L. and Gasser, L. (2008), 'Information Quality Work Organisation in Wikipedia', *Journal of the American Society for Information Science and Technology*, 59 (6): 983–1001.

Sugar Quill (n.d.) *The Sugar Quill* [website], http://www.sugarquill.net/index.php (accessed 3 October 2009).

Sussman, M. B. (1965), 'Relationships of Adult Children With Their Parents in the United States', in E. Shanas and G. Streib (eds), *Social Structure and the Family: Generational Relations*, Englewood Cliffs, NJ: Prentice Hall, pp. 62–92.

Swisher, K. (2003), *There Must be a Pony in Here Somewhere: The AOL Time Warner Debacle and the Quest for the Digital Future*, New York, New York: Three Rivers Press.

Tancer, B. (2007), YouTube and Google: Quantifying the Synergy, *Hitwise Intelligence*, 29 January, http://weblogs.hitwise.com/bill-tancer/2007/01/youtube_and_google_quantifying.html (accessed 3 October 2009).

Tapscott, D. and Williams, A. (2006), *Wikinomics: How Mass Collaboration Changes Everything*, London: Atlantic Books.

Techtree (2008), 'Facebook: Largest, Fastest Growing Social Network', *Techtree News*, 13 August, http://www.techtree.com/India/News/Facebook_Largest_Fastest_Growing_Social_Network/551-92134-643.html (accessed 3 October 2009).

They Work For You (2009), 'Are your MPs and Peers Working for You in the UK's Parliament?' *TheyWorkForYou*, [website], http://www.theyworkforyou.com/ (accessed 3 October 2009).

Thomas, A. (2006), 'Fan Fiction Online: Engagement, Critical Response and Affective Play Through Writing', *Australian Journal of Language and Literacy*, 29 (3): 226–39.

Thompson, C. (2005), 'The BitTorrent Effect', *Wired*, 13.01 (January) http://www.wired.com/wired/archive/13.01/bittorrent.html?pg=2andtopic=bittorrentandtopic_set= (accessed 3 October 2009).

Tosenberger, C. (2008), 'Homosexuality at the Online Hogwarts: Harry Potter Slash Fanfiction', *Children's Literature*, 36: 185–207.

Turing, A. (1936), 'On Computable Numbers, With an Application to the Entscheidungsproblem', *Proceedings of the London Mathematical Society*, series 2, (42): 230–65, http://plms.oxfordjournals.org/cgi/reprint/s2-42/1/230.pdf (accessed 3 October 2009).

Twittervision (n.d.) *Twittervision*, [Website] http://www.twittervision.com/ (accessed 3 October 2009).

UN (2009), *United Nations Member States*, United Nations, http://www.un.org/members/list.shtml (accessed 3 October 2009).

UNESCO (2002), *Universal Declaration on Cultural Diversity* http://unesdoc.unesco.org/images/0012/001271/127160m.pdf (accessed 3 October 2009).

van Dijk, J. A. G. M. (2005), *The deepening divide: Inequality in the Information Society*. Thousand Oaks, CA: Sage.

Vise, D. A. (2006), *The Google Story: Inside the Hottest Business, Media and Technology Success of Our Time*, London: Pan Books.

Voss, G. (2007), 'The Dynamics of Technological Change in a Socially Stigmatised Sector', DRUID (Danish Research Unit for Industrial Dynamics) Winter Conference, 25–7 January, http://www2.druid.dk/conferences/viewpaper.php?id=1072andcf=10 (accessed 3 October 2009).

Vossen, G. and Hagemann, S. (2007), *Unleashing Web 2.0: From Concepts to Creativity*, Burlington, MA: Morgan Kaufmann.

Wajcman, J. (1991), *Feminism Confronts Technology*, Sydney: Allen and Unwin.

Wajcman, J. (1994), 'Technological A/Genders: Technology, Culture and Class', in L. Green and R. Guinery (eds), *Framing Technology: Society, Choice and Change*, Sydney, Allen and Unwin, pp. 3–14.

Wajcman, J. (2004), *Technofeminism*, Cambridge: Polity Press.

Walsh, J. (2001), 'Language, Citizenship and National Identity', *Language and Citizenship*, London: LSE Language Centre, London School of Economics, pp. 1–4, 24 October.

Wang, T. Wu, L. and Lin, Z. (2005), 'The Revival of Mozilla in the Browser War Against Internet Explorer', *ACM International Conference Proceeding Series, vol. 113, Proceedings of the 7th international conference on Electronic commerce*, China: Xi'an, pp. 159–66.

Warschauer, Mark (2003), *Technology and Social Inclusion: Rethinking the Digital Divide*, Cambridge MA: MIT Press.

WB Press Release (2008), 'India Top Receiver of Migrant Remittances in 2007, Followed by China and Mexico', *World Bank Press Office*, 19 March.

Weber, T. (2006), 'Now on YouTube: Google's Gamble', *BBC News*, 10 October, http://news.bbc.co.uk/1/hi/business/6036023.stm (accessed 3 October 2009).

Weise, Elizabeth (2001), '"Potter" is Still the Muggles' Domain', Cyberspeak, *USA Today*, 24 April, http://www.usatoday.com/tech/columnist/cceli000.htm (accessed 3 October 2009).

Whitlock, G. (2007), *Soft Weapons: Autobiography in Transit*, Chicago: University of Chicago Press.

Widyanto, L. and Griffiths, M. (2007), 'Internet Addiction: Does It Really Exist? (Revisited)'. in J. Gackenbach (ed), *Psychology and the Internet: Intrapersonal, Interpersonal, and Transpersonal Implications* 2nd edn, Amsterdam: Elsevier/Academic Press, pp. 127–49.

Wikipedia 'Salam Pax' (n.d.), 'Salam Pax', *Wikipedia, the Free Encyclopedia* [website], http://en.wikipedia.org/wiki/Salam_Pax (accessed 3 October 2009).

Wilbur, S. (1997), 'An Archaeology of Cyberspaces: Virtuality, Community, Identity', in D. Porter (ed.), *Internet Culture*, New York: Routledge, pp. 5–22, http://project.cyberpunk.ru/idb/archeology_of_cyberspace.html (accessed 3 October 2009).

Wired (2005), 'Feds Urge Delay for .XXX Domain', (Associated Press), *Wired*, 16 August, http://www.wired.com/techbiz/it/news/2005/08/68545 (accessed 3 October 2009).

Wired Safety (n.d.) *Wired Safety: The World's Largest Internet Safety, Help and Education Resource* [website], http://www.wiredsafety.org/index.html (accessed 3 October 2009).

Wohl, A. (2006), 'How We Process Words: The Marketing of WP Software', *IEEE Annals of the History of Computing*, October–December, 28 (4): 88–91.

Wolak, J. Finkelhor, D. and Mitchell, J. K. (2004), 'Internet-Initiated Sex Crimes Against Minors: Implications for Prevention Based on Findings from a National Study', *Journal of Adolescent Health* 35 (5): 424.e11–424.e20.

Wolak, J. Mitchell, J. K and Finkelhor, D. (2003), 'Escaping or Connecting? Characteristics of Youth Who Form Close Online Relationships', *Journal of Adolescence,* 26: 105–19.

Wolak, J. Mitchell, J. K and Finkelhor, D. (2006), *Online Victimization of Youth: Five Years Later*, Alexandria, VA: National Center for Missing and Exploited Children, #07-06-025, http://www.unh.edu/ccrc/pdf/CV138.pdf (accessed 3 October 2009).

Wolf, G. (2004), 'Weapons of Mass Mobilization', *Wired*, 12.09, September, http://www.wired.com/wired/archive/12.09/moveon.html (accessed 3 October 2009).

Wong, J. and Nah S. L. (2001), *China's Emerging New Economy: The Internet and e-Commerce*, Singapore: Singapore University Press/World Scientific.

World Bank (2008), 'Migration and Development Brief 8', 11 November, http:// siteresources.worldbank.org/INTPROSPECTS/Resources/334934-1110315015165/ MD_Brief8.pdf (accessed 3 October 2009).

Ybarra, M. and Mitchell, J. K. (2004), 'Youth Engaging in Online Harassment: Associations with Caregiver-Child Relationships, Internet Use and Personal Characteristics', *Journal of Adolescence*, 27: 319–36.

Ybarra, M. and Mitchell, J. K. (2008), 'How Risky Are Social Networking Sites? A Comparison of Places Online Where Youth Sexual Solicitation and Harassment Occurs', *Paediatrics*, 121 (2): e350–e357.

Yin, R. K. (2003 [1984]), *Case Study Research: Design and Methods* (3rd ed.), Thousand Oaks, CA: Sage.

Young, M. and Willmott, P. (1957), *Family and Kinship in East London*, London: Routledge and Kegan Paul.

Zetter, K. (2010), 'Google to stop censoring search results in China after hack attack', *Wired*, 12 January, http://www.wired.com/threatlevel/2010/01/google-censorship-china/#Replay (accessed 6 February 2010).

Zonday, Tay (n.d.), 'Chocolate Rain' [Music Video], *YouTube*, http://www.youtube.com/ watch?v=EwTZ2xpQwpA (accessed 3 October 2009).

INDEX

This index has avoided, where possible, terms beginning with internet, virtual, cyber and online. For example: Internet access is listed as Access; Online games and gaming as Games and gaming; Virtual community as Community; and Cyber stalking as Stalking.